SPELLWORKING
FOR
COVENS

ABOUT THE AUTHOR

Edain McCoy became a self-initiated Witch in 1981 and has been an active part of the Pagan community since her formal initiation into a large San Antonio coven in 1983. She has been researching alternative spiritualities since her teens, when she was first introduced to Kabbalah, or Jewish mysticism. Since then, she has studied a variety of magickal paths including Celtic, Appalachian folk magick, and Curanderismo, a Mexican-American folk tradition. Today she is part of the Wittan Irish Pagan tradition, where she is a priestess of Brighid and an elder. An alumnus of the University of Texas with a B.A. in history, she is affiliated with several professional writer's organizations, is listed in the reference guide *Contemporary Authors*, and occasionally presents workshops on magickal topics or works individually with students who wish to study Witchcraft. This former woodwind player for the Lynchburg (VA) Symphony claims both the infamous feuding McCoy family of Kentucky and Sir Roger Williams, the seventeenth-century religious dissenter, as branches on her ethnically diverse family tree. In her "real life," Edain works as a licensed stockbroker.

TO WRITE TO THE AUTHOR

If you wish to contact the author or would like more information about this book, please write to the author in care of Llewellyn Worldwide and we will forward your request. Both the author and publisher appreciate hearing from you and learning of your enjoyment of this book and how it has helped you. Llewellyn Worldwide cannot guarantee that every letter written to the author can be answered, but all will be forwarded. Please write to:

Edain McCoy
℅ Llewellyn Worldwide
P.O. Box 64383, Dept. 0-7387-0261-7
St. Paul, MN 55164-0383, U.S.A.

Please enclose a self-addressed stamped envelope for reply,
or $1.00 to cover costs. If outside U.S.A., enclose
international postal reply coupon.

Many of Llewellyn's authors have websites with additional information
and resources. For more information, please visit our website:

HTTP://WWW.LLEWELLYN.COM

Spellworking for Covens

MAGICK FOR TWO OR MORE

Edain McCoy

2002
Llewellyn Publications
St. Paul, Minnesota 55164-0383, U.S.A.

FIRST EDITION
First Printing, 2002

Book editing and design by Rebecca Zins
Cover design by Lisa Novak
Cover photo © PhotoDisc
Interior illustrations by Kevin R. Brown

Library of Congress Cataloging-in-Publication Data
McCoy, Edain, 1957–
    Spellworking for covens : magick for two or more / Edain McCoy.—1st ed.
        p.   cm.
    Includes bibliographical references and index.
    ISBN 0-7387-0261-7
    1. Covens. 2. Charms. 3. Witchcraft. I. Title.

BF1572.C68 M373 2002
133.4'3—dc21

                                                                2002067110

Llewellyn Worldwide does not participate in, endorse, or have any authority or responsibility concerning private business transactions between our authors and the public.
    All mail addressed to the author is forwarded but the publisher cannot, unless specifically instructed by the author, give out an address or phone number.
    Any Internet references contained in this work are current at publication time, but the publisher cannot guarantee that a specific location will continue to be maintained. Please refer to the publisher's website for links to authors' websites and other sources.

Llewellyn Publications
A Division of Llewellyn Worldwide, Ltd.
P.O. Box 64383, Dept. 0-7387-0261-7
St. Paul, MN 55164-0383, U.S.A.
www.llewellyn.com

Printed in the United States of America

OTHER BOOKS BY EDAIN MCCOY

Witta

A Witch's Guide to Faery Folk

The Sabbats

How to Do Automatic Writing

Celtic Myth and Magick

Lady of the Night

Entering the Summerland

Inside a Witches' Coven

Making Magick

Mountain Magick

Celtic Women's Spirituality

Astral Projection for Beginners

Bewitchments

Enchantments

Ostara

Dedicated to all the covens who worship,
celebrate, and make magick together
as the deities intended:
with pomp, and feast,
and revelry . . .

◆   ◆   ◆

And pomp, and feast, and revelry,

With mask, and antique pageantry,

Such sights as youthful poets dream

On summer eves by haunted stream

—JOHN MILTON (1608–1674)

CONTENTS

PREFACE

Even with all the good information on Pagan and Wiccan practice available today, there remains a persistent but detrimental belief among modern practitioners that a coven *must* consist of a specific number of people to be effective. This mistaken idea has kept small groups from doing good work together because they've been taught they have no right to call themselves a coven or to engage in covenlike activities. Some of these small groups have even been brainwashed to believe their magick cannot be successful because of the number issue.

Ask around and you'll get dozens of different answers about that "right" number. Some will say you must have at least three. Why? No one seems to know for sure. Some say you must have thirteen, the supposed traditional number of coven members, dating from Middle Age practices. So strong is this belief that some people will not consider any group to be a coven that does not have exactly thirteen members. Others insist you must have an equal number of male and female practitioners to balance the coven's energies—of course, having equal numbers of males and females is impossible in a coven of either three or thirteen. Still others have been influenced by a popular Hollywood film that leads them to believe they must have four people—no more and no less—to represent each of the four elements.

Are these number "rules" starting to sound as silly to you as they do to me? And what do any of them have to do with making successful magick?

For those who doubt that only two can be a coven, consider for a moment that covens of two have a notable history, one that makes sense magickally and mythically.

Consider first that the best energy flows between people who share a close bond, the kind that occurs most often in a true friendship or tight familial bond. The famous royal magicians John Dee and Edward Kelly worked together with legendary success in the sixteenth-century court of England's Queen Elizabeth I. High priests and high priestesses often work together, away from the rest of their covens, in rites where they embody the creative essence of the God and the Goddess.

Similarly, domestic partners often form covens of two, creating rituals and spells that they alone can work because the imagery they employ is unique to their shared view of the world. They also have the added advantage of using their established bonds of physical intimacy and a shared vision of deity to enhance their spellwork.

The idea that two people are a special magickal team was also evident in the Celtic traditions. In old Ireland, a friend to whom you bared your deepest secrets while mentoring each other through life's trials was given the honored title of your *anamchara*, or your "soulfriend." This person was as much your other half as any lover or domestic partner, and it was accepted that the power of magickal potential flowed between soulfriends as naturally as lightning flows between water and metal.

For almost two years I worked or worshipped on an exclusive basis with my best friend. We were novices for a great deal of that time and so we did not think of ourselves as a coven, yet that's what we were. The root word of coven is *con*, meaning "to come together," and that's what we did on all levels of our being. Yet we let ourselves miss out on many special rituals and spells we could have done together because we'd bought into one or more of the silly number theories.

The spells and exercises in this book are meant to be used by at least two practitioners, though more are welcome, and even encouraged. Just remember that building a group mind and blending your energies with others is tricky and not always successful, even among people who are otherwise close. If you are lucky enough to have even one person with whom you can do these things, it is a blessing and you should not waste time looking for others who may only disrupt your energies. Enjoy what you have right now and, if more good working partners come along, that's great; if not, you're not lacking anything.

I receive inquiries on a daily basis from Witches, Wiccans, and other Pagans. The two most often-asked questions concern the practice of magick and the availability of covens (see Appendix B for my detailed answers). Just as the adherents of Pagan religions have increased tenfold over the past decade, so have covens and study groups aimed at teaching, sharing, magick, and worship. Clearly, group worship and magick is a desirable goal for many who choose the Old Ways as their spiritual path.

Most of the focus of coven work is on ritual and, so far, the available books on coven practice have focused in depth on formation, organization, and ritual. None address group magick in serious detail. I believe that, so far, this has been a good oversight as Paganism has grown up and come into its own. It must always be remembered that

Witchcraft, Wicca, and other Pagan spiritualities are first and foremost *religions in which the worship of, and union with, the divine creator(s) is the primary goal.* Covens exist to facilitate that worship and union, not to seek magickal solutions to everyone's problems. Still, many mature covens are now more than ready to begin crafting magick together in addition to their ritual work.

The art of coven magick is a more advanced practice than coven ritual. Almost anyone can worship in a Pagan format with little guidance, but not everyone can make successful magick without training and practice. It surprises some newcomers to Paganism that covens tend to attempt spellworking later in their association than almost any other art. This is just the same as the student Witch who is taught the art of magick much later in his studies than other practices.

This is because magick is not a requirement for any form of Pagan practice, and because it builds on other skills one must learn for basic ritual and meditation. Magick also requires the spiritual maturity to be done in an ethical manner and to have its greatest chance of success. We who follow these nature-based traditions believe in the energies of the universe that make magick possible, and we use them when necessary, but they are not our first line of defense for every problem we face.

Magick is not and never has been the sole reason our religions or our covens exist. Those who find good covens willing to teach them the Craft will be disappointed if all they are seeking are other warm bodies to provide a constant feed of magickal energy for their problems and the coven wants to spend time paying homage to and serving its patron deity instead. If a coven senses that magickal work is the only goal of an applicant, entrance to the group is often denied.

Because group magick provides a different set of advantages (i.e., potent group energy) and disadvantages (i.e., creating a group mind and the tenet of "keeping silent") over solitary magick, sometimes even very experienced and skilled practitioners are unsure of how to make an effective translation of one to the other. *Spellworking for Covens* has been written to help bridge that gap in the current annals of Pagan literature. Written at the intermediate skill level, it seeks to provide a format and stepping-off point for exploring group magick. If you already have magickal methods that work for your coven, please don't feel the need to change them to conform with what you find here. There are many methods of raising energy and creating magick. This book was written for the coven just beginning magickal exploration, and for the seasoned coven looking for fresh ideas, not replacement practices. Take what works, adapt it, mold it, meld it, and make it your own. The text is culled from over twenty years' experience in crafting magick as a solitary and as both a member and a leader of covens.

If you or your coven don't feel you're at that intermediate level of practice or understanding yet, please see the Annotated Bibliography at the back of this book for some suggested reading. You'll find there are many texts that cover various Pagan subjects in detail, and they can be found in almost any bookstore.

If you're seeking to connect with other Pagans or Wiccans for friendship or coven work, you'll find that many books on basic Wiccan or Pagan practice make some mention of networking, or "webweaving" as it is sometimes called. If you are seeking to find or form a coven or magickal study group, I suggest looking into Judy Harrow's *Wicca Covens*, Amber K's *Covencraft*, Maria Kay Simms' *The Witches' Circle*, or my own *Inside a Witches' Coven*. Amber's and Maria's books also delve deeply into the art of ritual, the spiritual heart of Pagan worship that should be the first goal of any working coven.

Spellworking for Covens is written from an eclectic Wiccan perspective, but should be adaptable to other traditions since the art of natural magick is a universal practice. Wicca is but one tradition under the Pagan umbrella, and even it has many different subsets. Within Wicca we usually call the groups we form for worship a coven, but there are many other labels a group may give itself. They are synonymous, but may be very different in practice. Other popular names for spiritual groups are circle, sept, touta, tuatha, cîrculo, spiritual family, famtrad, clan, grove, kin group, cove, village, temple, study group, covenant, aquelarre, croî, and hearth friends.

Throughout this book I use Wicca, Witchcraft, and Pagan without much regard to their more precise shades of meaning. Pagan is often used to refer to Earth- or nature-based religions in general, while Witchcraft and Wicca are often used to denote Pagan paths more Anglo-Celtic in orientation. I apologize in advance to those who are offended by this imprecise use of language. I also have chosen to follow the lead of many modern authors who are shunning the use of "he or she" or "him or her," or using the grammatically incorrect "their." Instead I randomly use the feminine and masculine pronouns, and it must be understood that, unless otherwise stated, they have no bearing on which gender may perform a specific action. I have chosen this style as a device to get my point across without cluttering the text, and because I refuse to give in to the endless debate on gender semantics.

Being part of the right Pagan group is a rewarding spiritual experience and, having worked and worshipped both as a solitary and as part of study groups and covens, I can assure you that each path offers rich spiritual blessings and pathways to knowledge and growth. It is my dearest wish for you that magick shall follow each step you take, and that the Lord and Lady of Creation shall illuminate and bless your path back to them.

Covens and Group Magick ♦ 1

1

THE MAGICK OF THE COVEN

High priestess Snow Owl kept her eyes focused on the star-spattered sky as she lowered her arms with deliberate slowness. She could sense the last remnants of the coven's cone of power spiraling into the unseen realms. The spell the group enacted to help heal a rift in their town felt good—successful—and the familiar thrill of excitement from a job well done rippled up and down her spine, igniting the power of each of her chakra centers.

Snow Owl smiled at the other seven faces in the circle, noting their beams of joy. No one had to say a word. She knew they were all feeling the same things as she.

This was the real magick of their coven: their community of love and trust.

Cheers and infectious laughter erupted from the group, and she turned to accept a bear hug from Red Wolf, her high priest.

"Party time!" Greenwood said, flashing his characteristic elfin grin. He uncovered the table laden with potluck snack food as Rain picked up her Irish drum and began beating a lively rhythm, inviting them all to dancing and merriment.

"Hey, Snow Owl, did your little girl get over her flu?" Red Wolf asked.

"She's back in school. The healing spell we did last week helped her so much."

"Blessed be, babe."

"And you? Are you getting along any better with your boss these days?"

"Would you believe she got transferred to another department right after we did that ritual for contentment at the last full moon?"

Snow Owl almost laughed. "You're kidding! That is a good thing, isn't it?"

"Perfect. She's happy and in a job more suited to her personality and—best of all—I don't have to deal with her anymore."

"As it harms none . . ."

". . . do what you will."

Red Wolf grabbed her hand. "Come on, let's dance."

Snow Owl joined in with the seven other coven members in a spiral dance to celebrate the miracle of life, death, and life renewed, and felt their energies meld again as one.

◆　◆　◆

The true magick of any coven is its spirit of community, the sense that the bonds uniting you are ones as close—or closer—than those of family. With your coven, you merge your energies in ways as intimate as those of lovers. You share with them your innermost secrets and desires, you bare your soul in ritual, you cry, laugh, teach, learn, eat, drink, love, trust, worship, and make magick as a single unit.

It is not easy to develop this sense of united community, or group mind, that allows true coven magick to happen. This is why covens tend to keep to themselves. They cherish their privacy and are cautious in the extreme about admitting new members, or even about opening an outer circle for teaching. Unlike churches, synagogues, and the settings of other mainstream religions, covens cannot easily replace members who must move away or whose spiritual needs take them elsewhere.

Unlike the mainstream places of worship, covens rarely get to celebrate centennials. They are formed and disbanded and reformed again as the spiritual needs of those who are a part of them change. This fluid setting for our worship reflects our belief in the eternal cycles of existence as seen in nature, where life, death, and rebirth occur in endless cycles. The same is true of our covens.

No Witch is ever required to become a part of a coven, and many choose not to, even though they may have close bonds to others within the local Pagan community. These people are usually referred to as "solitaries by choice," as opposed to "solitaries by chance," or those who have not or cannot find the right group with whom to merge their spiritual paths.

From my observation of the Craft for the past twenty-plus years, it seems that the majority try working with some kind of group at least once. The lure of a coven is easy to understand. A coven can be a center for our spiritual lives, a focal point for expressing those religious impulses with which we are all born. It can also be the best way for many Wiccans to grow and learn. We all learn in different ways, and solitary book learning and private experimentation does not work for everyone.

Yet when all these reasons are sifted down to their essence, there remains one reason for a coven's existence. We form or join covens for the primary purpose of worship, the goal of which is to bring us closer to the Goddess and the God, whose union created all things, including us. We serve them to the best of our abilities and try to be good children who do them honor. We believe that the God and Goddess are our spiritual parents and, as such, part of their power flows through our spirits, just as part of the DNA of our birth parents flows through our blood. Because they created all things, we believe a part of them exists in all things. We accept that what is in the macrocosm, or universe, is replicated within the microcosm, or within ourselves. With training and practice, we have learned we are able to tap into that creative power within our spirits to perform what we call magick.

MAGICK IS NOT SUPERNATURAL

Spellworking with other Pagans is a bonus to being part of a coven, but it is never its reason for being. All members of a working coven need to be grounded in the magickal basics and have an understanding of how energy flows through the universe in order for spells to work their best. This means taking the romance, but never the mystery, from our perception of magick. Optimally each coven will also have at least one strong leader skilled in the art of magick to help guide the others.

As reflections of the God and Goddess, we accept that we are born with the ability to act as a channel through which creation can manifest. We do this by taking the energies around us and shaping them to our will. We can raise these energies, collect them, magnify them, and direct them by using the will of our spirit. This is not an evil practice, as our detractors have tried to have the world believe. It's no more than using what's available to us in order to invent something new, something that has been done for centuries to create our modern wonders. Besides, how can a divine gift be evil? Magick is just energy that's been raised, collected, magnified, or directed, similar to the way a radio wave is collected, magnified, and directed to manifest as sound. The deities created that energy, so sending out magickal energy is no more evil than sending out a radio wave.

Magick is many things, but it is not supernatural. Think about how nonsensical that word is. Stop right now and really think about it. Put this book down and focus on the word. Break it down and relate it for a moment to all you know about the magickal arts and Witchcraft.

"Supernatural" refers to something that exists contrary to all laws of the universe, including all those of nature, biology, and physics. Therefore, by logic, nothing super-natural can exist. All matter—both the seen and the unseen—acts in accordance with the laws of the universe. Matter has a density, a vibrational rate, a molecular structure, and an essence all its own. We can change it, move it, and shape it, but, as our high-school physics teachers told us, we can neither create nor destroy it.

We may not understand the scientific or natural laws under which everything oper-ates, but we know that those laws must exist and are only waiting to be named, just as those previously mentioned radio waves were once named. When that happens, magick becomes science and its taint of evil is removed. Many Witch burnings of the past no doubt persecuted someone who did no more than accept and work with the natural energies they discovered surrounding them every day. Imagine what would have hap-pened had two German men named Daimler and Benz lived in the fifteenth century instead of the nineteenth. The creation of the internal combustion engine would have been feared, declared a heresy, and two inventors would no doubt have died at the proverbial burning stake for bringing a "tool of Satan" into the world.

Witches know that by taking the energy around us and shaping it to our will, we are acting as what we are by nature: small reflections of the powers in the larger universe. An oft-heard old magickal adage is "As above, so below; as without, so within." To us this means that there is nothing existing anywhere that does not exist within us as well, and nothing we can imagine that cannot be made manifest on some plane of existence.

Sometimes this concept of "As above, so below; as without, so within" is a bothersome point to those from other religions, even when they are sincere in seeking to understand basic Pagan ideology. It stems from the two distinct ways we view deity. Pagans see deity as being indwelling as well as outdwelling, while the Judeo-Christian faiths see deity as transcendent.

A woman from a liberal Christian sect once asked me if I didn't think it was arrogant to believe I had the same power to create as God. In turn, I asked her if she believed she was created in God's image. Of course, she said. Then I asked her if God could create, why couldn't or shouldn't she if she was but a microcosmic version of her God?

She thought about it and, not having a good answer, told me she just felt that magick wasn't something God wanted people to do, even if they had the power to do so.

I explained to her that Witches accept the use of magick as their right, a gift from the deities. It is natural to want to use it when we train ourselves so diligently to sense and move in harmony with the Earth's rhythms. Then I told her my personal feeling was that it was the ultimate sin to take a divine gift and refuse to use it. I explained that I viewed the power to create as a gift that some of us were able to sense and use more easily than others, just like the gift to be a great artist or to have a good head for business or to play the violin. She then asked me how I believed this gift was given to me. I replied that it was given when I was created. It was passed to me the moment I was given life.

She was baffled and began accusing Paganism of believing in predestination. One of the first lessons every Pagan learns is that we are wholly responsible for our actions. I knew I had to find some way to relate this gift at birth to an image that she could understand.

I asked her if she was familiar with any of the more famous vignettes from Michelangelo's famous paintings on the roof of the Vatican's Sistine Chapel. In one panel, known as the Creation of Adam, a host of angels are bearing the Judeo-Christian God toward a waiting Adam, who lies almost lifeless with one limp hand raised, his index finger pointed outward in expectation of receiving the touch of his approaching God. God's arm is also outstretched. Compared to Adam's it is strong, muscular, and pulsating with power. His finger is also outstretched, only inches from Adam's. The idea is that by God's touch Adam will be infused with the creative energy of God and brought fully to life. A part of God—part of the life force of which he is capable of creating and gifting—will be transferred to Adam, his creation and son. And this, I told my friend, was how I saw people as being gifted with the same creative power as the deities.

"The life force of the deities sparks us to life and a part of their power is always within us," I said.

Then she asked me why Witches use herbs and stones and other items to help make their magick if the power to create is within them. I had to admit she asked good questions; better than some from my Craft students. I explained that these items are catalysts that help us focus our energy, and that they also contain specific energies gifted to them from the creator that we can draw from to help make our magick work.

also
Good
Points.

MAGICK AND THE CRAFT AS A RIGHT AND A RESPONSIBILITY

We Wiccans do not question that magick works, and it is that unshakable confidence that has always inspired fear in our detractors. Perhaps this is because they sense that they would abuse any power they had over others, so Witches must seek that as well. It's true that all religions have their loose cannons, and those who crave power for its own sake will always abuse it. It's also true that Witchcraft has some loose cannons, but few of them stay with the Craft for the long haul. In a short time their selfish efforts rebound on them and their power bases crumble. They then move on to the next venue they feel will provide them a platform for their narcissistic desires.

Witchcraft is a religion, and as a religion it is governed by ethics. At its heart is our Rede: *As it harms none, do what you will.* The penalty for violating this ethic is the Three-fold Law: *The energy you send out will return to you threefold.*

The Threefold Law is not a scare tactic like the Christian Hell that is used to keep adherents toeing the line. It is only another reflection of our acceptance of the natural energies surrounding us. We see things occurring in cycles: time, tides, the moon, the seasons, life, death, rebirth. Nothing in the Pagan worldview is ever linear.

In this same manner, we envision the great wheel of existence constantly spinning around the universe. The energy and intent we put onto the wheel goes out from us only as far as the wheel's edge, then it begins its path back to us. The energy we placed on board is shaped and magnified by the will of other energies on that wheel, and has attracted to itself sympathetic energies. In other words, positive energy accrues positive energy, and negative energy accrues negative energy. By the time it comes back to us, we reap what we have sown. This is why Witchcraft is the ultimate religion for the self-responsible. There is no one to blame but ourselves for what returns to us as the result of our magick.

PERFECT LOVE AND PERFECT TRUST

The same woman who asked why I believed I had the power to create like God was finally able to understand—though not accept—my point of view on an individual basis, but then she asked me, "How do you make all that effort to come together to work within a coven?"

Even those who are new to magickal religions have heard the phrase "perfect love and perfect trust." This is the frame of mind in which we are obligated to enter the group's sacred space. By the time a coven is ready to craft spells together, the bonds of trust and love should be well forged.

It's a fantasy—albeit a pleasant one—that perfect love and perfect trust are both present from the beginning of a coven's formation. This is just not possible. Perfect love and perfect trust are not present at the start of any other of life's relationships and, though you may feel an instant kinship and find you "click" with the other group members as soon as you meet, the true bonds of love and trust must be forged with time and with visible commitment to the group's goals. For some covens these bonds develop more quickly than others. For others it never happens as it should, and the group either splits into smaller groups or disbands.

Magick is usually one of the last practices into which a coven ventures because of the love and trust issues, and because there is probably no trickier blending of energy than that which occurs when two or more people are involved in manifesting a magickal goal. Many Witches who will gladly blend their energy with that of strangers in open seasonal rituals will think thrice before doing so in magick, even when working with close friends.

To blend energies successfully within a group you must be able to rely on one another's integrity, good will, honesty, personal efforts, ethics, and their spirit of team unity to not have your goals thwarted or go awry. This is a lot to ask of others, particularly if the goal you seek is a personal one or one that does not affect all members of your group in equal proportion.

STRONG MAGICKAL FOUNDATIONS
EQUALS STRONG COVEN MAGICK

The art of magick has its prerequisite needs and skills, just like any other art. If you want to be a concert pianist, you must first practice scales. If you want to be a surgeon, you must first master high-school biology. If you want to be a good police officer, you must attend the police academy with an open mind, then work with a mentor who has already mastered the necessary skills. Being a competent practitioner of magick is no different.

Magick is not easy. The explosion of interest in the religions of Paganism has produced lots of books on magick and spellwork that are eagerly read by both Pagans and non-Pagans, many of whom are looking for a quick fix to a problem. They mix up a few herbs, chant some words of power, then look to the heavens for the answer to their prayers to rain down upon them. When their desires refuse to manifest, or when they manifest against expectations, newcomers get frustrated and either think magick is a crock, or else start to believe that some secret to magickal success is being withheld from them.

Repeat: Magick is not easy, and it never has been and never will be. Since this book is aimed at intermediate practitioners, this is a statement reiterated for novices reading this book. The only "secret" we have is this: Successful magick is hard work—much more so than many people realize.

This "secret" should not surprise anyone with even a modicum of common sense. If magick were easy, we'd all be rich, beautiful, famous, and cruising the Mediterranean on our private yachts with our perfect mates. You would not be reading this book because you'd already have figured out how to make it all come together by yourself, and you'd be willing into being every whim that hit you faster than Endora on the old *Bewitched* television series.

Magick will not work without a combination of physical, emotional, and mental effort that may need to be enacted over and over again, both within and outside the boundaries of the actual enactment of the spell. Magick is an excellent support for our efforts to create change, but it is not a panacea for all our ills or a wishing well for all our desires. And it never works without expending some serious personal effort on the goal.

The creation of magick becomes both harder and easier within a coven, for reasons to be discussed at length in a later chapter. Yet one fact about coven magick remains paramount: To make even the simplest spell work, everyone in the coven must have some functional knowledge of the basic arts of magick. This does not mean everyone has to be at the same level in their magickal skills. One of the great things about a coven is that those who are skilled in one area can help teach the others, and vice versa. What it does mean is that everyone should be able to demonstrate that they are able to understand, create, and work simple spells using the long-accepted principles that drive natural magick.

This book is written for intermediate-level practitioners and is not a replacement for a good text devoting itself to natural magickal practices. If you are a newcomer to the magickal arts, it is recommended that you seek out at least one—and more are better—of these books and learn and practice all you can. Among the books available right now that teach magickal basics are Amber K's *True Magick*, Doreen Valiente's *Natural Magic*, Marion Weinstein's *Positive Magic*, Raven Grimassi's *Wiccan Magick*, and my own *Making Magick*.

Finding a good teacher or teaching coven can help you progress even faster, but you'll find you have a better chance of being accepted into a teaching coven if you already have a good background in current Pagan literature. If you don't like to read and study, you may want to rethink your desire to be a Witch. This is part of the hard work already mentioned that makes us successful with magick.

MAGICKAL PREREQUISITES

A spell is not a holy object with which you cannot tamper. It is only a blueprint, an outline for creating the reality you want. You can, and should, shape it to suit yourself. This is done by understanding the basic principles that drive a spell to success.

There are several recognized steps to successful spellwork, and there are hundreds of variations on this format. Many long-term practitioners add extra steps of their own. But for all practical purposes, these remain much the same from Witch to Witch, tradition to tradition, and from past to present. Why? Because the structure works, and this is why it has lasted throughout the centuries. Magick does not work like firing off a shotgun, hoping something will splatter onto your target. In magick you get your target in clear sight, aim with a slender arrow at the precise point of your desire, and then release the arrow with practiced care.

The magickal prerequisites are:

1) Having the desire and a real need.
2) Possessing a strong emotional involvement in the desire.
3) Having the knowledge to work the spell and realistic expectations for its outcome.
4) Having the conviction and faith that your spell will work.
5) Knowing how to keep silent about your efforts.
6) Having the willingness to pursue your goal in the physical world, including periodically reenacting the spell if necessary.

With these prerequisites, we come back to our basic belief that all things are cyclical, and what we send out returns to us on that great wheel of existence. Notice how each of these steps makes a full circle, with one feeding off the other and leading into the next. Without a desire born of need, you will not have the necessary emotional involvement. Without emotional involvement, you will have no desire to fuel the spell. Desire without knowledge is useless. Knowledge without faith in your success will only act as a counterspell that will negate your efforts. Keeping silent—a problem in group spells— prevents the loss of power that should be channeled into the spell, and keeps those with a vested interest in your failure from countering your efforts. Working in the physical world makes your efforts present in both the seen and unseen worlds, further driving your desire and heightening your emotional stake in the outcome.

Then the cycle begins again.

DEVELOPING BASIC MAGICKAL SKILLS

Any spell requires you to have basic magickal skills already in some stage of development. As children of the deities, the ability to develop these skills is inborn within all of us. Some of us are more talented in one area than another, but none of the skills are out of reach for anyone willing to put forth the effort to learn them. If someone in your coven is struggling with one or two, have someone else in the group who excels in those areas offer to be a coach.

1) The Skill of Visualization

Visualization seems to cause a lot of problems for those first learning magick. From the mail I get, I sense that novices try to make it harder than it is. Everyone can visualize. Everyone does it all the time. The only skill to develop here is holding the desired image in your mind for long periods of time.

Therefore, visualization is no more than focused imagination. It is the art of "seeing" your goal within your mind as a completed action, something you now have in your life. All magickal envisioning must be done as if the goal has already been achieved. The image is empowered by your desire. The energy of your desire helps you make it real on the planes of existence where our thoughtforms come alive. Enough energy creates a density for your vision that makes it so heavy that it slips into the material world intact. That may be an oversimplified explanation, but it's one most newcomers can understand.

Visualizations take on the character of the person creating them. Someone very visual will see her goal as a mental movie in which she is the star. Others see a series of still-life images, sort of like looking through a photo album, or they focus on one image that they feel sums up the essence of the desire. Aural-oriented people hear things others will say to them when their magick manifests, and empaths will sense what the goal feels like to themselves and others. Some people combine several of these techniques. They are all correct.

Which one works best for you? You might consider what runs through your mind when you daydream. Do you see things or hear things? Do you get flashes of images or whole movies playing before your mind's eye? Or you might try thinking about how you visualize a project given to you by a teacher or boss. How do you imagine yourself achieving the goal? How do you imagine yourself having finished the goal? This should give you an idea of how you naturally visualize. Start with that process until you feel good about it before trying another process or becoming frustrated. The human mind is easily bored, and you will have to force it to focus on one thing at a time until it's disciplined enough to conform to your will.

Visualization is the skill on which your most intense efforts should center. No spell or ritual will ever be its best without good visualization skills. They are vital. Don't skimp on the process of perfecting it to the best of your ability.

2) The Art of Centering and Balancing

These are the twin skills that allow you to pull all your energies and all surrounding energies deep within yourself. Once you have them captured, you can mold them to your will and send them back out into the universe as an empowered version of your magickal desire.

Balancing and centering must be accomplished on both the emotional and physical levels. You must be in balance and harmony with the energies around you before you can mold them to your will and bring them back into your life in the shape you choose. This is one of the primary reasons why magick doesn't work as a panacea for all our problems. In contrast to what your high-school science teacher told you, opposites *do not* attract in magick. In magick, like energy attracts like energy. They unite and magnify themselves. This is why we never step into magick without centering and balancing first. When either our inner- or our outer-world is in disorder, or we are upset or angry, our energies are scattered, and this only brings back to us more disorder, so that we are in worse shape than when we began.

Learn to ground and center by experimenting with visualizations of yourself as a large tree. Know your roots and feel your branches. This is a popular visualization exercise that works wonders when you feel scattered and out of balance.

3) The Art of Raising and Sending Energy

In a group setting, the raising and sending of energy takes on a different format and feel than when one works alone, and this will be discussed in depth in the next chapter. For now, simply understand that this skill means you have the ability to build up those energies you've collected. As you collect them, you infuse them with your magickal will. Visualization plays a large role in this process. When the energy feels it has reached a peak, you must have the skill to send it out, directed toward the goal.

Remember the "As above, so below; as within, so without" adage? You want your will to be projected into all worlds, and the unseen worlds are places where thought is action and where all magick first takes shape. You will want to direct your sent energy into these worlds so that you can build on them and pull them into the physical world, where you want them.

4) Charging, Enchanting, and Empowering Magickal Catalysts

Inanimate objects and magickal tools contain no power in and of themselves, though they will collect your magickal energies over time. These items are chosen to assist us in magick because they share affinities or sympathetic energies with our magickal goals. Some catalysts have a history of use in specific types of magick, such as lavender in love spells, frankincense in spells for exorcism, and double-edged blades for casting ritual circles.

Energy directed to your goal may be channeled through those catalysts, but you are the source of the power that drives the spell. You take that energy from many sources. You take some from yourself, but even more from the Earth, the heavens, and the deities. You use the catalyst to help support and direct your will.

5) The Ability to Alter Your Consciousness

This is the art of being able to change the focus of your mind, to slow its pattern of energy so that it connects you to all other worlds and beings. You do this naturally when you concentrate, read, watch television, or sleep. In magick you learn to control it at will. In this respect it is much the same as learning to visualize. You must attain the skill of holding one image in your mind for a long period of time.

Entire books have been written on the art of meditation, which is no more than a sustained altered state of consciousness that is under your control. This is not mysterious or difficult. In fact, trying too hard to alter your consciousness can do more harm than good. You don't have to force yourself into an altered state when you read or watch television. Use the same process for learning to meditate. Relax and focus your mind on one idea or object and, when you feel a sensation similar to that when daydreaming, your consciousness is altered. Don't become frustrated when your mind wanders. That happens to all of us sometimes. Just bring it back to where you want it and keep it there as long as possible.

Regular meditative practice, or studying with a book of meditation exercises, will allow you to go deeper and reach further each time you try. There are four levels of consciousness, as defined by the measurement of brain waves during each level. Your normal waking consciousness is called beta. The daydream, reading, and television-watching level is alpha. In this state you often retain a dual awareness of the worlds you are in. On one hand, you will be fully absorbed in your magickal vision, but you may retain awareness of where your physical body is and what is happening around it, too.

Anyone who can achieve an alpha level can work magick with success. So keep in mind as you practice that if you can focus on a book or movie, you ought to be able to focus on your magick.

The next slowest level is theta, a level associated with deep sleep and Zen-master meditation. Many advanced magickal people work exclusively in this level and produce excellent magick. They are usually skilled at astral projection and psychic healing. Just know that it is not required that you regularly reach this level to be a magickal success.

The slowest level is delta. This is a level of very deep sleep, or even unconsciousness, which is not part of most magickal practices.

6) The Skill of Grounding

Grounding is often overlooked as a magickal skill, yet it is as necessary as any of the others if you want to be successful and not have otherworldly trouble spilling over into your everyday life. Remember that magick is about the control of energies. Grounding allows you to take unused or excess energy and send it harmlessly back into Mother Earth, where it can be used again when needed.

Failure to ground yourself after magick or ritual will allow excess energy to frazzle you or, worse still, will allow you to become a portal from the astral world for all sorts of odd creatures and energies that you will just have to banish back to the astral later. They are not harmful but their presence can be disturbing, and they will suck up any energy they can in order to stay alive.

Like most newcomers, I had to learn a few things the hard way, including the fact that grounding was important. I had this "creature" who became attracted to my ungrounded energy and would follow me around the house and even watch me sleep. I didn't sense anything malevolent—it just seemed curious about this unfamiliar world it was in, and the person with the interesting energy that had given it a portal to this world. It loved my vacuum cleaner and would follow right at my back as I cleaned my house. That was the breaking point for me, and I banished it back to its own realm—and have never forgotten to ground after magick or ritual since.

Grounding is both a mental and physical action. If you are a beginner in magick, you should ground by visualizing the energy in you flowing out through your palms or feet as you place them on the ground or floor. Later on, your visualization skills and your will alone will direct the energy out of you, if you'd rather not actually touch the ground for any reason.

CREATING AND USING WORDS OF POWER

Creating and using words of power is not a specific step in magick. It fits in with both the visualization and with the charging and empowering steps. Words of power support your visualization by stating your goal in concrete terms. They also spark life into your visualization.

The idea that there are ancient and secret words of power that work all on their own has caused them to take on a mysterious shroud over time. Many nonmagickal people believe this, as is exemplified in their fear of uttering the name of a demon three times in a row for fear it will appear. In the Judaic mystic text known as the Zohar, this belief is codified in the myth that God created the universe by uttering the Torah, or first five books of the Bible, as one single word, thus bringing all things into being. Enochian magick teaches that vibrational recitation of the proper names of angelic beings makes them immediately manifest, and many superstitious Christians will not speak any of the names given to their antigod Satan for fear they will evoke his presence.

The truth is that most words of power just aren't that powerful on their own unless they support your goal and work to help keep your mind focused and your desire in sight. To be fair, there are few ancient doggerals we utter in magick, but most words of power we use for spellworking—the successful ones, at least—are created each time they are needed so they best fit the goal.

Words of power are often written in rhymes or are sometimes set to music. The reason for this is twofold. First of all, rhymes are easier to remember than straight prose. Second, they give a rhythmic quality similar to chanting that helps feed power into your magick by allowing your mind to slow into those alpha levels in which your mind becomes receptive and better able to communicate with other areas of itself and with beings from other worlds.

Words should be chosen carefully for both the images they evoke in your mind and what they ask to be made manifest. Now here's one of those magickal secrets that anyone who has been practicing magick for a while already knows: You should be clear and precise without dictating to the universe how it is to do its job. This is a tricky line to walk without losing your balance. You must also make sure your words do not violate anyone's free will or cause harm, yet you must be clear in what you want in order to avoid a magickal mix-up that gets you what you asked for but not exactly what you wanted.

Divinations are invaluable at this point in a spell's creation. They help you discover any hidden negative aspects. Divination for group situations is often done as a group and the outcome discussed at length before the spell is enacted. Your coven needs at least one person with intermediate-level skills in at least one divination art to help you prepare your spells. These can be learned through books or classes given at occult shops where these items are sold. After that it's a matter of practice and developing your magickal intuition. Popular divination methods include tarot cards, rune stones, augury, I Ching, Wiccan wand casting, and dream magick.

It should be noted that spells do not require words of power to work, but in coven settings they are almost always a part of the magick because it helps keep everyone focused on the spell and in the precise place within the power-raising process everyone's mind should be. It can be a great feat of diplomacy to construct words of power upon which everyone in a group agrees and that are void of harmful side effects. A good leader can guide you through this maze to successful spellworking as a working coven. In the end, everyone should be happy with the words, or the one who isn't could take power away from the spell, even without intending to do so.

SPELL FAILURE

Often I'm asked what went wrong when a spell is perceived as having failed. The first thing I ask is if it really has failed. This is as simple as taking a good look at what you asked for and seeing how it may be manifesting. For instance, if you tried to manifest a new car and received a toy model, then you got what you asked for, regardless of what you expected.

Like any energy, magickal energy flows through the path of least resistance. If you give it an easy route to its end, then that's the path it will take. This is why it is important not to take just any spell you find in a book or get from someone else as a piece of rare porcelain to be protected and kept in its original state. Spells are scattered energies brought to unity and directed to their goal by our willpower and our precise need. They work best when modified to meet your specific need and situation. In the example of the new car spell, it might have included lines about needing reliable transportation to and from work, or to help get you in and out of town to assist with the care of a sick relative on weekends. Doing so would have taken the car from the toy ideal to that of a mode of human transportation.

Spells fail for only two reasons:

1) Because not enough energy and effort were put into the spell in the first place (including not making the goal clear), or

2) Because there is a stronger opposing force to your spell.

The opposing force does not have to be magickal in nature. It can be no more than the will of an individual to maintain the right of free choice. You can redesign a spell to overcome the first impediment; the second impediment usually cannot be overcome. Sometimes the free will of an individual cannot be broken, no matter to what length you're willing to succumb to the temptation of negative magick. To stand strong in the face of your magick and not succumb to it is that other person's right, and to continue to interfere with it will only rebound on you in unpleasant ways later on.

You must also have realistic expectations about what magick can and cannot do for you, and you must have enough common sense to know when magick is not needed. I once received a letter from a young woman who asked me for a spell to change her eye color. She insisted that this desire was no whim, but was something she'd thought about for a long time. The first problem with this is that no spell alone can permanently alter physical appearance. There are spells known as glamouries that can create a temporary illusion, but it would not realistically extend to one's eye color. The other problem is that the magick to make this change already exists in the physical world in the "magick" of tinted contact lenses. The only logical way to make this goal a reality was to spend the money and effort to be fitted with the tinted contacts.

In keeping with the natural laws of the universe, magick will not make you fly, but it can help you find the money to take a plane trip or assist your learning to astral project or soul travel. Magick will not force someone famous that you've never met to fall in love with you without ever meeting you, though it can call attention to you in positive ways and create a fertile garden in which love can grow. Magick will not make you smarter, taller, more witty, more popular, et cetera, but it can temporarily project these images of you to others. It can also enhance what gifts you do possess and give you the self-confidence to overcome physical or emotional barriers to these goals.

IS COVEN MAGICK WORTH THE EFFORT?

With the magickal blessing of perfect love and perfect trust built by your prior association, spellworking can take on a potent new meaning and offer the lives of everyone in the group a chance to achieve their fondest dreams and desires.

Sharing needs and desires within a family-like setting is a rare treat in life, one not to be missed if this is the setting in which you wish to worship and work your magick. There will be times when you will have to compromise, bite your tongue, or give up getting your own way, but the others will all have their turns feeling this way too. For most of us who are or who have been a part of a good coven, the outcome is always worth the effort.

2

Raising and Sending Energy As a Group

The keen eyes of high priest Red Wolf met those of his high priestess, Snow Owl. He saw the otherworldly twinkle in them that let him know she was connected to powers far beyond her own body. His well-developed priestly intuition sensed the coven was ready to begin the power-raising ritual. Red Wolf took a deep breath to make sure he was centered, ready to perform the power-raising ritual that would conclude the coven's spell and send their collective will into the universe.

His right arm arced in a graceful swing over his left as he grabbed the left hand of the person to his own left in the circle next to him. In a loud, clear voice he yelled out loud, "The fever breaks."

The swift, firm movement of his hand made it clear to all that he was not only passing along the force of his words, but his personal and raised energy as well. The circle of power was starting to take shape.

Standing next to him, Moondancer felt that power enter her arm. Following his lead, she swept her right arm over her left to grab the hand of the next person in the circle. In the same clear voice as Red Wolf, she cried, "The headache flees."

Around the circle the hands linked with hands as the power was passed, each person contributing their personal energy and healing energy to the spell.

"The ears are clear."

"The stomach is soothed."

"The pain is gone."

The energy passed through the members of the coven in rapid succession, soon returning to Red Wolf.

As soon as he felt the energy he had sent out return to his left hand with the full weight of the group will behind it, he sent it around again, confident that they could build the energy even higher.

'Round and 'round the circle the healing magick swirled, gathering momentum and strength. Red Wolf could actually hear it, like a low electrical hum in the background, as the healing chant they'd prepared was started by Snow Owl. He murmured the chant along with the others while their collective energy spun overhead like an inverted cyclone. It was coming to a peak soon. He could sense it, and his stomach clenched in an anticipation that was almost sexual.

Snow Owl's voice grew louder and faster, and he knew it was about time to send out the magick. He watched with his inner eyes as the circle of healing energy spiraled around them, humming its own song, seeming anxious to be on its way.

"By our will, so mote it be!" he shouted above the roar of the chant.

Moving as one, each coven member turned 180 degrees to the right. Turning under their own right arms, they faced outward and, with their turning, released the spiral of energy they had created.

Red Wolf felt himself go limp as the force of the group will left them. Then he smiled. Windwalker's child would be healed. The group will had been perfect. The spell would succeed.

◆ ◆ ◆

HOW DO YOU KNOW WHEN YOUR COVEN IS READY FOR MAGICK?

Even though it's been stated that this is a book aimed at the advanced beginner to intermediate-level practitioner, it's not realistic to assume that all members of a single coven will be at the same magickal skill level at the same time. Not all coven members will ever excel at every magickal art, though all can become proficient at each one with guidance and practice.

This is one of the great advantages of working magick within a coven. The art that one member is skilled at and another is not provides you with a willing and trusted teacher available to help you learn all you can. At various times all members of the group will be teachers and all will be students. You may be the group's best tarot reader, the one they turn to for divinations before spells are cast. You may be the most skilled seer, the one who can gaze into the balefire and see the prophetic visions others miss. You may be the coven's faery charmer, the one who can connect with the spirits of the land and garner their assistance. You may be the animal totem advisor, the one who instinctively knows which animal spirit to call upon to assist with a problem and how best to ask for that animal's help.

Over time, a good coven finds it has someone to cover all its needs. Even more important, it will have a leader or leaders wise enough to know when to let coven members use their special skills to do what needs to be done for the sake of the group. This is a theme you will hear repeated often throughout this book. A coven is not the place for a big ego to show off. It is a place for a balance of talents, cooperation, and reciprocity. Only in this harmonious environment will a spiritual community be built in which magick flourishes for everyone.

There is some contention within the Pagan community about what constitutes beginner, intermediate, and advanced levels within the Craft. Much of this ruckus has to do with people not realizing that we all have different talents and that none of us will be advanced practitioners of all the arts, no matter how long or hard we try.

For example, in my book *Astral Projection for Beginners*, I wrote that remote healing via astral projection, or out-of-body or consciousness projection, is considered a more advanced skill. A few weeks later I received an angry letter from a reader who wanted to know where I got the idea this was an advanced art since she'd been doing it naturally since she was a teenager.

Point made!

I receive many letters and e-mails from other readers frustrated because they cannot astral project, no matter which method they work with or how hard they try. The idea that they could appear at someone's bedside in astral form and assist in a healing is beyond their imagination. I hope the writer of the angry letter has learned how blessed she is to have been given two special gifts: the skill of a healer and a facility for astral travel. For many others these are not easy tasks.

There are almost as many ways to work and worship together as there are covens. The Old Religions, such as Witchcraft, have had to adapt to fit the needs of each generation of practitioners in order to remain accessible and of value. If they did not, then they would have died out centuries ago, forgotten at worst or, at best, remembered as some primitive faith long ago abandoned in favor of things that worked better.

If you find your group is not working precisely as outlined in this or any other book on coven practice, or as prescribed by any other coven with whom you are friendly, don't worry about it. Don't waste time trying to assess who is right and who is wrong. If the ritual and the magick are positive and the spells are working, then the practices are fine just as they are, and they do not need or deserve anyone's value judgments.

It is fine to have magickal beginners in your coven as long as you have more experienced members to balance and guide the energy of the group. Still, it is better that a beginner who wants to work magick within your coven must be past the "I'm so over-awed 'cause everything is new" stage. Otherwise they will be of little assistance in making your group magick work. A raw recruit could even hinder your efforts. You don't want a weak link in your circle of energy siphoning off the power you're trying to build simply because they have not developed the skill to sense and pass along the energy within the circle. All six of the prerequisites for successful magick are important, and everyone in your coven should be able to demonstrate that they can work with each at at least a basic level if magick is to be performed. This means everyone should be able to perform these prerequisites with at least a rudimentary skill level and possess an understanding of the concepts behind magickal operations and why they are important to the overall magickal working.

An intermediate-level practitioner has usually been studying the Craft for at least a year and a day and undergone some form of formal initiation into the Craft, though some initiates will progress faster in their studies than others. They will be able to enact, talk about, demonstrate, or understand most of the items on the list below. They may excel at some to an advanced level, and may know little about another, but it will be clear to the coven that the time they have spent within the Craft studying has been put to good use.

Intermediate-Level Craft Skills

1) Understands and can perform all of the six magickal prerequisites: Having the desire and a real need; possessing a strong emotional involvement in the desire; having the knowledge to work the spell and realistic expectations for its outcome; having the conviction and faith that your spell will work; knowing how to keep silent about your efforts; and having the willingness to pursue

your goal in the physical world, including periodically reenacting the spell if necessary.

2) Understands what magick is, what it can and cannot do, and adheres to an ethical standard in its enactment.

3) Has developed an interest in at least one form of divination and has achieved a skill level beyond basic in its performance. This can be tarot reading, rune casting, augury, star gazing, fire scrying, stone casting, crystal gazing, or any other form of divination.

4) Has a solid sense of the properties of the four elements of earth, air, fire, and water, and how they relate to magick and to magickal catalysts.

5) Has an interest in and knowledge of Craft history, and can accept differing viewpoints without feeling threatened.

6) Has developed a personal relationship with the God and Goddess and feels comfortable calling upon them during ritual or prayer.

7) Understands how different cultures have influenced magick, Paganism, and its various traditions, and has developed an interest in learning about at least one of them and its pantheon in depth.

8) Contributes to the group's efforts to raise and send energy and appears to be developing a sense for knowing at what level that energy is working at in any given moment.

9) Displays a greater interest in the advancement of the group than of herself, and is both proud of her developed skills and humbled by them.

10) Demonstrates an understanding that there will always be more lessons to learn and skills to develop, no matter how far one goes in the Craft.

11) Understands why groups have leaders, whether they are the same leaders each time or those roles are rotated or shared with all.

12) Understands the nature and purpose of ritual and works well with the group in seasonal or lunar rituals.

13) Shows promise in at least one magickal skill. There are hundreds of these: kitchen witchery, astral projection, guided meditation, spirit contact, magickal herbalism, stone magick, power raising, divination, candle magick, weather witchery, et cetera.

14) Clearly loves the Craft and tries to embrace the lifestyle it prescribes.

For the purposes of coven spellworking, your own coven may waive certain standards if it has large numbers of advanced members, or it may set other standards in addition to, or in place of, those on this list. This may be especially true if you are part of a teaching coven that has a large number of very new Witches coming into the circle on a frequent basis. It is each coven's right to decide when a new member is ready to join in the more advanced workings, or if they should even be allowed to be present while they are being enacted. No one should feel slighted by this decision. This is just a way of protecting the group's hard-won knowledge, secret rituals, and magickal energy. Those of you who are new to the coven will come to appreciate that decision once you've attained greater skills and are working with the coven on a regular basis.

The rest of this chapter will discuss the advantages and disadvantages of group magick, and offer practical exercises to help your coven develop its ability to raise and send energy together.

WHERE DOES MAGICKAL ENERGY COME FROM?

Those six magickal prerequisites each have their advantages and disadvantages within a group setting. The one that could ultimately cause coven magick to stumble is the raising and sending of energy step. No matter how well the group mind is honed, if you are unclear or untaught in raising and sending the magickal energy your group raises, it will come to nothing.

Before your coven attempts magick of any kind, it is wise to begin having everyone work both together and in small groups to learn to raise energy, shape it, and send it. This not only builds a necessary magickal skill, but it strengthens the bonds of love and trust and boosts the confidence level of each member of the group as they realize their energy is important to the desired end result.

Magickal energy comes from two sources:

1) The Witch doing the spell, and
2) the environment where the Witch is doing the spell.

The environment provides the major energy source, but the Witch provides the direction in which it flows, and controls that with her personal energy.

Important

Did I hear a big "huh"?

All matter vibrates. It has an energy all its own. The rate of its vibration comes from the movement of the molecules that make up the object and determines its solidity and how much it is or is not able to merge with other objects. For example, water molecules are not tightly bonded. They are fluid and can blend with most other substances. You can drop an object into the water and, depending on how porous the object is, the two can blend or even merge into a new substance. On the other hand, a desk made of wood has a slower vibrational rate. Its molecules have a tight bond and an object placed onto the desk will not sink into the desk itself, nor will part of the desk seep into the object. Without hammers and other major efforts, the two will not blend.

This is why various catalysts have an affinity for different types of magick. The vibrational rate of water makes it a good catalyst for magick involving blending and fluidity, while wood—governed by the element of earth—is a good catalyst for magick involving stability and safety. We can use these catalysts to help us focus on our magickal goal and to draw energy from them to empower that goal.

Human beings also have vibrational rates; some would say we have a physical one, which is determined by the density of our physical bodies, and a spiritual one, determined by the character of our souls. Through power-raising rituals, such as dancing or drumming, we can cause these molecules on both levels of our being to speed up to the same level and blend. This creates a smooth pathway for energy to flow through us, making our magickal will the path of least resistance.

In order not to deplete our personal energy stores, we must also learn to draw energy from other sources to support and feed our own magickal energy needs. Think of it like charging a good battery. You know there's a certain amount of energy potential stored within the battery, but you also know that it's not unlimited. Repeatedly using the battery alone will eventually drain it of its power. You will do better to support that battery with some other source of power to keep it strong, so it will not conk out on you just when you need it most.

The two most popular methods for drawing in outside energy are: one, to draw it up from Mother Earth below us, or two, to draw it down from the sky above us. Both of these sources represent to our subconscious and superconscious minds the infinite realm of the divine and the unseen worlds. To do either of these effectively we must use visualization to drive our magickal will.

Crown
(just above the head)

Third Eye
(between and just above
the eyes)

Throat
(center of the hollow
of the throat)

Heart Center
(middle of the breastbone)

Solar Plexus
(center of the solar plexus)

Navel
(just below the navel)

Root
(at the base of the tailbone)

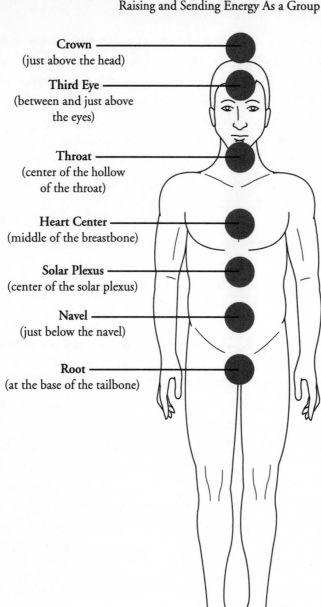

Chakras of the Human Body

As you stand in your circle, imagine that from the root chakra—or energy center at the end of your tailbone—there is a channel that extends down deep into the womb of the Earth from which you can draw up her energy. Visualize it moving up the channel and into your body, filling all levels of your being with an electric charge of vibrant, moving energy that you can shape to your will. Participants can envision this as coming from the heart of the Earth's core, from the Mother Goddess of the Earth, or from the element of earth. Whatever mental imagery works to get the energy up to the participants is all that's important at this point. Experimentation with other forms of visualization can come later.

You can also picture the same channel going up into the infinite universe above you. This can be envisioned as coming from the deities of the otherworld, the element of air or water, from the sky or planets, the wind, the collective unconscious made up of all thoughts of all people, or from the infinite power of the universe itself. Again, whatever mental imagery works for now is the method each person in your coven should use to draw in that energy to help boost their own.

Another popular energy exercise combines both the above and below imagery. Almost every coven uses it at some point. To do this you must imagine yourself as the trunk of a great tree. With your arms extending into the heaven and your roots deep into Mother Earth, you become the mythical world tree, the center point of all time and space, which is exactly what you are when you're inside the sacred space of your coven's circle. Your branches above reach into the infinite heavens. Reflected below you, in perfect reflection of what is above you, is your intricate root system reaching deep into the heart of Mother Earth. In this way you can draw energy from both above and below. This can feel more balanced to some than merely drawing from one direction. A tree is also an object to which everyone can relate. Sometimes this makes the tree visualization easier for newcomers to the Craft than the more abstract idea of channels reaching into worlds that have been unknown before.

More abstract energies can be drawn from the deities you invite to your circle or through the energies set in motion via dance, drumming, or music. Your coven, and each individual member, will find the balance that works best for themselves and for the group as a whole.

SENSING AND USING EACH OTHER'S ENERGY

Before you can shape the energy of many parts into one part, you must first develop a feel and appreciation for the components that will make up the whole when the coven begins making magick together. One of the best ways to develop a sense of your group's energy, and to help train those still struggling with the process, is to borrow an exercise from the American Kennel Club's Utility Dog Level Obedience Trials. This exercise involves having a dog pick out an object that has been handled by its owner using scent discrimination. For your coven it will involve having individuals select an object that has been handled by all members of the group using energy discrimination.

No barking allowed!

For this experiment, you will need about a half-dozen identical small objects. It is best if they are made of a natural material, such as wood, since natural objects absorb and hold our energies easier than synthetics. Select one member to turn his back while all the other members of the group handle one of the objects. Each person should place as much personal energy into the object as possible. The object should then be placed randomly back among the others. The person whose back is turned must then turn around and, using his magickal senses, pick out the object containing the group's energy.

Allow the person doing this experiment to use whatever method works best for him. No one way of sensing energy is better than another. We all have our own magickal talents and skills and we must work to develop them as they are given to us. Some practitioners will hold their palms down a few inches above the objects to feel their energy, similar to someone warming their hands over a flame. Others will need to hold each object to get a sense of who has been handling it. Still others will want to place that object against a chakra or energy center of their own bodies, such as the forehead or solar plexus, to get a sense of its energy. One or two people in your group may be highly skilled in spirit vision and will actually be able to see the group energy emanating from the correct object by using a meditative technique and gazing at the objects through soft focus.

When you have the next person turn her back, be sure to pick up the exact same object to handle as you did for the first person, or the energies on the objects will begin to get confusing and the experiment will grow harder instead of easier with each attempt.

The ones who went first may want to try again at this point, especially if they did not do well the first time, since the accumulated energy on the object will be stronger now than it was when you began the experiment.

DIRECTING ENERGY AS A GROUP

For this exercise you will need to divide your coven in groups of two. Have partners sit on the floor facing one another. Shoes, socks, gloves, or anything else covering the hands or feet should be removed. Partners should position themselves so the soles of their feet are touching. Then have them lean forward and place their palms together, with fingers pointing up. Emphasize that it is less important to have the fingers in contact than it is to have the whole palm in contact. This is where your energy will be sent and received.

Direct all participants to visualize drawing up energy deep from within the Earth beneath them. If they are unsure how to visualize this, have them see it coming from the core of the Earth—the womb of the Earth Goddess—and have them mentally pull it in through the root chakra at the base of the tailbone, as they did in the previous energy-raising exercises.

It is important that the partners not be allowed to speak to one another at this point. You want them to learn how to sense the flow of energy between them, not to tell each other what they are or are not doing. They may make eye contact to get a sense of how their experiment is progressing, but no verbal cues are permitted.

Tell the partners not to try to send or receive any energy just yet, but to only prepare to do so. Direct them to allow the energy they have drawn in to fill their spines, then work its way throughout their bodies, filling them to capacity. They should hold the drawn-up energy within themselves, blending what they've drawn in with their own innate magickal energies. Instruct them to feel this as a ball of potential energy at the center of their being. When you have a sense that everyone has done this, you may start the main part of the experiment.

Tell the partners that, when they are ready, they should begin to will the energy they have taken into themselves to move between them. They are not to speak or gesture to indicate which direction it will be moving, but should begin to move their energy though one person's palm and into the other's, where it will pass through them and come out their palm and into the first person's. It does not matter if the partners begin directing energy in a clockwise or counterclockwise motion. Allow each group of partners to find their own way. The look on their faces will tell you when they have found their balance and can feel the energy flow between them.

Some newcomers to magick worry about making any type of counterclockwise motion, and perceive it as the direction of negative magick. The group's leader should put this idea to rest as soon as possible because it is just not true. Both directions have their uses in positive magick. In general, a clockwise motion is used for magickal goals to gain or increase something, and a counterclockwise motion is usually used for magick to lose or decrease something. Only the goal of the spell determines whether that magick is positive or negative in nature. Energy is energy. We are the ones who shape its character. Remember: The Craft is the ultimate path for the self-responsible.

After the partners have had a chance to work with this energy for a while, have them take turns changing the direction of the energy flow at random to see if they can sense when the other person is making a change in the flow.

When you can see they have gained proficiency in this area, make it even harder. Have them try to keep track of two separate energy flows: one through the palms and another through the feet, or use palms and feet. The feet seem to be less sensitive than the hands at sensing magickal energy, and will really test the partners' sense of energy flow. You can even have those two flows—hands and feet, or left hand and foot and right hand and foot—going at the same time, or going in two different directions when your partners gain skill.

Another variation on this theme is to have the partners stand back-to-back with their feet apart and heels touching. Have them turn their hands backwards and place their palms together. Without the advantage of eye contact and facial expression, it becomes harder to sense the flow and counterflow of energy, but this is a great exercise to help develop the magickal senses.

As your group gains skills, have them change partners. Then have them move into larger groups, such as groups of three or four, depending on the size of your coven.

Eventually you will want to practice these exercises with your entire coven. When working with these exercises as a coven, one of your leaders should select an individual to direct the energy. The group may speak or make comments if they wish to as the director of the energy sends it first one way and then another. Everyone should get a turn and you should keep working with this until you have all developed your energy-direction skills to a high level.

TRADITIONAL POWER-RAISING TECHNIQUES

When crafting magick by yourself, often called working as a solitary practitioner, it is common to use chanting, dancing, or drumming as a power-raising catalyst. These techniques are also used in group settings to help raise and shape the energy surrounding us.

A chant is a rhyming couplet or quatrain recited over and over in rhythm. It is best if it is written out beforehand by the group and memorized. Spontaneous chants don't always meet the group need unless they are drawn from a collection of chants the group uses on a regular basis. This is common within covens who have been together for a long time. If this is the case, then having someone start a spontaneous chant during a power-raising exercise works well.

The chant may either strengthen the goal of the spell, enhance the garnering and sending of energy, or both. This is another reason why generic chants, like generic spells found in books such as these, are best if tweaked by those who will use them. It personalizes them to the situation in which they are needed.

Magickal goals have changed little since humanity first discovered its ability to use energy to help shape reality. Common magickal goals include:

Love and romance

Lust and passion

Mental prowess

Employment

Money

Healing

Comfort and consolation

Justice

Truth and divination

Warding and protection

Psychic self-defense

Giving blessings

Overcoming obstacles

Faery and elemental contact

Invisibility or high visibility

Working with animal or plant totems

Otherworld journeys

Gaining knowledge

Viewing past lives

Fertility

Eco-magick

Peace and tranquility

Sleep and dreams

Creativity and inspiration

Psychic enhancement

Spirituality

Beauty and appearance

Balance and harmony

Communication

Connection with elementals

Spirit contact

Astral projection

Self-transformation

Friendship

Binding

Courage and strength

Victory and success

Abundance and prosperity

Your group's chant may include one of these needs. An example of a chanted couplet that would include a goal—in this case, the goal of friendship—within its power-raising words might sound something like the following.

Friendship binds us closer still,

We raise the cone to work our will.

Drumming and dancing often work together to raise energy for magick and ritual. If you don't have anyone in your group who is skilled with percussion instruments, you can purchase drumming music to be played during your spells. Drumming need not be done with a drum. Hand out castanets, rattles, bells, et cetera, and allow your group to build its own rhythms as you dance.

I once attended a Pagan gathering at a small coffeehouse in a nearby city. After a few hours of watching people stay in their own groups and not mingle, the organizers handed out some rhythm instruments and the drumming began. Suddenly everyone in the room was on their feet, even the shy people, and we began dancing in a clockwise circle around the room. A young woman lit a white candle and placed it at the center of the dancing circle. In our minds this was the balefire, the center of the universe, the presence of the divine. I have no idea how long the group danced together. It may have been one hour or four. In the heightened state of ecstasy brought about by circle work, time has no meaning. We danced to celebrate the deities and our coming together as their children, and they rewarded our efforts with joy and fellowship.

While dancing to raise or shape energy, the members of your coven should be visualizing culling energy from the environment and blending it with their own, which in turn is being blended with that of everyone else. Often the dance takes the form of a spiral, mimicking the DNA molecules that are the building blocks of life.

The use of spiral imagery in magick far predates humanity's knowledge of DNA. Cave paintings from thousands of years ago and coven dances from the early twentieth century all employed spiral images. Spirals are featured in the artwork of the Celts, the Saxons, the Norse, the Aryans, the Asians, the Polynesians, and the Aborigines, and has been depicted as the snake emerging from the egg of creation that sparks all life.

Allow your drumming and dancing to be creative and to fit the needs of your group and its magickal goal. Drumming may start slow and gain in speed as the energy starts to peak. The dance may be led by one person, or everyone may be free to do their own thing, or you may want to move in a circle or spiral.

THE HAND-OVER-HAND ENERGY GENERATOR

The hand-over-hand method of passing energy is depicted in the scene opening this chapter, and will be used in spells in the Grimoire section of this book. I have believed in the power of the hand-over-hand method of passing energy since childhood, when two separate events hinted to me of its power. An experiment in my elementary school science class showed me that when one person was hooked to an energy generator and held the hand of the person next to them, then that energy would pass rapidly through the group. It would flow through everyone and back to its source so long as the connection of everyone present remained unbroken. Then, in a brief experiment with Girl Scouts, the symbolism of hand-over-hand was used as a method for projecting the group energy outward at the meeting's end. The combination of these two experiences has served me well in group magick ever since.

Which hand or hands are used can make a difference to the feel of the energy flow. The right is considered the direction of projected energy and the left is considered the direction of receptive energy. In other words, it is traditional to send energy from your right side and receive it from the left, though for those who are left-handed, the opposite often works better. Whether you are right-handed or left-handed, these standard directional ideas should be kept in mind for your initial experiments. Of course, if you are standing in a circle facing outward to begin with, all these guidelines are opposite. And they are ONLY guidelines. They can be adapted as your skills increase or your needs change.

You may wish to first experiment with just holding hands as you stand in a circle and practice getting the feel of sending energy in both directions. Try this both facing into the circle and facing outward. Each has its own feel that may be useful later in a particular spell or ritual.

When you are ready for the hand-over-hand method, have everyone stand in the circle facing inward. Have everyone cross their arms in front of themselves, with the right arm over the left. Everyone's right hand should be grasping the left hand of the person to their left. Now allow energy to flow through the right hand and into the left of the person to the left, who will in turn send it through their own right hand into the left of the next person, and so on. The right hand should be visualized as passing along drawn-in energy and the left hand should be perceived as receiving it.

If using hand-over-hand seems too confusing, go back to simply holding hands, facing each other, before going back to the hand-over-hand method. The only advantage of the crossed arms in this case is to facilitate the image of sending out the energy when the group turns out. It does not affect the passing of the energy from person to person.

Do the turn out when you're ready to send out raised magickal energy. To do this, everyone must turn in unison. At the cue of the leader, and without letting go of each other, have everyone raise their right arms and pass their heads underneath. Turn 180 degrees until you're all facing out of the circle, still holding hands. Raise them skyward while still clasped and feel the energy flow from you toward its goal.

THE CHILD'S PLAY VERBAL POWER-RAISER

Many youth groups play a game where one person says a word, then another repeats it and adds a word of their own. This is usually done rhythmically so that the person who breaks the rhythm must step out of the circle. A similar exercise works well to build group energy and, later on, will assist in the development of the group mind, since word association is revealing of the psychological state in which the group is functioning.

To do this, you should all sit comfortably in a circle facing one another. Start a steady rhythm of four beats per measure by slapping your thighs with your hands on count one, clapping your hands on count two, snapping your left fingers on count three, and snapping your right fingers on count four. The rhythm will be:

Slap, clap, snap (left), snap (right).

Slap, clap, snap (left), snap (right).

Slap, clap, snap (left), snap (right).

Et cetera . . .

Have the leader begin on count four by saying a single word, preferably the name of one of the four elements: earth, air, fire, or water. The person on his left will repeat that word on count three and add a word of her own on count four. The third person in the circle will repeat person two's word on count three and add a word of his own on the fourth count. Words may be repeated, and you'll find the words circle back to the same elements over and over.

This exercise reveals how your group thinks about magick and about which elements relate to what type of magick through the keywords they trigger in everyone's minds. This is how a simple game can both build energy and help develop the group mind. Notice that the spoken words always come on counts three and four, or the snaps.

A typical round might start out something like the following.

Slap, clap, snap, "water."

Slap, clap, "water," "cold."

Slap, clap, "cold," "dark."

Slap, clap, "dark," "night."

Slap, clap, "night," "moon."

Slap, clap, "moon," "dreams."

Slap, clap, "dreams," "visions."

Slap, clap, "visions," "prophecy."

Slap, clap, "prophecy," "understanding."

Slap, clap, "understanding," "peace."

Slap, clap, "peace," "goddess."

Et cetera . . .

SENDING MAGICKAL ENERGY AS A GROUP

As the energy the group draws in and magnifies reaches a peak, it is often conceptualized as a cone rising over the circle. This is called the cone of power. Some people have hypothesized that this is the origin of the pointed hat often depicted on the heads of wizards and Witches. Though the cone is a popular image, and one to which novices can relate, this is not the only way to picture raised energy. Some people prefer to see it as a spiral or inverted cyclone rising over their group, or as a swirling mass moving in a circle around them.

This is where a coven leader skilled in magick is invaluable. Someone has to be in charge of sensing where the magickal energy is moving and when it has reached its peak. It must be directed outward toward its goal by everyone at the same time, and that requires doing it at someone's cue. If everyone were to siphon it off as they felt it best, it would weaken the overall effect, like punching holes in a fire hose would weaken the final stream that must fight the fire.

A leader skilled in sensing and sending magickal energy can feel when the magick has reached its peak and, by prearranged signal, let the other members of the group know that it is time to send it out. At this point all members should send out the energy with the visualization or physical gesture they feel best represents the sending of energy for them. The hand-over-hand method is one of the exceptions to this "do your own thing" rule, since everyone has to make the same physical motion to send out the energy, but all sending out of energy must still be backed up with clear visualization and intent of will.

Individuals may see that energy projecting from their arms or chests, or rising above the group and taking off like an inverted tornado. Some people let their arms fly upward, other fall to the ground as the energy leaves their bodies. Some shout, some wail, some droop. No way is right or wrong.

The leader should also keep an eye on everyone after the energy is sent. People should feel energized and in tune with one another. Someone who seems depleted or withdrawn may have been using too much of their personal energy and not drawing in enough from other sources. This is not a good magickal skill and will not add to the group effort over time. That person will need some individual attention to help him or her learn how to use what nature has provided for making magick.

These exercises, experiments, and games should not be seen as a chore, but should be a fun way for your coven to develop both individual and group magickal skills. As you grow together as a spiritual family, you will find many uses for these games in ritual and magick, and they will both be stronger for your efforts.

3

Group Magick and the Group Mind

Windwalker had been speaking for a long time, but high priestess Snow Owl resisted looking at her watch. She knew it was growing late, but it was important that everyone have the chance to say what was on their minds. At least now she was getting a sense that the group was coming closer to an agreement on the format and method for enacting the spell to help Oakman find a new job.

No one was arguing that the layoff was in any way Oakman's fault, or that he had not been working diligently with his own spells and backing them up in the physical world by sending out résumés and going on job interview after job interview. So far, he'd had no luck. Now he was turning to his coven for help.

"We must word the spell so that the right job for Oakman comes along, taking away nothing that was intended for someone else," Windwalker insisted before passing along to Moondancer the feathered talisman that allowed its possessor to address the group uninterrupted.

"And that no one loses a job just to make one for him," Moondancer added. "And I think that's all I have to add at this time."

No one else reached for the feathered talisman.

Snow Owl almost sighed out loud. "Okay. To recap, are we all in agreement that the spell will take place on Sunday near the full moon, and that we will use candles and coins as catalysts? And that the words of power will be crafted to take nothing away from anyone else?"

The coven nodded with enthusiasm, as anxious to finish the details as Snow Owl.

"Good. Now who would like to write out the words of power for us, and then who wants to do the divination to make sure that we are okay in terms of 'harm none'?"

Storm Willow raised her hand. "I'll do a tarot reading, but I'd rather not write the words of power."

"I'll do the words right now," Greenwood volunteered. "Then we can all at least agree on a rough draft before I go any further."

"I'll help," Rain offered.

"And I'll cast the runes after Storm's tarot reading to see what details I get," Red Wolf offered.

Snow Owl continued to discuss fine points of the spell with the others while Rain and Greenwood put their heads together over the words of power. Several times they interrupted the group to ask about a single phrase or mental image. The input everyone gave was excellent, and Snow Owl knew that they would have a terrific spell when they were done.

As they continued to hone the specifics of the spell as a group, Snow Owl could sense their minds were merging into a single unit with a single purpose. She was sure Oakman would have a job—one he really liked—before the next lunar cycle ended.

◆   ◆   ◆

After covens learn to raise energy as a single unit, the next step is to develop a sense of group mind that allows the energy to be directed successfully to a cohesive magickal goal. Successful group magick requires that all members of the group participate in the creation and execution of the spell; to that end, they must achieve a sense of singular purpose that forces their collective will to function as one when enacting the magick.

The prerequisites for successful magick, as discussed in the two previous chapters, have advantages and disadvantages within group settings. Many of the problem areas can be overcome over time as the bonds between individual members grow stronger. Other issues must be worked through as a group for each and every spell done, and with the full cooperation and input of each member.

When people think of coven magick they immediately assume that any spell worked by a group is automatically enhanced because of the number of people putting energy into its outcome. In one way, this is true. More people sharing one vision means stronger magick. However, it only takes one person in the group who does not share the group vision, or who feels anger or resentment toward the spell, or feels he was not allowed to give his full input, to slow or even block the magickal efforts of the rest of the coven.

Presumably everyone in your coven is part of the group because you trust one another and have not been afraid to blend your energies in worship and ritual. It can also be assumed that the perfect love we seek in our working partners is growing as the group continues to work and worship together. If this is the case, and there have been few issues arising that have been difficult to resolve, then you should be able as a group to come to consensus on the way the prerequisites for successful magick will be handled in any given spell.

Consensus is a term often misunderstood. It is not a democratic process in which the vote of a majority dictates with a tyrannical hand the course of events. This causes nothing but resentment in the minority, and will only cause your magick to backfire and your group to fragment. In a coven, everyone is of equal importance and their proposed ideas, unless manipulative or negative in nature, should be given a try at some point. Consensus means that you talk yourselves into agreement, perhaps with contingencies. It can be a time-consuming process, but one that is vital to both the casting of successful spells and to the future of your coven. For example, if you use someone's preferred spell-casting method this time, you'll use another's the next time. Or if one set of words of power don't manifest results within one lunar month, you'll try the set that the minority likes best. Sometimes one person will have a vehement dislike for a word, image, or method about which everyone else is enthused. This does not mean that the majority should try to sway the lone hold-out, but that give and take are offered so that the dissenter feels able to put the full strength of her efforts behind the spell.

Through consensus everyone's way gets to be "the way" at some point, and this allows everyone to feel they are an integral part of the group's efforts. It also creates good will between members, strengthens your bonds and sense of group mind, allows everyone to feel their ideas and thoughts are important to everyone else, heightens that all-important sense of love and trust, and makes everyone more willing to put their full magickal effort into each spell.

PREREQUISITE I: DESIRE AND NEED

Desires are as personal and individual as our dreams. Desires are not always needs, though the one desiring them might think otherwise. Does everyone enacting a spell have to have the same level of desire for the goal in order for the spell to be successful?

No. This is an unrealistic expectation.

What is necessary for success is for everyone to desire the one who has the goal to be successful and to see that desire as a need of some kind for that person. We must all get into the spirit of the spell and want what our fellow coven member wants for himself, then throw the full weight of our collective magickal will into its execution, just as we would a spell for our own desire.

This mutual concern for each other's desires is part of the familial relationship that should develop in a good coven. We shouldn't be in a coven if we don't care about the happiness of our fellow members. This does not mean we have the right to judge their desires beyond deciding if the spell requested is one that is negative or harmful to others. A desire that will clearly cause harm to someone else is not one any group should be asked to back. We must see the desires of our fellow members as steps on their own path through life; a path that is between that person and her deities, and is not for us to alter. For instance, a coven is a family, but no one is a parent to anyone else, and we do not have the right to say, "You know, Oakman, I know you think you want this really badly, but I don't think it's the best thing for you, so even though there is no harm in this spell, I won't be part of it for your own good."

As your coven begins its discussions toward consensus, keep these points in mind. Write out these "cans" and "can'ts" on a big piece of posterboard and place it where everyone can see it if you have to, but your discussion must be limited to the spell's ethics and mechanics. None of us has the right to judge the suitability of a goal desired by someone else. We all must make our own mistakes and learn for ourselves what it is we want and don't want, and what will make us truly happy in the end. Certainly if you have doubts, you might remind the petitioner of the old adage, "Be careful what you wish for, since you just might get it." But that is where your input should end. A coven with a condescending attitude toward its members is doomed from the start. If you're in one . . . run!

As mentioned before, all it takes is one jealousy or one resentment to cause a counter energy that could lessen the effects of the spell or prevent it from manifesting altogether. That jealous person might not realize on a conscious level that her feelings are at odds with the group goal, but even without a concerted effort at a counterspell, the energy can be thwarted.

This is why talking out *everything* when the spell is in its planning stage is a crucial extra step in the prerequisites for magick when working with a group. It's up to the person or persons with the desire to convince the others that theirs is a goal of which they are deserving and that is worthy of group time and energy. It is up to the group to decide if the spell might be harmful to others and to help hone it into a format that everyone can agree will work.

Keep in mind that resentment comes in many forms. For instance, say you need a new car to get to work because bus service is being discontinued in your town, but another member of the coven has been having constant maintenance problems with his car. This could cause resentment, even if the owner of the car in constant need of repair has not asked the group for help. Another example is if someone wants the group to do a healing spell to help a relative with a serious disease, but your group was unable to assist another coven member's relative with the same illness. Even when an unsuccessful result is in no way the fault of the coven, a later success with the same spell could still cause someone to feel resentment, even if that someone is aware that his feelings are unreasonable.

No one is proud of having these negative feelings. We tend to deny them, but as humans we all fall prey to them, even within an environment of love and trust. It can be hard to watch someone else—even someone we love—get what has always eluded us.

If you have a desire and need that you are sure might not be appreciated by someone else within the group, then you may be better off to keep this to yourself and work toward it on your own. Giving up the energy of seven other people is worth it if you feel the eighth will not be able to overcome her resentment toward your goal. If you feel you can trust your high priest or priestess, you may wish to discuss your feelings with them in confidence to see how they feel your request will be accepted before making your request to the entire group.

PREREQUISITE 2: STRONG EMOTIONAL INVOLVEMENT

It can be difficult to get others to feel the same emotional connection to a spell being enacted for the benefit of only one or two people. This is why spells that benefit the entire group, or a goal the entire group holds dear, work best in coven settings. This is often the only way to whip up the requisite strong emotional tie to the outcome.

Emotion is the driving force behind any spell, which is why spells worked in anger are always a bad idea. That whirlwind of feeling gives a potent boost to your magick, but may also push you over the edge into the world of negative spellwork, which will rebound on you in unpleasant ways later. It places a negative emotion on that great wheel of life that will eventually return to you threefold.

The anger someone feels, whether it is a righteous anger or one fueled by resentment toward the goal of someone else's desire, is an emotion that must be kept out of the circle. The sacred space of your coven's circle magnifies energies, and as you build the energies of the magick you are working, you will also build the anger and resentment. It doesn't take a high priestess to understand how dangerous enhancing these emotions are for both the spell and for the welfare of the group. All negative emotions must be worked out, grounded, or dealt with before stepping into sacred space. This is another aspect of the self-responsibility each Witch must accept for herself and for the coven in which she works and worships.

If you are the person for whom the spell is to be worked, explain as best you can to the group the emotional involvement you have. Try to inspire the others with your words. Weave a magickal net like the storytellers of old in order to garner an emotional response. Not only will this place others in sympathy with you, but you will help them gain the emotional stake in your need necessary for them to feed your goal with their finest magickal energy.

The greatest emotional distance comes when you are trying to work magick for someone who is not within your circle. For example, if your great-aunt Sarah has asked you to do a spell to help heal her rheumatism, it can be difficult to garner the proper emotional connection if no one else in the group has even met Sarah. For this reason, some covens have strict rules about if and how often they will perform magick for anyone not part of the coven. Exceptions are usually made for sick children or difficulties with significant others, but most of the time a coven will not take magickal requests from the outside. Doing so opens you to a barrage of requests from people who can't seem to solve their problems on their own, and don't really want to try. Soon you will be doing nothing but magickal requests for others. This will drain your energy reserves and take away from the worship and ritual that is your purpose for being in the first place.

PREREQUISITE 3: THE KNOWLEDGE TO WORK THE SPELL

Knowledge is an arena where group work can have its biggest advantage. We all have our individual talents and strengths, and this is as true in our magickal lives as in any other aspect of ourselves. Some Witches are skilled herbalists; others have an affinity for candle magick. Some are born healers; others can astral project with ease. Some read tarot intuitively and can make the cards work magick; others can connect with animal or plant totems to find solutions to problems.

Take advantage of everyone's skills to put together the best group spell you can craft. If you are unskilled, unknowledgeable, or unfamiliar with a specific area of magick, or unused to working with a specific catalyst, you may find that the suggestions of someone who is gifted in this arena to be both effective for your magick and a great learning opportunity for everyone.

Be fair about sharing your skills, too. Don't hesitate to offer suggestions or help to another coven member for whose goal you may have a great catalyst and with which you can offer a great boost of energy. Support your fellow coven members like you would family, and be willing to close ranks in each other's defense when necessary.

Groups seem more willing than the solitary practitioner to experiment with new magickal or ritual formats or to work with unusual or unfamiliar catalysts. Perhaps this is because we feel if the others think it might be worth a try to see how it works, then maybe it just might be so. As with any type of group, we tend to go along with the majority when new ideas are suggested, so long as they don't violate the rights of another. This is similar to the peer pressure that often gets young people in trouble when their group leaders are not mature enough to come up with positive ways to pass leisure time.

When you're talking out the mechanics of your spell, don't feel you cannot or should not suggest an unusual format or catalyst. If it feels right to one person, it might feel right to others, and you will all gain in knowledge from the outcome of the spell.

PREREQUISITE 4: CONVICTION THAT THE SPELL WILL WORK

In the four-step prerequisite often taught by longtime practitioners of the Craft, this is the step "to dare," as in:

To will, to know, to dare, and to keep silent.

We must have the confidence to dare the universe with our desires, almost taunting it to not comply with our goals. Practitioners of magick have long known that what the mind is convinced is real becomes our reality. Without delving into an esoteric discourse on the nature of reality—which can be as entertaining as it is maddening—please know that no spell works if you doubt its outcome.

Faith is another word for this conviction, and there is not a religion on Earth that has not taught its followers that true faith is rare but, even in small amounts, it will make anything you desire become your reality. The most famous of these teachings comes to us through Christianity, whose savior-God Jesus told his followers that if you have faith no greater than the size of a tiny mustard seed, you can move mountains. Another example comes from the early twentieth-century writings of Englishman Sir James M. Barrie, who in his children's classic *Peter Pan* (1904) tells us that to save the faeries, such as Peter's faery friend Tinkerbell, we must demonstrate our belief in them, otherwise they will perish.

It helps most of us to back up our convictions with words of power and an intense visualization that we can fall back on when our confidence in the spell's outcome starts to waver. These two elements are always constructed in the present tense, as if the goal were a current reality. We don't want words and imagery always phrased as tomorrow's reality. That only keeps them locked in a tomorrow that never arrives.

PREREQUISITE 5: KEEPING SILENT

Of all the prerequisites for magick, this one presents the greatest problem in group magick. To work successful spellwork as a group, you must have lots of discussion about goals, needs, methods, catalysts, formats, words, and so on. Gaining consensus on each point is tricky and there is always the real threat that someone will not agree with the spell's goal or with the method through which the group will achieve the desire.

This also brings us back to the idea of resentment. One person who has a stake in seeing the spell not succeed can slow it, harm it, or even stop it from manifesting. The person who is blocking the effort may not even realize how he feels, which is why all aspects of a spell must be talked out in advance to the point of consensus. In this way, everyone is involved and can work through their problems with the spell before any magick is attempted.

Group magick can be strong. If you want group help, you have to open up and share your needs with the group in an atmosphere of love and trust. When someone feels there is something wrong with doing the spell—usually an ethical concern—you should not take it personally. Later on in this chapter we will discuss ways to work through these inner-group difficulties.

No matter how much or how often you discuss magick or personal issues about magick with your coven, the coven's magick should never be discussed with anyone outside of the coven. This means never, and it means with no one else. No exceptions. Most covens consider discussing magickal operations—or other coven issues—with others to be grounds for banishment. That's how important it is to keep the power from being harmed or drained away.

PREREQUISITE 6: WILLINGNESS TO PURSUE THE GOAL IN ALL WORLDS

Unless you're working a spell that is a personal goal for all members of the coven, then it is up to the person for whom the magick has been enacted to back up the magick with effort in the physical world. For example, Oakman will never find that new job he really likes if he hides in his living room waiting for a job to come to him. Windwalker's child will not heal without the help of a doctor, and Stormwillow will not find her perfect mate by hiding out at home, waiting for him to ride up to her house on his white horse and knock on her door. With the power of magick behind them, all these people will find their search for their desires more fruitful, but they must still search. Magick opens the door, but the magician must have the courage to step through it and seek out the new reality.

Spells sometimes need to be reworked to keep their energy going until it manifests. If the spell is being done by an entire coven for the benefit of one person, that's a significant outlay of time and effort. Please be sure that the primary beneficiary is doing her part before putting more energy into a need.

DEALING WITH THE PERSON IN CONSTANT CRISIS

What do you do if Oakman doesn't seem to be putting forth any effort on his own to find that job he claims to need? What if before the job crisis he had one problem after another with his personal relationships that he kept asking the coven to fix? What if you had to also find him a place to live? What if his next request is your help in finding a new car to drive to the job interviews he so rarely attempts? What if after that he needs money to pay the rent, and help with medical bills, and then some healing spells for a distant cousin? What if after the healings he needs help with his next girlfriend and her medical problems and her bills?

Vampires are real. They exist as surely as you and I. Oh, not the blood-drinking, Dracula kind that are the staple of bad horror films, but energy vampires who suck the life essence from any group of which they are a part, draining its resources with their incessant needs for problems that never go away. These vampires are attracted to strong sources of energy like Dracula to a blood bank. You find them not only in covens, but in churches and synagogues, community outreach programs, in the halls of social service providers, and their names are well-known to those who work on crisis hotlines.

Vampires always have some pressing problem that everyone else must solve. They never tire of expounding on all the details of each issue, even when it is clear that there is no longer a willing ear to listen. Talking to them about commonsense self-help measures makes no impression. Their arguments for their woes are not logical. They take no responsibility for their situation and there is no way to fight their conviction that they are somehow targeted by the cosmos to have a bad life. They cannot see, and will never see, that most of their problems are of their own making, and that simple lifestyle changes would solve the majority of their problems. Most irritating of all is that there is usually a "pity poor me" undertone to their whining that soon grates on the nerves of the group as if the whiner were running his fingernails over a blackboard, creating an energy drain on your group as effective as a black hole. If you keep working with this person, soon everyone's energy will be sucked into a void and there will be nothing left for anyone else—not even the deities, whose worship and honor should be your primary goal.

When you recognize this destructive pattern in someone in your group, you must stop offering magickal help immediately or this person will drain you all dry. Explain to the person that the group cannot at this time devote any more resources to the personal problems of one individual. That's not harsh. It's just tough love.

These vampires have lived their entire lives in crisis. In spite of all protests to the contrary, they enjoy their problems. They revel in them. They create them both consciously and subconsciously. Their problems bring them attention and fill a void in their otherwise empty lives. It quickly becomes clear to the coven that these vampires will never make any effort to create a better life for themselves, but they will let you and everyone else in their lives pour vast amounts of time and effort into trying to do it for them.

So what do you do with this poor creature? Do you banish this person from your coven? Not necessarily. If this person is interested in the religion you practice, he will stay even after the steady supply of energy is cut off. Be aware that this person feeds off your energy input and, like an addict, he will redouble efforts to get you to provide the fix. If you really care about this person, you must resist listening to the bitching and moaning, hard as it may be, and you must not offer any sympathy or magickal help. Cut off the energy supply now. If the person is sincere about practicing with you in a spiritual setting, his magickal requests will lessen, but chances are the vampire will move on to a more fertile feeding ground.

DEALING WITH DISSENTERS
WITHOUT DESTROYING YOUR COVEN

What happens when one or more members of your group feel the spell you want to do is unethical, or if they find themselves dissenters for other reasons, such as they feel the problem under discussion should best be handled through nonmagickal means or by the individual who is making the request?

You must decide as a group how to handle the problem when you first come together so that you have a plan for coming to consensus on sticky issues that will not destroy what is otherwise a solid working coven. Do you leave someone out of what is usually a group event in order to do a spell the others want to do? Do you allow someone to volunteer to abstain from a spell? Do you ask the one who wants the magick to do the spell on his own? Do you try nonmagickal means first?

Like vampires, covens may also attract those individuals with contrary personalities who can wreak just as much havoc and prevent anything positive from ever being enacted by keeping every issue that arises in an eternal, interminable discussion phase. The psychology of these perpetual dissenters eludes most of us. Perhaps they are trying to take over the leadership role. Perhaps they just aren't advanced enough to discuss magick in any greater depth and are trying to hide that fact. Perhaps they just enjoy creating discord, or being the center of attention, or pretending to know more than everyone else, or perhaps they don't want to see anyone else have something they do not. Whatever the reason, the constant dissenter must be brought under control or your coven will never get any work done.

The first course of action must be to decide if the dissenter is a valuable member of the coven. If he contributes on a regular basis and, in general, has a good relationship with everyone, then banishment from the group should not be a consideration. In fact, banishment should always be the last consideration for even the most serious infraction of coven trust. In this case it might be best if the group as a whole challenges him to come up with concrete reasons for his dissent, not just vague "it feels wrong" comments.

The problem becomes harder to handle if your constant dissenter has caused nothing but discord among coven members since he became part of the group. In this case one of the leaders should have a friendly discussion with him about his constant dissent. He may have a good reason for it, such as a concern that all magick suggested may harm someone. In that case, you can explain that this issue is dealt with in all spells and his input is welcome. If he can't identify a good reason, then you have the right to tell him that he is hindering the coven's efforts at magick and that he needs to rethink why he is part of your group. Make it clear that he is valuable to you and is still wanted as part of the group, but that you feel he slows or blocks your goals. In counseling anyone on any issue it is always wise to point out someone's strengths and good points before bringing up the issue that is the sticky point. This softens the blow and lets the person being talked with know that they have made valued contributions and that they are not being personally attacked.

If the dissenter becomes defensive or angry during the discussion, then he will probably move on to another group; if not, then he may not have realized how frequent or vociferous his dissenting comments were, and how much they were holding back the group.

The occasional dissenter is most often sincere in her concerns, and she most often voices them about an ethical issue. If this is the issue, you might see if there is a way to reword or rework the spell to overcome the problem area. An evening spent in reworking the spell and doing some intense divinations can usually overcome this problem. It's traditional to do divinations before enacting a planned spell anyway, just to make sure there are no hidden repercussions. Allow several members to give input. Among your ranks, you probably have a skilled tarot reader, rune caster, augury master, dream enchanter, or fire scryer. All these methods can work together to give you a full picture of the spell's strengths, weaknesses, and current probable outcome. Best of all, it will start a positive discussion of the issues raised by your dissenter.

Talk out the problems you've identified after each round of divination and see if you can move any closer to consensus. If not, you must choose the path that is best for the group as a whole.

Sometimes the best path is not to do the spell as a group, and the one making the request should not take this as a personal slight if she is committed to the best interests of the coven. Sometimes a coven just is unable to agree on the ethics or mechanics of a spell, and in this case it's best to ask the person making the request to handle the issue on her own. Certainly those who want to may send good wishes and energy that person's way, but it's never a good idea for other coven members to volunteer to assist the petitioner in person. This will only cause a schism in your group later on, when the giving of help is discovered. And don't think it won't be. Doing things behind your coven's collective back is like trying to have an affair with your boss's spouse. Someone, somewhere, somehow will have her binoculars turned on you at the worst possible moment.

The answer to a lack of consensus that cannot be overcome should never be offering one person abstinence from the group as a whole while the rest continue on with the spell. Never leave anyone out of any major coven event. That only stirs up the same feelings of inadequacy and hurt you felt when you were picked last when teams were chosen in elementary school gym class. It stings and only makes the dissenter want to get even for the pain he feels.

Magick is not what your coven exists to do. Keep your priorities in order and try not to take group decisions personally. You can always go home and work magick on your own if the spell means that much to you, but you must not try to force it on an unwilling group. There's no room for petty bickering. Your spiritual family is at stake. No matter how you want the decision to turn out, try not to whine about it or, worse, make accusations or threats. The integrity of the group is more important than any magickal need. Keep focused on what's most important.

HELPING DISCUSSIONS FLOW

Many groups find their open discussions are productive and easy to work through without any arguments or issues that cannot be handled in a mature manner. Some groups who find they have trouble making their discussions productive or cannot keep them from becoming shouting matches have borrowed an idea from Native American councils. They use a "talking stick." This is an object that allows the person holding it to speak without interruption until he passes it along to the next person who wishes to be heard.

Your talking stick can be a wand, a branch, or even a bowl taken from your kitchen. It doesn't matter what it is as long as all members recognize that possession of it means a speaker may talk uninterrupted until she gives it away.

The rules are simple:

1) Your talking stick can be any object you choose.

2) One of the leaders starts the discussion, then passes the talking stick on to the next person.

3) No one may interrupt someone who holds the stick.

4) If anyone has a question for the speaker, it may not be asked until the speaker is ready to pass along the stick. No interruption of the speaker is allowed until the question is answered. At that time another can be asked, if needed.

5) Anyone may reach for the talking stick to make a point or add to the discussion, but only *after* the stick has first made one full round of the circle so that everyone has a chance to have some initial input.

6) The leader or leaders should be aware of any attempt by the group to keep someone else out of the discussion.

7) The leader has the right to take back the talking stick if an argument ensues. The leader must then pass it back to the combatants so that they may continue to work out their issues in a more productive manner.

8) Grabbing for the talking stick, or wrenching it out of someone else's grasp, should not be tolerated. Make that person wait an extra turn to have the stick back to reinforce that this is not an acceptable use of this device.

9) The discussion is ended only when the talking stick is passed once more around the circle and everyone has said they have nothing more to add to the issue at hand.

Not every coven will need to use a talking stick, and not all will need to use one every time they discuss a spell, ritual, or other issue. It is still good practice to have one nearby just in case it is needed.

CENTERING AND BALANCING AS A GROUP

Coven spellworking takes place inside sacred space. No one should ever come into that space with emotional, psychic, physical, or mental turmoil. That's a broad statement, and one that often seems impossible to achieve when each passing year of life both scars and blesses us with new baggage to carry through each day of our lives. This is why many books on basic Pagan practice talk at length about preparing to enter the circle.

Often a ritual bath, anointing, private meditation, or some other type of purification ritual is prescribed for individuals. Once coven members reach the ritual site, often referred to as a covenstead if the group meets in the same place every time, there will be time for meditation so that everyone can get in the proper frame of mind. Sometimes this is done as individuals, other times someone will lead a group meditation that culminates in a visualization of the desired outcome of the spell or ritual about to be undertaken. Sometimes this time is given over to everyone holding hands while quietly gazing into a fire or lake.

Whatever form this premagickal or preritual balancing takes, its goal is to begin removing us from the worries of the everyday world so that we can better connect with the energies we hope to raise and direct. We must enter in a harmonious state of mind. As mentioned earlier, all energy is magnified within the sacred space of the coven's circle, and any anger, resentment, jealousy, worry, hatred, prejudice, fear, or other negative emotions will be magnified as well. These can turn a simple ritual into chaos if even one person does not let these feelings go before stepping into the sacred space.

Most covens begin any gathering with a ritual that opens their sacred space, also called casting their circle. Ritual is one of the first exercises most groups undertake, and it is integral to Pagan worship practices. Some of the basics of this art will be discussed in the next chapter, but if you do not yet understand basic ritual, then you need to back up and start to learn and practice this basic art before you leap into magick. One thing at a time. Ritual before magick. Practice before performance.

Also keep in mind that, in many ways, ritual is magick. If magick is defined as change in accordance with will, then ritual, which changes the mind-frame of its participants, is also a magickal operation. Ritual is basic magick. Don't skimp on learning it well.

As soon as the coven gathers to cast their circle, the magick begins. As the elements and their associated directional energies are called upon, and the deities are invited to be present, the group mind starts to form around the planned spell. It's usually at this point where the more experienced members of a coven will know if the working will be successful or not, for they can feel the group mind emerging and the group energy already blending. They will know if there's a blockage even if they are not sure who is the cause. It cannot be hidden forever . . . especially not from Witches trained in the art of sensing and seeing energy patterns.

GROUP VISUALIZATION AND WORDS OF POWER

Learning to visualize magickal goals as a group is easier than it sounds. Naturally, the closer you have grown as a group and the more love and trust you've built, the better your efforts will be.

Much of how you visualize will depend upon your group conception of the desired outcome. This conceptualization will have been developed in your discussions when the ritual or spell was being planned, and will influence your words and mental images.

If you're still somewhat new to magick, it is important to keep in mind that we always visualize magick the same way we create words of power. They are always set in the present tense as if the goal is a fact in the here and now. To see it as something in the future will keep it in the future, always just out of reach of today. Your coven's leader(s) will no doubt remind you of this as the spell is being planned and the details pinned in place.

If you find you have trouble keeping your words of power in the present tense, and want to slip into future-tense phrases such as "will be" or "shall be," then think through your visualizations first. One of the reasons words of power accompany visualization is that visualization, like a mind movie, has an immediacy that is almost always in the present tense. If we make our words conform to this, then they will strengthen and feed off each other. It is a lot easier to write words of power in the present tense if you are simply describing what you see in your head rather than trying to see in your head the words you've already written.

Words are also more concrete to our conscious minds than images, and words put into firm form our nebulous desires. Spells without words often wander in the subconscious not fully formed because we have not given a concrete image for it to form around. These words allow us to give life to our visions without dictating to the universe how our desires should manifest. Words and their accompanying visions will often determine if the spell is harmful or not. Adding a line about "with harm to none" or "as it benefits all" can make a big difference in the end.

Let no one tell you that words have no value to the subconscious mind. Certainly symbolic language, such as imagery and pictures, are an easier way to communicate to the subconscious, but words have great power in any culture because they are part of that culture's first language. Single words conjure up images that create symbolic images in the subconscious. In magick or ritual, when the subconscious is open to the conscious and superconscious minds, the image becomes a catalyst for your goal.

For example, think of a few simple nouns and see what comes to mind: Door. Star. Moon. Peace. Fire.

A door is a portal that allows us to move between worlds. A star is far away, but hot and bright and part of the universe, usually symbolic of the goal we strive to reach. The moon is the light of the night sky, representing the Goddess and the psychic. Peace means different things to all of us, but we all know it as a calm sense of contentment and rest. Fire is heat and light, movement and transformation, and it has the power to destroy, create, or transform.

Words are as symbolic as pictures and they are a fuel source for power in our magick, whether we want them to be or not. Craft them with care.

CHOOSING AND EMPOWERING YOUR CATALYSTS

The method you choose for your spell will be determined by three considerations.

1) The magickal skills of your individual members.
2) The affinities and governing elements of your goal.
3) The availability of catalysts and their ease of use where your coven will be working.

This means that if you have people skilled in kitchen witchery or herbal magick, you use these methods more often than not. You usually use water for dream magick and candles for spells of transformation, and you don't put off an important spell because you do not have a certain ingredient. You learn to understand the energies of catalysts and you find a substitute.

There are hundreds of suitable substitutes for almost any catalyst, and practicing magick on a regular basis will help you learn to spot these. And whether you have chosen a wand, blade, herb, stone, kitchen recipe, metal, gemstone, candle, bowl of water, salt, food, or any other item for a catalyst, it must be empowered to its goal. This is an area few people seem to have trouble with when practicing magick alone. As a group it seems to create difficulties, and it shouldn't.

Just as each person in the group participates in the creation of the spell, each person should assist in empowering its catalysts. This helps each person make an energy connection to the catalyst when it is time to draw upon that object or objects to assist in your magick. It may not be pretty to pass around a bowl of dirt for each member of the group to handle or place against their body while they add their will to the mix, but it is a necessary step. One or two people cannot adequately prepare a catalyst that all of you will be using and have it work as well as you'd like.

You also need to choose how many catalysts you will have. For example, if you will be using candle magick, will you have a candle for each person present or will you use only one? Will everyone bring their own magickal tools—such as wands and athames or ritual knives—to use in the spell, or does the group have one set everyone uses? If you're making a talisman, will everyone make one or will there be one for the whole group? All these decisions affect how the spell is enacted, how members interact with and empower the catalyst, and how their energy will flow to and from the catalysts during the working of the spell. No single way is right or wrong but some methods work best for some covens and other methods work best for others.

Another point to keep in mind is that the more different types of catalysts you have present, the harder it is for the less-experienced member to connect with their energies and meanings. This can weaken your efforts. If everyone is using their own candle, then it's easy for a beginner to focus on their own, but if you have candles, charm bags, several herbs, three or four stones, and two tree branches, the beginner is not yet intuitively in tune enough with their symbolism to keep connected to all these energies at once.

Unless you have a coven made up of very advanced magicians, in which case you're probably not reading this book, then simpler is better.

GROUNDING IN A GROUP SETTING

As mentioned in chapter 1, grounding is the last action performed during the act of magick or ritual, one that is often overlooked as unnecessary until someone grows in knowledge and understanding of energy manipulation and finds that not taking this last step can cause problems. In a group setting it can be overlooked even more easily because everyone is excited about the working that just took place and gets busy talking or eating and does not take the time to let go of the excess.

Even group leaders sometimes forget to direct everyone to ground themselves, especially if dancing and drumming continue afterward, and the energy that clings to you is needed to feed your physical self. Hold on to that energy as long as you like, but once the circle is opened, everyone should be encouraged to ground before leaving the sacred area. If your group leaders tend to forget, then appoint someone who has a good memory and seems to have a strong need to ground after magick or ritual to remind everyone.

No my
Name is
DAN.
No

4

Coven Magick and Ritual

Red Wolf felt the power of the ritual rise around them, engulfing their circle in a cloak of golden blue flames. He listened as Stormwillow called upon the energies of the west and water, and felt the watery softness of those powers wash over him and fill their circle with their blessings.

One by one, each of the elements was evoked: north and earth, east and air, and south and fire. Red Wolf felt a sense of wholeness of being as the full circle of the elements was completed and Snow Owl connected them with her call to the powers of spirit that united them.

He stepped forward to begin the spell they had prepared for the evening. "We are gathered in this sacred place, which is not a place yet is all places, at this time, which is no time and yet is all times, to raise a spell of fertility for Rain and Greenwood. They are the God and Goddess incarnate, and we shall open the pathway to the creation of new life within them—as above, so below; as within, so without. Rain and Greenwood, approach the altar of the deities as the deities you are."

Rain went to the altar and lifted up the chalice, symbol of the womb of the Goddess. She was joined by Greenwood, who came to take up the athame of the God. Red Wolf was joined by his priestess, Snow Owl, and they began the age-old invocation of the deities into the bodies of the waiting couple.*

◆　◆　◆

* The complete text of this ritual spell appears in the Grimoire section of this book.

Ritual is an integral part of all spiritual expression and is central to the Pagan and Wiccan experience. In fact, it is hard to imagine how Pagan religious expression could be enacted without practical ritual. Yet how much is ritual the same as magick in our worldview? Are they two functions, or are they simply two components of the same magickal process?

Magick is often defined as a change in one's perception of reality manifesting from a change in one's consciousness. Through this mechanism, what we believe or envision becomes real in the unseen world, and then it manifests in the physical world. It is part of the ever-turning wheel of energy that twirls around us at all times, taking our will with it into the universe and, eventually, returning it to us in a form altered by the will of the strongest minds.

Because the circle is a place of all time and space, ritualizing a spell gives us an immediate link to the creative forces of the universe. Ritual is sometimes rushed through by newcomers to the Craft, yet it is the basis for the most potent changes within the mind. It is repetitive for a reason. Ritual patterns allow us to connect to archetypal patterns within the larger universe. Those repetitious patterns trigger our subconscious to move in a specific direction, allowing us to accomplish the goal of the ritual more easily. Over time, the repetition evokes a powerful response from us on all levels of our being so that just the act of thinking about ritual begins a chain reaction of magickal change within the self.

Change is the goal of magick. Change is also the goal of ritual. In this respect, magick and ritual are indistinguishable. If you expect everything to be the same both before and after your efforts, why bother? One of my favorite arguments for the power of ritual was written by Lady Sabrina, a longtime priestess and Wiccan teacher. She encapsulated her rationalization for ritual in her regrettably out-of-print book *Reclaiming the Power*:

> Ritual magick is the creation of a specific ceremony . . . to create or force a change
> to occur in accordance with your will. The only reason for doing ritual magick is
> to change something, even if the change is only one of personal attitude (p. 38).

PAGAN RITUAL MAGICK

Pagan ritual involves the casting of a circle of energy that both contains raised energy until it is ready to be used and protects those within its perimeters from stray energies or entities who are attracted by the bright power of the raised magickal energy. It provides a setting in which all time and space are one, where the elements and powers that help drive magick can converge and blend, each lending their efforts to the desired goal.

When the goal of ritual is to enhance or enact a spell, the ritual provides a setting in which the practitioner can spend more time within a magickal frame of mind, which strengthens the energy placed into the spell. When enacted in a coven setting, this strength is magnified by the number of participants lending their will to the group effort. This makes potent magick.

It's probably safe to say that most coven magick is performed within a ritual format simply because covens meet at times when ritual for worship is required, such as for the sabbats (solar festivals at the changing points of the year) or esbats (lunar rituals at the full or new moon). Spellwork is often done after the primary ritual purpose is complete. However, effective coven spellwork does not require a full ritual treatment.

As with any group effort, group ritual should involve all members of the group. This is one of our primary distinctions from the mainstream religions. In our observances, we are all participants and we all contribute to the end goal. This is why it is essential to master ritual basics early in one's study of the Craft. It is the foundation of almost all other explorations and efforts.

A BASIC RITUAL FOR OPENING AND CLOSING A CIRCLE

Because this book is aimed at an intermediate level of practitioners, we will skim the basics of ritual as we skimmed the basics of magick. If you are ready for group magick, then you should already be skilled in group ritual, and most of your members should be able to take on any ritual role necessary.

The terms "opening" and "closing" confuse many Pagans, in part because they are used interchangeably to mean the creation and grounding of the circle, or sacred space in which the coven will work, and also because the terms "open" and "close" do not make sense in our world of form as they do in the unseen world where the circle lives.

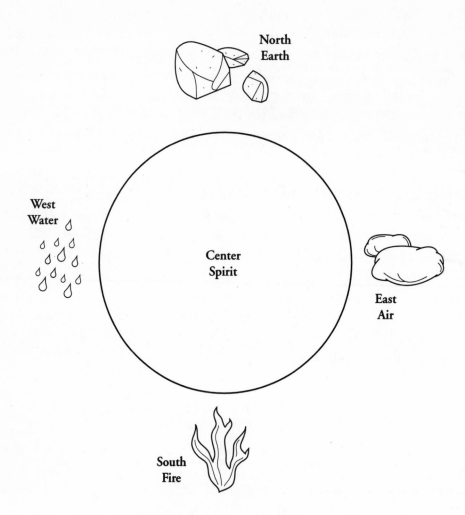

Basic Wiccan Circle Correspondences

When a circle is created or cast, it is often said to be opened, meaning that the sacred space is now a viable place to work. It is also sometimes said to be closed, meaning that the sacred space has been closed off from the mundane world and contains all time and space within itself. And to the contrary, when the circle is dismantled or grounded, it is often said to be closed, meaning that it is no longer a viable place for magick and no longer considered sacred space. By contrast, some say that a grounded circle is opened, meaning that it is no longer a boundary between the worlds of form and spirit. A popular saying at these moments is "The circle is open but unbroken."

You may take your pick of terminology. I tend to use the term "opening" when casting a circle and "closing" when I ground it, but both terms are correct.

Before you begin any working within sacred space, you should have inside the circle area all accoutrements you will need to accomplish your planned workings. These can be held by participants or arranged on an altar. The altar may be in the center, or facing the direction corresponding to the element that seems to best govern your magickal goal.

The circle is cast by projecting energy along its perimeter. This can be done with a ritual tool, a finger, or by mentally pulling into place the energy as you walk the edges of the circle area. The ritual use of the circle symbolizes completion, eternity, and containment. It represents our worldview that all things are cyclic in nature, each being born, dying, and then being regenerated once again in a never-ending circle of time.

One of the first lessons a newcomer to the Craft learns is that the circle is real, even if unseen, and it must be respected. The circle has three functions:

1) To protect those inside from unwanted outside forces that may be attracted to the energies raised.

2) To contain raised energy until it is ready to be directed toward its goal.

3) To mark off a place in between the worlds of matter and spirit, a space that lies outside the confines of our normal perception of space and time.

Starting at any one of the four cardinal direction points, next you will call the quarters. Directional and elemental correspondences can vary depending upon the cultural basis of the individual or of the coven but, in general, the Wiccan correspondences usually apply:

West = Water

North = Earth

East = Air

South = Fire

There is a fifth element called spirit or "akasha," which is viewed as a force that is within all of the elements and that unites and animates them. Some traditions see spirit as the center of their circle, others see it as above or below, and others honor it in all three places.

Quarter calls can be lavish or simple, and different groups have different styles. Neither is right or wrong. Simply facing the proper direction and making an invitation—never a demand—to the corresponding element is all that is needed. More formal covens will combine their quarter call with a tool or catalyst of that element. Some of the traditional tool correspondences are listed here, and some can be assigned to more than one element. Again, this is a matter of preference and no single way is right or wrong. These tools can help you keep in mind just who and what you are calling on.

Earth Tools or Symbols

Disks, wood, pentacles, tiles, hammers, stones, clay, bowls of soil, salt, sand, a double-headed axe, shields, wheels, necklaces, clubs, roots, drums, bronze or copper items, animal pelts, mallets, flint, ashes, nuts, shovels, hoes

Water Tools or Symbols

Cups, chalices, cauldrons, hollow horns, bowls, pitchers, goblets, rings, barrels, tridents, wine casks, silver items, convex shields, tea kettles, sea shells, paint brushes, bollines, sickles

Fire Tools or Symbols

Candles, matches, athames, swords, wands, iron or gold items, red or orange stones, pikes, claymores, torches, bracelets, crosses, brooms, spears, scourges

Air Tools or Symbols

Staves, lariats, whips, tridents, stangs, athames, swords, wands, feathers, incense, slings, claymores, pikes, single-headed axes, daggers, spears, javelins, earrings, brooms, wind instruments, broaches, ram's horns, smudge sticks, letter openers, pens and pencils, fans, pipes, arrows

Spirit Tools or Symbols

Cloaks, perfectly clear crystals, black eggs or ovals, deep empty bowls, black glass, mirrors,

A simple quarter call for each element, and for the union of the spirit within them, might sound like the following examples. Please feel free to take these and use them to create your own invitations to the elements. There are lots of books containing sample quarter calls, some simple and some lavish. All of them can inspire you to choose or create the right words and atmosphere for your coven's opening rituals.

Water Call

Powers and spirits of water who reside in the west, wash over this circle with your blessings of fertility, psychism, and mystery. We ask you here to join in our celebration and magick. Welcome and merry meet again.

Earth Call

Powers and spirits of earth who reside in the north, we ask that you lend to us your stabilizing energy, that which connects us to our mother, the Earth. We ask you here to join in our celebration and magick. Welcome and merry meet again.

Air Call

Powers and spirits of air who reside in the east, we ask that you blow to us your powers of communication, intellect, and reason. Bless us with the joy of your changeable nature. We ask you here to join in our celebration and magick. Welcome and merry meet again.

Fire Call

Powers and spirits of fire who reside in the south, we ask that you burn brightly in this circle with the force of your passion. Bless us with your transformative powers. We ask you here to join in our celebration and magick. Welcome and merry meet again.

Spirit Call

Blessed be, spirit, that is in and of all things. We ask you here to unite the elements and us with all that is so that this sacred space may be a true meeting place of all time and space; a place wherein magick is inherent, waiting only to be shaped by our will. We ask you here to join in our celebration and magick. As above, so below; as within, so without. From macrocosm to microcosm, you are welcome. Merry meet again.

After calling the quarters, a coven will usually invite their God and Goddess and ask their blessings on the proceedings. Candles or incense are often lit to both honor and symbolize their presence. Sometimes offerings of food or other sacrifices—never living ones!—are made to them at this time.

The ritual and magick then begins.

When the purpose of the ritual is ended and any spellwork is complete, the circle may be closed, or "opened," as some would prefer to say. Thank your deities and, if candles or incense were used to symbolize their presence, they should now be extinguished.

In the reverse order that you called the quarters, go to each and thank them for their presence and assistance. Offer your blessings upon them and tell them they are free to leave at will. This is sometimes referred to as "dismissing" the elements, but this is a harsh term. They were invited and, by some natural law of the magickal universe, seem compelled to come. But if you want to keep their good will and have them give you their best, you will treat them with respect as sentient beings who have a free will just as valuable as your own.

WHAT DOES RITUAL HAVE TO DO WITH OUR COVEN'S SPELLWORKING?

More often than not, covens do their spells after other ritual work, so the spell takes on a ritualized format. This can help bring in all the power of the elements and deities to the working and enhance its effort. It also means more time and energy has been put into the preparation for the spell and that the group mind is well into a receptive state for magick.

For these reasons some covens will ritualize all spells they do, even if no other reason for ritual exists at that time. This is a choice for the coven to make. Ritual can be added or taken away from any spell, and this should be kept in mind when reading through the spells in this or any other book on magick, or when your coven is creating its own spells.

5

The Diversity and Spontaneity
of Group Spellwork

High priestess Snow Owl heard the laughter of Rain and Greenwood as they searched through the thicket on the far side of the creek for magickal catalysts. The coven decided they needed a spell for protection since one of their members had received an anonymous threat, probably from someone who did not understand what Wicca was and, as was usual in these cases, probably did not wish to be enlightened.

"Hey, look." Moondancer ran over with a prize clutched in her fist. "This looks like pyrite."

Snow Owl leaned over the small nugget and nodded as she noted the shiny gold particles adhering to the orange stone Moondancer found.

"I think Rain found some acorns and Stormwillow looked through her backpack and found some cinnamon sticks."

Smiling, Snow Owl said, "That's probably plenty. Why don't you go get the circle set up for our warding spell?"

Snow Owl stood and called to their summoner, Windwalker, to gather the coven at the covenstead so the rite could begin.

Nodding for the ritual to begin, Snow Owl attuned herself to each element as the coven called the quarters. She made a special offering to the element of fire to assist them in the spell of protection, then stepped into the center of the circle near the altar.

"Friends, tonight we make the spell of warding to protect us and our homes from harm. To that end nature has provided us with pyrite, cinnamon, and acorns, all items governed by fire, the element that transforms and protects. As I pass these items around the circle, please add your energy in the way you feel is appropriate."

Snow Owl could not watch as the three catalysts made their way clockwise around the sacred space. She needed to focus on projecting her own need for protection into the items as they came to her. She saw them wrapping her, her coven, and each of their homes in a wall of white-gold protective light, then she passed them on.

When the items had made the rounds, Snow Owl led the coven to the center of the circle, where they held the objects together in their right hands, hand upon hand, empowering the catalysts with their collective will.

◆ ◆ ◆

Solitaries and covens can both create variations on their usual magickal themes, but groups have the advantage of being able to use the diversity offered them to both help each other increase magickal skills and to forge the ties that bind them to one another.

Just as raising and sending energy, divination practices, and ethics are all different in group magick, so are the variety of ways in which magick may be enacted within a coven. Some of these are as fun and joyous as a game, even though the goal is serious business. There are also ways to craft spells unique to groups, such as working with spells using litany or those requiring a spiritual scavenger hunt to seek out the right catalysts. These spells serve a dual purpose:

1) They make the magick stronger through everyone's participation in all aspects of the spell's creation and execution.

2) They strengthen the bonds of perfect love and perfect trust as you build your team spirit and group mind.

USING LITANY IN GROUP MAGICK

A litany is a group ritual practice used in all spiritual settings, including that of the mainstream religions. It is sometimes called a "responsive reading." It involves a leader reciting a ritual phrase and the congregation responding with another. In mainstream religions these are usually printed out in hymnals or other ritual texts to be read aloud by leader and congregation. The leader chooses a reading based on the season or the subject of the sermon or lesson for that gathering.

Most Pagan litany spells are preplanned with either set responses that are the same each time, or with memorized lines being used in a quick and rhythmic nature. Examples of these types of spells appear in the Grimoire section of this book.

In Pagan practice, the litany spell takes one of three forms.

1) Leader speaking followed by coven responding

In this format there is a planned response either to every single line or to a specific phrase. The "merry meet, merry part, and merry meet again" phrase used to end coven rituals in Wicca is an example of this type of planned response litany. It sounds like this.

LEADER: **And so we thank the elements and deities.**

COVEN: **Merry part.**

LEADER: **As we ground our circle . . .**

COVEN: **Merry part.**

LEADER: **. . . which is open but unbroken. Merry meet.**

COVEN: **Merry part, and merry meet again.**

2) Everyone speaking in turn ad hoc

This type of litany spell is done with slower, more lengthy prose, and is sometimes called a blessing spell. Each member in turn is allowed to step forward from the circle and offer a blessing or verbal gift related to the spell. This practice is most often done at life cycle events such as presenting a newborn to the deities, initiation into the Craft, memorial rituals, and the like.

One of the best examples of these spells of blessing can be found in the faery tale *Sleeping Beauty*. Faery tales have been used to conceal and preserve Witch lore. Reading faery tales, Mother Goose rhymes, and popular children's tales can all reveal magickal teachings, and some Wiccans make it a major focus of their studies. In this faery tale, Sleeping Beauty's birth is attended by several faery godmothers—from three to thirteen, depending upon the version you read—who offer a blessing for her future. One of the godmothers curses her to prick her finger on a spinning wheel and die at age sixteen.

This type of litany or blessing might sound like this:

> SNOW OWL: I wish for you peace and harmony, a life in balance with the elements and Mother Earth.

> RED WOLF: I wish for you the gift of far sight, the power to see behind you and in front of you.

> RAIN: I wish for you the gift of health and vibrancy, so you will have the strength and courage to see yourself through any storm life throws in your path.

3) Everyone speaking in turn preplanned

This type of litany spell is usually done in short, rhythmic bursts, and it is usually used to raise magickal energy. This eliminates surprises that can disrupt the group mind and keeps the group focused on the goal. In other words, it can all be part of the planning stage of the spell.

The surprise "blessing" of the faery godmother who cursed Sleeping Beauty to death is not pleasant, and is one reason why these types of magickal rituals are often pre-planned. Whether you act in a planned manner or allow each person to improvise will depend upon how well honed your group mind is, how much perfect trust you've built, and how comfortable your group is with improvisation.

The advantage to this type of litany is that it can move quickly once it is set and memorized. It can be started slow and sped up, being used to build the magickal energy you desire. It is one of my favorite forms of group magick, but it is one that takes time to create and absolutely must be memorized by everyone participating. A tip that will help you keep it in rhythm and make it easier to memorize is to create it in rhyme.

This type of rhythmic litany might sound something like this spell of protection.

> SNOW OWL: By our will the wall we raise.

> RED WOLF: God and Goddess we do praise.

> MOONDANCER: Protected, warded, are we all.

> WINDWALKER: On the power of fire we do call.

> RAIN: Safe from harm from spirit and man.

GREENWOOD: **Summon we the protective hand.**

STORMWILLOW: **We each have power to call our shield.**

OAKMAN: **Protective magick we do wield.***

* The full text of this spell appears in the Grimoire section of this book.

COVEN SPELLWORK AND THE SPIRITUAL SCAVENGER HUNT

Sometimes magick can be needed in a hurry and all the tools or catalysts aren't right at hand. Or sometimes it may just feel best to let nature provide the best catalyst for your magick. To that end, a coven may embark on a scavenger hunt through the area where they are working to find the proper catalysts for their goal.

The quest to find the right catalyst is like a spiritual scavenger hunt in which members of the group must rely on their wits, on nature, and on each other. All members must trust the universe to provide the right catalyst when the need arises. You may wish to begin this quest within the circle, then go out through a cut doorway to seek the catalysts, returning to the circle when a find has been made. This is an excellent exercise for developing group mind and for learning to trust in the bounty of what the deities have provided. The best way to do this is to fall back on your elemental teachings. An item that corresponds with a specific element that also corresponds with your goal is usually a good catalyst.

For those new to magick, please be aware that there are several books on the market to help you explore the elements and their relationship to magick, including my own *Making Magick*. Any of these guides can help you learn more about how the elements feel and function, so long as they include practical exercises to assist you in learning about these correspondences the way the elements wish you to learn.

These spiritual scavenger hunts are microcosmic examples of the great macrocosmic quests in mythology where a spiritual symbol is sought that will heal or make whole the people and their land. The most obvious example of this is the search for the Holy Grail of Arthurian legend. The Grail is a chalice, a symbol of the womb of the Goddess from which all life is born again and again. When the desired object is found and returned to the people, healing and wholeness occur, and the people are reconnected with the powers of the deities that had been severed.

What happens if no suitable catalyst can be found? If this happens, then you should trust that the deities may be telling you one of two things:

1) Rethink the spell and its goal, checking to make sure it is what is really wanted and that it is free from harm to any being.

2) You need no tools but the energy you can raise yourselves. After all, the power is not in the catalysts, but in the Witch who uses them.

The scavenger hunt can take place indoors or outside, or within a combination of both. Some covens set boundaries for how far members can venture looking for catalysts, others do not. Time constraints or the circumstances of where you meet may dictate how this will have to work.

Sample objects of easily found items that might have a magickal significance could include:

Bark: Stability, healing, communication.

Belts: Binding spells, appearance spells.

Berries: Abundance.

Books: Communication, mental prowess.

Broken glass: Protection, meditation.

Calendars: Time magick.

Computer disk: Communication, mental prowess, creativity.

Eggshells: Fertility, transformation.

Envelopes: Communication, astral projection.

Feathers: Astral projection, communication, mental prowess.

Garden tools: Growth, protection, abundance.

Grain: Abundance, fertility, home and children.

Hollows (as in a stone worn by wind and water): Dreams, love, fertility, psychicism.

Kitchen tools: Transformation, growth.

Leaves: Communication, astral projection.

Light bulbs: Transformation, passion, energy, stamina, courage.

Moss: Eco-magick, dream magick.

Nuts: Fertility, stability.

Pillows: Dream and sleep magick, psychicism, peace.

Pine cones: Fertility, money, employment.

Rocks: Stability, fertility, eco-magick.

Roots: Stability, fertility, home and animal magick.

Sand: Protection, grounding, transformation.

Sticks: Protection.

Toothpaste: Truth, communication, attraction.

Vines: Binding spells, love magick.

Water: Romance, psychicism, childbirth, fertility.

Use caution when using any wild herbs or plants found on the scavenger hunt unless the person who finds them is an expert botanist. Even if you're 99 percent sure what the plant is, it is wise not to ingest it or allow it to come into prolonged contact with skin. Many poisonous plants look like harmless weeds. This is Mother Nature's way of protecting her babies from harm. Magickal herbalism is an art unto itself, and while there are several good books on the subject that will help you sort through the intricacies of herbcraft, they still will not make you an expert on discerning between plants that are deadly and those that are harmless.

Stones and gemstones also have specific magickal properties depending on type, color, and origin, and several guidebooks are available to help you sort these out. Small stones for magick can also be found in most occult shops.

When in doubt about the properties of any herb or stone catalyst, always remember that they both come from Mother Earth and they can be used for any earth-related spell such as fertility, stability, or home and animal magick.

As with any catalyst, all those who will be putting their energy into them should help empower or program the found objects to the group's desire. This can be as simple as passing it around the circle to have everyone touch it and project energy into it in their own way.

MAKING MAGICK WHERE YOU ARE

Sometimes you may find yourself in a strange setting and want to enact a ritual, or you may find nature giving you a setting for which you did not plan. An example of this is the weather.

If you work outdoors most of the time, you already know the weather is not always cooperative. Instead of fighting with the elements, try seeing them as a gift instead. If it rains, employ water magick, or see it as a baptism of water energy upon your coven. However, if it storms, have enough sense to seek shelter for everyone's safety, but use the power of the storm to fuel your spells. Storms are a combination of all four elements and can make a powerful setting for any spell. If it snows, bring some inside in a bowl and place it at the center of your circle, where you can honor the winter-born God and his mother, the Goddess. If it's not too cold, go outside and worship in the snow. Make snow people as a means of building magickal energy, shaping them to represent the reality you want as the result of a spell or ritual.

Sometimes you might find yourself in an unfamiliar setting and need to orient yourself for magick or ritual. This often happens to covens who enjoy meeting in public parks or who go camping together. You can find the best place for your circle in an unfamiliar setting by allowing nature to show you where the best place for creating sacred space is to be found. Look around you. Where is the water? The fire? This is a great exercise in group mind, and makes a good lesson for students if yours is a teaching coven.

Examples of items or areas that make good orientation points outdoors include:

Earth and North

  Large oak tree

  Large rocks

  Piles of stone

  Rocky outcroppings

  Limestone formations

  Moss

  Cave entrances

  Statuary

Gardens
Crops or fields
Flagstone walkways
Small animal feeders
Burrowing animal holes

Air and East

Feathers
Bird's nest
Roosting owl
Bird houses
Bird feeders
Windchimes

Fire and South

Fireflies
Privacy fences
Outdoor lanterns
Grills and barbecues
Hot or sulfur springs
Sundials

Water and West

Creeks or rivers
Lakes or seas
Moss
Willow trees
Wet leaves
Waterfalls
Cold springs
Water fountains

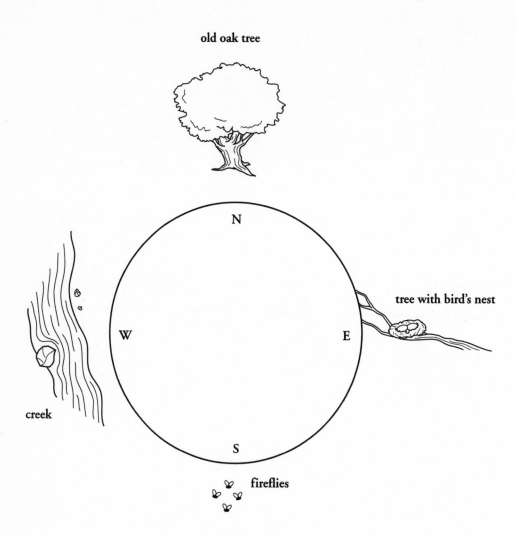

Example 1 of Making Magick Outdoors

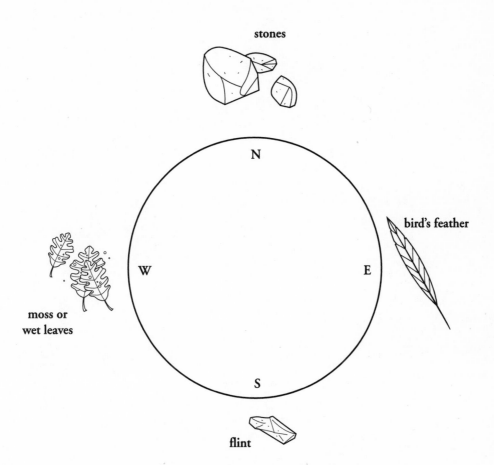

Example 2 of Making Magick Outdoors

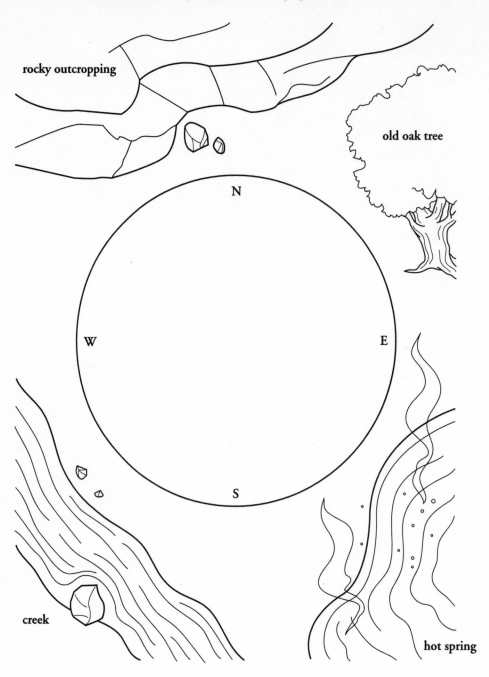

rocky outcropping

old oak tree

N

W

E

S

creek

hot spring

Example 3 of Making Magick Outdoors

Covens who work indoors can try this experiment as well. Space may be limited, but you should feel free to try casting your sacred space in another area of your meeting place if it is practical. Try to find a place oriented toward objects in your home or from the construction of your home that correspond to the proper elements and their directions. Let the deities guide you and you may be surprised at the power to be found in another place.

Examples of indoor orientation points are:

Earth and North

House plants

Terrariums

Animal doors

Basement door

Food pantry

Crystal decorations

Glassware collections

Stoneware collections

Statuary

Clay planters

Children's play area

Air and East

Atriums

Staircases

Bookshelves

Open windows

Paintings

Potpourris

Desks

Screened porches

Barometers

Windchimes

Censors

Ionizers

Fans

Air conditioning units

Door harps

Bells

Home offices

Fire and South

Solariums

Portable heaters

Door harps

Stoves and ovens

The kitchen

Fireplaces

Flashlights

Lamps

Sun catchers

Sun streaming through windows

Thermometers

Water and West

Sinks and tubs

The bathroom

Moon through the window

Desktop waterfalls

Dream catchers

Bedrooms

Lunar decor

Punchbowls

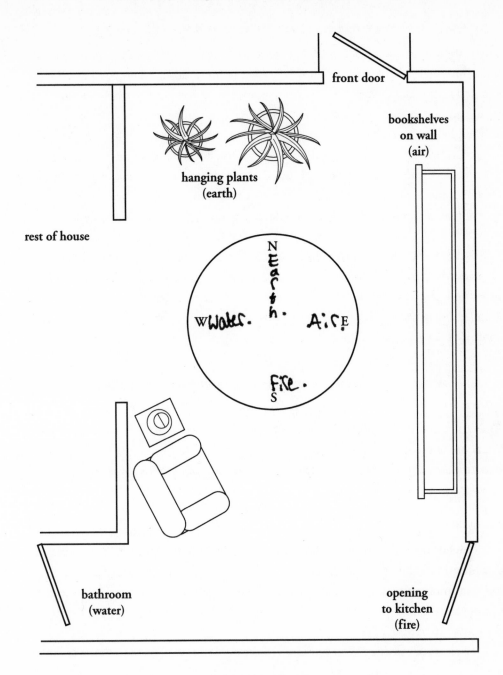

front door

bookshelves
on wall
(air)

hanging plants
(earth)

rest of house

N
Earth
W Water   .   Air E
Fire .
S

bathroom
(water)

opening
to kitchen
(fire)

Example of Making Magick Indoors

SPELLWORKING TOGETHER WHEN YOU'RE APART

There are lots of so-called rules for magickal timing, and they can help enhance any spell, but magick works best when it is needed because this is when you have the drive and desire to make it work. Sometimes you may find you need the help of your coven for a spell but you are unable to physically meet. This can be overcome by setting a time aside and allowing each coven member to enact a spell on their own for the goal.

Start your long-distance magick by setting a time for meditation, when you mentally connect with the energy of your group. The closer you are emotionally to the other members and the better developed your group mind, the easier this will be.

You may plan how the spell is to be done, or you may each be free to work on your own.

Another variation is to do a round robin spell, where one person enacts the spell, then the energy is passed to another. A phone call or preset time can make this work. By the time the last person to work the spell passes the energy to the one who needs it, the group will has been built and the one who needs it can do the final step in the spell to compete the circle.

WHERE DOES THE DIVERSITY AND SPONTANEITY FIT IN WITH OUR COVEN'S OWN SPELLWORKING?

Any spell can and should be altered to fit the needs of the person or persons for whom you're doing the spell. Keep these ideas in mind when choosing or creating your spells. It doesn't matter if the spell is culled from this book or another book, or is one you created on your own or with your coven. The scavenger hunt, the litany, ritualization, and so on, can all be added or subtracted to make the spell what you want it to be.

This is why you will find the spells in the Grimoire section of this book referred to as "spell blueprints." You are the architect of your own reality and the spells should not be considered infallible, perfect, used by the ancients, set in stone, unalterable, or anything else that implies they are not to be tampered with. Spells for covens can be done by two or more, or they can be altered to the needs of the solitary practitioner. Spells written for the solitary practitioner can be altered for use by covens.

Magick is your divine right as children of the deities. Use all its tools to make the spell you and your coven need its strongest and most successful.

MAGICKAL BONDING RITUALS

One last thing you might want to do as a coven before enacting group magick is to create some type of bonding ritual or initiation rite into this next step in your spiritual lives. The true magick of any coven is its spirit of community, the sense that the bonds uniting you are ones as close—or closer—than those of family. With your coven you merge your energies in ways as intimate as those of lovers.

When you first came together as a coven, you probably enacted some kind of dedication ritual. You gave your coven a name, organized leadership roles, and probably did a ritual dedicating yourself to the service of your deities.

You do these rites of passage when you progress from novice to initiate and from initiate to priest/ess, so you should consider it also for your coven as a whole when it is ready to advance to a new level of awareness and practice. You do not have to do another ritual before you enact magick together, but it's a nice way of stating your new goal and for marking a transition to a new phase of your spiritual lives together.

Ritual in itself is a form of magick because it changes the focus of our minds. Rituals of transition impress upon our minds that we are at the door of a new threshold with yet new terrors, challenges, and rewards.

You might begin by having everyone make or bring a small talisman representing to them what this change symbolizes. For example, in the coven we're following in this book, Moondancer may have decided to weave together grasses or limbs to represent the power of transformation she sees each person undertaking as they make magick. She might know Oakman is truly strong as an oak, but she may perceive his strength in magick as his ability to bend and change with the forces surrounding him and choose for him the flexible willow branch.

Each person can explain their item, and it can be put in a bag that you bury near your covenstead or keep nearby when you do magick together.

The rite of passage ritual each coven designs will be unique, based on the overall experience of the group and where they see their magick taking them together. Suggestions for things to include are:

1) Rededication to the deities to reaffirm the coven's purpose as their servants. Never forget their worship is still your primary focus.

2) Having each person make a blessing or a statement about where they hope this new adventure will take you as a group.

3) Passing through a symbolic doorway where a personal terror or demon must be overcome. This can be acted out or done through a group guided meditation.

4) The passing of a never-before-used glass from which all drink. The glass is then destroyed, similar to what you see at the end of a Jewish wedding ceremony. The crashing sound drives away negativity attracted to your energy and creates an item in time that belonged to and was used by only those who chose to be bonded.

5) The dedication or creation of group magickal tools that are in addition to those possessed by the individuals.

6) If your coven has created an emblem or banner for itself, this might be a good time to add something new to it to mark this rite of passage.

7) Vows may be taken by the group as a whole, perhaps litany style, in which they affirm their decisions about the magick they will do. For instance, it will harm none, work for the good of all, be guided by divination, be honed by consensus, and so on.

Even if you choose not to do a special rite of passage ritual as your coven moves into magickal work, you should at least celebrate your first spell together as a special event. Have a feast, invite family, and enjoy revelry with the deities.

6

Converting Solitary Spells
for Group Use

High priestess Snow Owl scribbled furiously as Rain and three other members of the coven spoke in rapid succession, converting a solitary spell that always worked well for Rain into an effective spell for the coven's use.

They all had great ideas, and coming to consensus on the major points was swift and certain.

Snow Owl could sense the excitement growing within the room where they sat working, and repressed the urge to dampen the spirit of creativity by reminding them that they still had to go over all the minor details and do some divinations before they could be sure that this was the best spell for their need at this time.

When the difficult items came along, Snow Owl was delighted that the flow of energy that moved the group so far was still at work and there was little dissent. No doubt this spell was one that would work well for them, and everyone was excited about all the creative input that allowed them to add tidbits from their private spellwork to the group's effort. Of course, there were the divinations to come. One of those could always send the group into a one-eighty, but she sensed that this was one of those times when everything was coming together as it should.

If only it were always so easy.

◆ ◆ ◆

You no doubt know by this point in your spiritual life that there are many ways to construct a spell to bring you the goal you desire. There are also many ways to restructure spells to enhance them for better personal use. You can also use these same spells, written or intended for solitary use, so that they work just as well within a group setting.

Any spell can be converted to group use, though some goals will not work as well in coven settings as they would for the solitary practitioner because of their private nature. Personal goals, such as those for romance or beauty, are best done alone. However, they can be enhanced by a group willing to put forth the effort to back you up magickally. Just be aware that your coven may not think helping you appear prettier in the singles bars or get a date for Saturday night to be a goal worthy of their time and energy.

The following steps for converting a spell should be viewed as only generic guidelines. The precise details will vary with each spell. Your group may choose to add to, subtract from, or modify any of these steps as you see fit. If your coven does not have at least one person experienced in the spell conversion process, or does not have someone to guide you through it who has a firm understanding of magickal physics, these steps will help see you through, but they are not a replacement for experience. It needs to be reiterated at this point that having the majority of your coven practicing at the intermediate or beginning-intermediate level is essential to successful group magick. Please question whether your coven is ready to practice spellworking together if you don't have the input of at least one person you trust to guide you through the basics.

A CHECKLIST FOR GROUP MAGICK

This list is a starting point for your coven to look at while you are considering a spell. The list cannot include every scenario that may arise, but should still give you a set of guidelines to facilitate discussion and reach consensus. There are no right or wrong answers to the questions you will ask of yourself and one another, and there are no right or wrong ways to find consensus. Each group will have its own way of solving spell-selection problems, if it wants to remain viable. You may want to add, take away, or change your spellworking checklist as you grow together as a coven and as you discover what does and does not work for you as a group.

1) Does the spell ask for precisely what is wanted without dictating to the universe how it should be made manifest?

2) Is everyone in agreement about working the spell?

3) Have all dissenters been allowed to express their concerns and have those concerns been addressed?

4) Is the spell free of harmful side effects for all beings in all worlds?

5) Did you do any divinations to see how the spell will turn out? How many? Did everyone have access to the answers?

6) Did everyone get a chance to discuss their feelings about the outcome of the divinations? Were they all pleased with the probable outcome?

7) Is the goal too personal or the issue too private for working in a group setting? Will others be uncomfortable working with it or do they feel it's a waste of valuable coven time?

8) Is the spell best for solitary work? If so, the coven could select a time when every member will work the spell alone in their own home and blend their energies from a distance.

9) Could you agree on a time and place for the spell that makes astrological sense to your group? Is your coven willing to give up some astrological advantages to ensure that all members can be present?

10) Did one or more members still maintain a vehement dislike for enacting the spell, even after consensus was reached? Decide if the spell is worth the coven's effort if it risks causing a schism in your group bond.

11) Has everyone participated in the spell's creation and will they all help choose and empower the catalysts? Decide how that empowerment will be done: in the circle, before the circle, and so on.

12) Are the words of power in the present tense? Do they support the visualization most of you will be using? Are they in conflict? Are you asking for what you really need?

13) Have you decided who will perform what role during the enactment of the spell? Does everyone have a role they feel is meaningful?

14) Is everyone comfortable with their role in the spell and do they fully understand their function and its importance to the outcome? Coven magick is like a huge jigsaw puzzle: It cannot ever be completed if a single piece is missing.

15) Is the person or persons for whom the spell is being done willing to back up the magick with physical-world efforts?

STEP BY STEP: THE SPELL CONVERSION PROCESS

Step One

Ask yourselves who is achieving the spell's goal. Who is it being done for: one person, several people, the whole group, someone outside the group? Regardless of the answer, *everyone in the coven should be a participant, never only a witness, to the spellworking.* Those who don't participate get bored and their energies go elsewhere, defeating the purpose of the spell. This is one of those cases where it may be best to have everyone do the spell at home on their own at a preselected time.

> **Example:** Rain has a solitary spell that mostly works well for her, but she would like to have the coven's energy backing her this time. Having her stand at the altar and work her spell while everyone else is standing around, presumably watching with interest and inputting their energy, is not realistic.
>
> A better solution is to have Rain tell her coven when she will be doing her spell at home and to ask that any who wish to send energy her way at that time do so.
>
> If the coven does want to help Rain as a group, then there should be a role for everyone so that all members participate. This may mean having to rewrite large portions of the spell. You can stage a ritual drama, give everyone an accoutrement to work with, or have everyone except Rain work the spell and surround her with your own rewritten version.
>
> If Rain's spell is being converted for the benefit of the coven as a whole, it's even more vital that everyone have a role in the performance of the actual spell. Some may light or pass out candles. Others may chant or drum during the spell's enactment. Still others may play the role of deities, heroes of mythology, or one of the elements.

Step Two

Hold an informal group meeting to hash out the spell's details. Do this outside of your sacred space, or you may do it after a regular coven gathering when all your ritual energies have been grounded and you are thinking in your normal consciousness mode again.

During this time, discuss the appropriateness and ethics of the proposed spell. Make sure everyone has a chance to be heard. The leader or facilitator has the responsibility to draw out the reticent among you to make sure no one is holding back concerns or resentments that will backfire later.

> **Example:** Rain may have worked her spell dozens of times with no ill effects, but this time she is asking that others take the risk of harmful rebound with her. It's always possible in the rewriting processes that something could tip the spell to the negative. Even the change of one word or concept can make a big difference in the outcome.
>
> New divinations must always be done when even the slightest change is made in a spell. In a spell to be worked in a group setting, everyone must be satisfied with the probable outcome before you can consider the spell ready for the group to use.

Step Three

Make a detailed list of the items you will need for the coven to work the spell. Is it too much? Too little? Will everyone have their own catalysts, or will there be one set of items for all to use? Does someone in the group already have what you need? Can you substitute items? Can the spell be made more simple? More complex? More ritualized? Less formal? Is there just too much involved in the spell to make it worth the effort for an entire group?

Who will be responsible for finding or purchasing the items you don't have? Who will be responsible for getting those items where they need to be when they need to be there?

> **Example:** This step is self-explanatory. The more people who are involved with the spell, the more items you're likely to need if everyone is to fully participate. If there are so many items needed that it becomes cost prohibitive or just too complicated, then this may make a spell better for solitary use. An ambitious coven

may make it work out fine for them, but that will be the choice of the group to make. Sometimes something as simple as adding a litany or blessing to the spell makes it participatory enough that everyone feels involved. Of course, this addition requires another divination.

Someone in the coven has to be responsible for obtaining the items needed. Usually this burden ends up falling on the priest or the priestess, who ends up resenting doing all the work, and rightly so. This also brings up the question of who is to pay for the items.

Does the coven have a treasury it can draw from? If the spell is requested by one person for their own gain, should that person have to foot the bill for all the items needed? Should everyone pitch in their share and have one person make the purchases, or should everyone be required to seek their own catalysts, whether or not the spell is to benefit themselves or someone else?

These are sticky questions and, if it has never come up before, will set a precedent for all similar future situations. Make your choices with care.

Step Four

If your coven decides to proceed with a particular spell, now is the time to format the rest of the spell and hash out the finer points. How will the spell's catalysts be empowered? What preritual work must go into this spell before it is enacted? Does something need to be made, cooked, sewn, et cetera? What about visualization? Is there a need for a consensus on how things will be envisioned? Talk about it. Make sure you're asking for what you really want and need.

Next, create your words of power and assign roles, speaking parts, and so on. Does someone need to lead a dance, create a talisman, offer a blessing, pass out herb charms, light candles, write a part of the ritual? Who will keep any talisman created from the spell? Where will items be buried or burned when the spell is done? How will the energy continue to be fed into the spell until it manifests? Who has the responsibility for following the spell up in the physical world? Who will decide when the time has come to close down a spell that has not worked and lead the grounding process?

Example: Everyone may wish to work with their assigned accoutrements for the spell on their own for a week or so to fully empower them, while others may wish to pass them around the circle at the time the spell is enacted. The former works better for fully charging magickal items, but the latter can sometimes help bring the group mind into better focus for the spell.

Anyone who is the beneficiary of a spell should be the one who must back up the effort in the physical world. That's often the hardest step in magick, but it's one that no one can do for someone else.

Step Five

Decide where and when the spell will be enacted. Because modern living involves a great many personal commitments to many people and causes, there may not always be an ideal time that works for everyone. Some spells, such as those to protect someone's home, may not be performed at the covenstead and will require extra travel time for some members.

People have busy lives and sometimes standard meeting times must be fixed if a coven is to succeed, and you'll have to work with that fact. However, remember that words of power and visualizations can be altered to suit almost any astrological situation. For example, if you're doing a spell for prosperity, visualize wealth increasing if the moon is waxing, and poverty decreasing if the moon is waning.

> **Example:** Covens have limited time together, no matter how high a priority it is in the lives of the members. People live busy lives—usually not by choice—and often the time and place best for the spell is not ideal for the coven. So you work with what you have. There's also always the option of everyone doing the spell at their own home at an appointed time.
>
> Even if the coven uses a less than perfect astrological time for the spell, there is no reason Rain cannot do the spell again for herself as a solitary when conditions are better to back up the coven's work on her behalf.
>
> Even if the spell you are doing is not just for one person's benefit, everyone should feel free to do the spell as a solitary to enhance that energy. However, caution must be taken that no word or gesture be in conflict with the spell's original format, or you may unwittingly send out energy at odds with the group's effort. If you're in doubt about what you're doing, ask a more experienced coven member or one of the leaders for guidance.

Step Six

When the spell is fixed in complete detail, down to the last little nuance, and is exactly as everyone feels it should be, it should be written down in detail by your coven scribe or some other member who is charged with keeping these notes. This way, there can be no disagreement on what was decided.

At this point, at least one divination should be done to see what the outcome of the spell is likely to be, based on the energies that are currently in motion. Only when all the details of your spell are complete can you get a clear reading on its outcome and possible harm done. It's even better if you can do more than one divination and compare them.

> **Important Note:** Again, it must be reiterated that any change in a spell, no matter how insignificant it seems, be reevaluated by a new divination that everyone in the group finds satisfactory. Starting your spell with some unknown clinker built in will eventually lead it off course. Compare it to a plane that takes off from London with only a slight deviation between the instrument settings and where the plane intends to go. The farther it travels, the farther off course it goes. A small miscalculation can make the difference between the plane landing in New York or in Buenos Aires.

Step Seven

When your coven has gathered at the place where the spell will be enacted, one of the leaders, or an appointee, must make sure everything you will need is inside the circle or wherever you need it to be before any formal ritual or spellwork begins.

Use a checklist. You probably wouldn't go grocery shopping without one lest you forget something important, so why would you chance not having something you need on hand for your spell? Nothing spoils the energy more than someone having to cut a doorway in the circle right in the middle of a magickal rite to run out and fetch a forgotten item.

> **Example:** If the spell is being done for one person alone, that person should be responsible for seeing that all needed items are present.
>
> In a group effort, these roles can be assigned or rotated among members. In either case, a leader or someone appointed to the role should have the checklist nearby to compare to what is available before the group begins to form its circle and start thinking with their group mind.

Step Eight

Enact the spell according to the way you planned it, but don't be a slave to its formatting if your group as a whole feels moved to ritual drama, dance, song, drumming, or any other expression of the spell's energy. Go with your feelings.

> **Example:** The "go with your feelings" applies only after the spell has been done as planned by the group. It's true that sometimes a rush of divine creativity changes a spell's direction, but it's something that's felt by all and is not the same as one person taking it upon themselves to alter the predetermined course of the spell.
>
> If one of these divine inspirations occurs, you will all know it and flow with the energy to the direction you're being led. You'll smile at each other, sharing the excitement of knowing but not knowing what's happening, and no one will look offended or upset by the change of plans. The deities are at work, and you are their vessels. This happens occasionally to all good working covens. If you haven't experienced the exhilaration of divine intervention yet, you have something tremendous to look forward to.

Step Nine

Send the energy of the spell toward its goal as you planned, then ground yourselves.

If you have a coven scribe, or someone responsible for keeping track of your spells and rituals in a magickal journal or Book of Shadows, that person should make notes under the written details of the spell as soon as possible. Any notes about the atmosphere created, the weather, and so on, that could affect the spell should be noted.

> **Example:** Some covens designate someone for the role of scribe to attend solely to this task. This person attends all gatherings of the coven or its leaders and is responsible for keeping detailed notes not only of the proceedings but of the weather, astrology, place, time, and other information that might affect the outcome of a spell or ritual.

Step Ten

Those who are to follow up the spell with physical-world efforts should begin doing so that very same day, if possible.

DON'T FORGET TO FOLLOW UP THE FOLLOW UP

Step Eleven

Reassess the spell, its goal, and its outcome in one lunar month. Did it work? Why or why not? Do you want to try again? Why or why not? If you want to try again, go back to step one and try making some changes to make the spell better.

This is where the role of the scribe can come in handy. He can tell you exactly what was said and done, and when. Every nuance will be in his book of records and the spell can be picked apart for weaknesses and strengths. From this you may find out that your coven is strongest on a new moon rather than a full one, or that healing is not your strong point, or that the words of power contain an error.

Remember again that there are only two reasons why spells fail altogether: one, lack of proper effort, or two, a stronger opposing force. Either of these can be greater problems in group magick than in work done by a solitary.

Make sure everyone gets to express their view on the spell's success or failure. Keeping open and honest communication between your coven members is more essential in magick than in almost any other area of your work together. You all know you're there for the primary purpose of uniting with the divine. You'll find little to disagree about on how to go about doing that job, but magickal differences can tear you apart. Keep your higher purpose in mind at all times, and your vows to come together in perfect love and perfect trust, and your magick and your spirits will flourish together with the blessing of the Lord and Lady.

◆ ◆ ◆

The word *grimoire* is thought to be an old French word of hazy etymology. It refers to a book of magickal formulae. Even so, no spell in this or any grimoire should be viewed as a rigid guide for spellwork. Spells found in books such as these are merely blueprints showing their creator's vision of the overall theme and direction a spell should take. They work best when honed, tailored, and otherwise adjusted to suit the specific situation of the person or persons enacting the spell.

Nothing you'll find here is a direct dictate from any deity, tradition, or magickal guru. I have performed some of these spells and they have worked well for me. Others have been suggested to me by leaders of other covens, and I modified them into a format that felt right to me. This is how they work best. If your coven finds a spell format it likes, but its goal is protection and you want a spell for fertility, take all the creative license you want to change the words, catalysts, symbols, and so on. That way, you keep a format you like and still have a spell that works toward your chosen goal.

You may also incorporate any of the suggestions from the previous chapter into any spell. Seek your catalysts from Mother Earth, add a chant or litany, or try orienting yourselves someplace new to see what the spirits and elements of that place have to offer.

In the spells in this book, Snow Owl and Red Wolf have been designated as the leaders, and their names will appear with the initials HP (high priest) or HPS (high priestess) after them within the ritual text. Fixed leadership roles are usually part of covens and traditions known as hierarchical. In these, the leaders have put much time and study into reaching their positions. Because the leadership is consistent in these types of covens, I have chosen to use these designations to cut down on confusion, and as a device for showing how the specific spell might work in your group setting. Your coven may rotate leadership roles among many qualified people—known as a priestly coven or tradition—or an acting priest or priestess may be taking over for this spell. Don't feel you have to have fixed leadership to make your spells work. In fact, even those in priestly covens or traditions may find that for the purposes of magick, someone with a special affinity for the type of spell being enacted might lead you through it with better results than your usual leaders.

Each spell blueprint presented here opens with a brief statement of the goal, who the goal is focused upon, what items are needed for the spell, and some suggested "best times" to work the spell. Please don't be a slave to either the items list or the best times suggestions. Catalysts can be substituted in any spell, sometimes for the better. Timing of the spell is also a matter of personal taste. A word to the wise Witch is that you should do a spell when it is needed most. That's when you have the requisite emotional connection, and that is much more important than in which sign of the zodiac the moon is traversing.

In general, spells for increase or gain are worked on the waxing moon, and spells for decrease or loss are worked on the waning phase. Special holidays and feast days to specific deities can be used to boost certain spells, as can specific days of the week.

Each day of the week is associated with a different planet that makes it a stronger day for certain spells, but it never makes it a bad day for any spell. The following is a general guideline for spellwork correspondences for each day of the week.

Sunday/Sun

Employment, money, success, purification, the God, passion, protection, exorcism, banishing, fame, politics, curse breaking, performing, fire magick.

Monday/Moon

Psychicism, astral projection, guided meditation, the Goddess, fertility, love, reconciliation, divination, water magick, dream magick, sleep.

 Tuesday/Mars

Courage, strength, dance magick, lust, discord, sexuality, passion, overcoming obstacles.

Wednesday/Mercury

Communication, study, writing, travel, healing, games, air magick.

Thursday/Jupiter

Money, prosperity, abundance, legal matters, riches, career.

Friday/Venus

Romance, beauty, dream work, the home, peace, contentment, fidelity, friendships, children.

Saturday/Saturn

Past lives, the hidden, seeking truth, self-undoing, banishing, curse breaking, psychic self-defense, protection.

To fall back on a popular analogy: There are as many paths to a magical goal as there are highways to a physical location. All of them will get you where you want to go sooner or later, but each offers something different to see and learn along the way. Pick the route that you find most intriguing, and that will be the one that offers the most enrichment and the greatest success.

◆ ◆ ◆

♦ BURNING BAD HABITS ♦

Goal: To take a bad habit, compulsion, or other unwanted personal eccentricity and banish it for good.

Subject: Every member of the coven will work toward this for themselves. You may wish to add the goals of others who request your assistance, even though they are not present.

Items: You will need a central balefire (a magickal fire, usually lit for a solar festival ritual), a fireproof bowl or fireplace or an iron cauldron on legs, or some other place or receptacle where you can safely burn small pieces of paper.

Best Times: On a Saturday, a spiritual new year, or during the waning moon or a lunar eclipse.

This is a great spell for use during the major turning points of the year—in particular the new year, a time when everyone makes resolutions for positive changes in their lives. Depending upon your coven's cultural focus, you may view the new year as occurring at Samhain (October 31, or Halloween), Yule (the winter solstice), or Ostara (the spring equinox).

Before your coven comes together to enact this spell, instruct each member of your coven to meditate on what habit or habits they wish to banish. They may choose more than one, but everyone should have at least one thing about themselves they wish to change for the better. For example, the nail biter may also be a compulsive talker and want to work on improving both traits throughout the year to come.

When each member knows what they want to achieve, they should take their piece of paper and cut it into a circle. Inside that circle they should write what they wish to banish. It should be folded in fourths and kept near its creator until time to enact the spell. This is so the paper absorbs more of the energy and need of each person.

Each coven member should already know to spend as much time before the coven meeting as possible physically connecting the energies of their desire to the paper on which they've written their bad habit. They may wear it, carry it, fondle it, breathe on it, and spend time thinking about how the upcoming ritual spell will ease the need to engage in the problem pattern and make it simpler to overcome.

There are other ways to make the personal energy connection to the habit written on the paper stronger. It is traditional in many circles to paint the words on the circle of paper in liquid dragon's blood. The dragon's blood is best painted with a tapered, medium-width paintbrush (you can find those in most discount department stores, craft stores, or toy stores). This crimson plant extract has the look and feel of blood and can be obtained for little expense at any occult store or through mail order (see Appendix A). I'm fortunate to have a wonderful occult shop in the city where I live that sells dragon's blood in small vials that usually last me a full year and cost about four dollars.

While there are always "best times" for any spell, based on traditional astrological correspondences—some of which can be very complex—your coven may have to make do with the time when everyone can meet. Modern schedules are hectic and it can be a coven's greatest trial to accommodate them all. Remember that these "best times" do not mean the "only times." Yours may be different, but my hierarchy for selecting a time for coven magick follows:

1) When there is the most urgent need.
2) When everyone can be present to work the spell.
3) When the moon is in the correct phase.
4) When other astrological, calendar, or weather correspondences are at their peak for the spell.

When the leader, leaders, or acting leader(s) indicates that it is time for the spell to begin, everyone should gather in a circle and produce the paper on which they've written the habit or problem of which they wish to rid themselves. An example of how this spell might sound in a group setting follows.

> **SNOW OWL HPS: No religion is of much value to its followers if it cannot offer us the hope of being better people. Each religion prescribes ways in which this can be achieved. Some offer several methods, such as Wicca.**

> **RED WOLF HP: Now is the hour when we gather here in this sacred space to purge ourselves of the habits, patterns, thoughts, and practices that hinder us from being the best people we can be. For some of us these are spiritual issues, for others they affect our daily lives. All are of importance to whom they plague. None are too minor to be of concern to the God and Goddess, who love us and whom we serve.**

SNOW OWL HPS: We shall engage our self-transformation with the element of fire. We ask that our friend fire step forward and speak to us of his powers.

The person playing the role of fire should be standing in the south end of the circle, if you follow the traditional Wiccan directional correspondences. The role can be played by either a man or a woman, but since fire is a masculine element, I have chosen a man—Oakman—to play the part in this example. The person speaking should not be bound by a written script if he feels the spirit of fire moves him to speak of other aspects of himself.

OAKMAN: (Steps forward to stand in front of the central fire.) **Behold my brightness. Feel my heat. I am fire. Like my brother and sister elements, I am one of the four legs upon which all creation is built. I am the ruler of all creatures of the south: the salamanders, the drakes, the jack-o'-lanterns. I am the one that consumes and transforms. My passion is infamous. When I get excited and am fed well, I can rage out of control, gobbling up everything I touch with my insatiable lust. I can lay waste to monuments humankind has struggled to keep safe for centuries. I can also be stolid and provide warmth on cold nights when the Holly King, the ruler of winter, holds sway over the world. I transform raw meat into edible food. I can be a friend or foe. I can be wild or I can be controlled. I can help you if you bother to know me, and burn you if you misuse my power. What is it you ask of me tonight?**

SNOW OWL HPS: (Steps forward.) **We come here to perform an act of magick. We wish to use your power to consume and transform so that we may rid ourselves of bad habits and personal traits we no longer desire. We ask your help in making us better people.**

OAKMAN: **I am yours to command this night. Use me and accept the blessings of my transformative powers.**

Light the fire near the center of your circle or on your altar, if it has not already been done. The one portraying fire should stand as near the fire as possible so he can oversee the safe burning process of the pieces of paper.

One by one, the members of the coven will step forward from the circle and approach the fire with their slips of paper. Because many of the habits or issues that your fellow members may want to rid themselves of can be personal, no one should be required to detail these out loud. Any example of how this ritual might progress follows.

> **Snow Owl HPS:** Blessed fire, element of willpower, I toss into your depths my desire to rid myself of the habit of nail biting. It may seem a minor flaw to many, but I'm tired of the sore fingertips and bloody nail beds. I ask you to consume this habit as I work to overcome this lifelong compulsion.

Each coven member should make a gesture of "good riddance" as they toss their slip of paper into the fire. It can be any gesture that has meaning for them in relation to the problem, even if no one else understands it.

If you do not have a gesture in mind, I recommend using what is commonly referred to as the banishing pentagram. The five-pointed star, which is a both a symbol of modern Wicca and a magickal sigil all on its own, is often "drawn in the air" in a variety of ways to draw in or send away energy. Some traditions—notably the British Alexandrian traditions—have both a banishing and invoking pentagram gesture for each element. You may use these if you like, or keep it simple by starting at the base of the star to banish and at the top to draw in energies (see the illustrations on page 106 for examples of each).

> **Oakman:** (Watches Snow Owl toss her slip of paper into the fire and sees to it that it begins to be consumed.) **Blessed be your efforts as I consume and transform your desire. May your will be rewarded.**

> **Red Wolf HP:** (Presuming Red Wolf is the next person in the circle, he steps forward to the fire.) **Blessed fire, I toss into your depths my habit of smoking. I know my life and health depend upon quitting this dangerous addiction.**

> **Oakman:** Blessed be your efforts as I consume and transform your desire. May your will be rewarded.

> **Rain:** (Steps up to the fire. She is not yet ready to reveal to the coven what her problem is, and all respect that she chooses not to voice it in detail.) **Blessed fire, you and the deities know my compulsion. This problem must end, and I am now ready to work hard to defeat it. Please help me with your powers of transformation so I can overcome what has haunted me for years.**

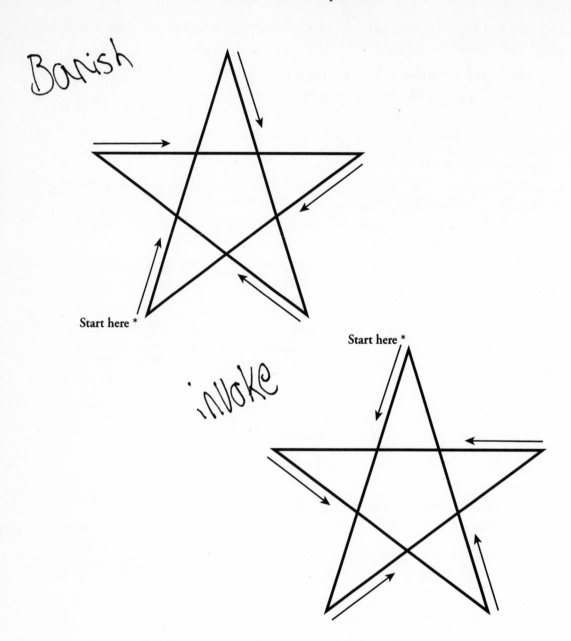

Banish

Start here *

invoke

Start here *

Banishing (upper left) and Invoking (lower right) Pentagrams

OAKMAN: **Blessed be your efforts as I consume and transform your desire. The deities who know you as their child will be your strength. Look to the ones who claim me as their patron element, and may your will be rewarded.**

The ritual should continue in this fashion until everyone has a chance to toss something unwanted into the fire. Some may toss more than one slip of paper into the fire, but remember that a desire to work on too many problems at once can scatter your energies in too many directions to be effective. Keep your issues to three or fewer for now.

The last person who gets to toss his problems into the fire will be the person portraying fire. In this example, Oakman's final speech might sound something like this.

OAKMAN: **On behalf of my friend Oakman, I toss into myself the compulsion to talk more than to listen. A wise man of another faith, a good man known as St. Francis of Assisi, once prayed to his God to help him to seek to understand rather than to be understood. Oakman wishes to be a more patient listener so he may be a better friend to all of you. I, fire, offer my blessing upon his and all your petitions. I will be as near as the south to assist you in achieving them. By the Lord and Lady who created us all, so mote it be.**

COVEN: (In unison.) **By earth, water, air, and fire, who bring us what we desire, and by the power of three times three, by our will, so mote it be.**

◆ **BANISHING BAD MEMORIES:**
A VARIATION ON BURNING BAD HABITS ◆

Goal: To take an unpleasant memory or other obsessive thought and banish it from your mind.

Subject: This may be done for one or more members of the coven during the same ritual. This spell may also be used as an adjunct to ending or breaking a spell.

Items: You will need a central balefire, a fireproof bowl, fireplace, or some other place where you can safely burn small pieces of string. You will also need some black string or thin cord.

Best Times: Saturday, Wednesday, or a waning moon.

Banishing memory is a controversial magickal issue. We not only contain within our subconscious minds the memory of all events that have transpired in this lifetime, but those of all the lifetimes we've ever lived. They may not always be conscious thoughts, and we may never uncover them all, but they live within us just the same and they affect our daily lives and thought processes. Some would argue to lose a memory may mean having to repeat a painful lesson you needed to learn. Sometimes a detrimental pain is given so that it can be used to our strength later on.

It is also true that memory can never be fully purged. We are the sum of who we are in all lives, forms, and dimensions. Many of us seek out those other selves to learn from them.

So can this spell even work? It can't if you want to wake up tomorrow morning with complete amnesia, but it can in that the memory's obsession can be lessened so that its impact is felt less in your everyday life. If the memory is crippling your day-to-day existence, you not only need magick, but should seek therapy as well.

In this variation of the previous spell, the person who needs to have the memory removed will stand or sit closest to the fire. The other members of the coven will each have with them a piece of black string or cord about two-and-a-half feet long.

In the secular world, black has been dubbed the color of evil. In magick, it is a color that absorbs other energies, just the way it absorbs light and therefore reflects no color back to our eyes. This is why black items become hotter than white items when placed in the sun; black is absorbing all that heat and light and holding it within, while white is deflecting it. It doesn't take a brain surgeon to conclude what the magickal possibilities are in such a color.

Each person in turn will step forward and tie his length of black cord around the head of the person who wants a memory or obsessive thought banished. As each person ties on the cord he will offer his best wishes for success, then step back into the circle while the next person comes to tie his cord around the petitioner's head.

There should be a few minutes of complete silence after all the cords have been tied. During this time everyone should focus on the image of memory or thought being pulled from the person requesting the spell and into the absorbent black cords.

When it seems enough time has passed, the person portraying fire should step forward and place a hand upon the cords over the head of the petitioner. Another person should join him. This one will be portraying air, the element governing thought. He should also place a hand on the head on the petitioner. Because air is the other masculine element, I have chosen another man—Greenwood—to portray air in this example.

> **GREENWOOD:** Behold me, I am air—rarely seen, yet always present. I am as fleeting as thought, but just as omnipresent. I am as changeable as the four winds, but each one is me. I bless your efforts to rid yourself of unwanted memories and obsessive thinking. Let them blow away with my winds, never to haunt you again.

> **OAKMAN:** Behold me, I am fire—the element that transforms, consumes, and changes all I touch. (Oakman removes the cords from around the head of the person for whom the spell is being enacted.) I feel in these cords the heaviness of your burden, and I cast them into myself to be changed into the life you want. (Oakman casts the cords into the fire and watches them burn.)

> **GREENWOOD:** When we change our thoughts, we change our whole reality.

> **OAKMAN:** When we transform our minds, we transform our lives.

> **OAKMAN AND GREENWOOD:** (In unison.) Blessed be your efforts to seek the better life you want. Go in peace, and so mote it be.

> **COVEN:** (In unison.) Memory deep in dungeons dwell, placed there by our magick spell. By the power of three times three, by our will, so mote it be.

◆ WITCH BOTTLE I: OF STICKS AND STONES ◆

Goal: To make a traditional tool for warding and protecting. In this case, we will be protecting the coven's meeting place.

Subject: Every member of the coven will work toward the goal using one bottle. The only time you may want more bottles is if you meet at different locations each time. Even then, it often works better to make one bottle together as a group and use it at your principle meeting site.

Items: You will need a clean glass jar (spaghetti sauce jars are perfect). You will also need some items culled from the area where you meet, which will be addressed within the spell text.

Best Times: On a Sunday, a full moon, or on Midsummer's Eve.

Witch bottles are believed to date back to the Middle Ages, when they were used as protective talismans by wizards. Because the availability of glass was not universal, it is doubtful that the poor—Witches included—used glass containers for these types of spells. Nonetheless, they have become known today as "witch bottles," and my own experiments have proven them to be powerful tools to protect or ward a person, group, home, covenstead, or other area.

When an individual Witch makes a witch bottle for her own use, it usually includes pins, needles, nails, broken glass, and rusty bits of metal. These are to protect and ward. It also includes ashes and salt to ground away negative energy flowing your way. It is traditional that the Witch top off the bottle with her own urine and, if female, a drop or two of menstrual blood.

When making a witch bottle with a group, it's necessary to make some modifications for sanitation's sake. It shouldn't need to be said at this point in time that blood rituals have almost vanished from Wiccan group practice since the advent of AIDS, and the covens who still use blood are careful not to come into contact with one another's bodies and to use only the sterile lancets purchased at pharmacies to prick the skin. Even with these precautions, the use of blood in a group witch bottle is not recommended. There are just too many substitutes for blood to justify taking risks with the health and well-being of your coven members.

Some of your coven members may wish to bring along a few items from home for the bottle before the spell begins. This is also one of those spells where sending the coven out to seek items culled from the environment the coven meets in adds a lot to the protection factor, simply because these found items have absorbed the energies of the area. Stones, sticks, and herbs may all be found that call out to one member or another as the perfect ingredient for a protective witch bottle. Instead of using salt or ash, using some dirt from the ground upon which the circle meets is more effective in this spell.

Another word of caution is needed about what items your coven members choose to pick up from the ground. It's a sad fact of modern life that people are litter-prone, and rusty metal and broken bits of glass are easy to find. Pulling these from where they are wedged in the earth could cause someone a nasty cut. Taking a fellow coven member to the hospital for stitches and a tetanus shot tends to take away from the magickal atmosphere. Use common sense when seeking witch bottle items in the outdoors.

When everyone is back at the circle and the group is ready to assemble the bottle, the leader should make sure everyone in the group has at least one item to add. The leader should go first, adding the salt, ash, or earth to the bottom of the bottle as the grounding element that will pull any negative energy away from your coven and meeting area and into Mother Earth. This might sound something like the following.

> RED WOLF HP: I place into the witch bottle the power of earth in the form of ashes from our balefire. These ground any negative energy and intent sent our way that is not deflected by the other items we are about to place inside. Come forward, everyone, as we grow a wall of protection around our covenstead.

The members of the group should all come and stand around the bottle. This is a fun spell and no one should feel silly about what they say or what they add. To the contrary, every anti-negativity spell I've done—no matter what the format—has worked best when I've been moved to laughter. Magick should be no more 100 percent solemn than ritual. Oftentimes the lighthearted touch works best. It took me a long time to learn this lesson. I was helped in this effort by a curandera, or wise woman of Mexican descent, when I lived in southern Texas. She would tell me when a negative energy or entity came my way that I was to look it in its metaphorical eye and laugh at its efforts to scare me or to cause me harm. It's a magickal truth that fear feeds fear and makes it stronger. The curandera was right. Nothing wilts negative intent quicker than a hearty belly laugh.

The ritual hodgepodge of items being placed into the bottle might sound like the following.

> MOONDANCER: I place in the witch bottle my broken compact. Not only is there broken glass inside that will deflect back to the sender any negative energy sent our way, but it symbolizes the fragility of the negative efforts of those vain enough to think they can harm us or weaken our faith.

> STORMWILLOW: I place in the witch bottle the nails I had left over from the birdhouse I built last week. They symbolize home and security, and they will prick and poke those who send us harmful intent.

> WINDWALKER: I place in the witch bottle some shavings from the salt lick on my grandparent's farm. Salt grounds and it represents both nourishment and the Earth that is our home, especially this small piece of Earth that is our covenstead.

> OAKMAN: I place in the witch bottle a rose quartz crystal I found over in the farm field across the street. It represents peace and harmony.

Snow Owl HPS: (Using tweezers to remove a small piece of plant from a plastic bag.) **I place in the witch bottle some nettles, a plant that causes stinging and itching to those who dare touch it. May it protect our covenstead and those of us who worship within.**

Rain: (Removing a small vial and pouring the contents into the bottle.) **I place into the witch bottle a mixture of rusty water found near the old shack with the tin roof down the road and some dragon's blood. The rust decays negative intent while the dragon's blood protects us and our sacred space.**

When the witch bottle has been filled, it should be buried a foot or so deep in the ground just inside your circle. It's best if it's placed at the directional quarter that your coven or tradition uses as a gateway. For many Wiccans, this is the eastern quarter. For some Celtic covens, it is the west. For covens who meet indoors, the witch bottle should be buried near the front door of the home or building where the meetings are regularly held.

Everyone should take a turn with the shovel and turn up the earth and, if possible, everyone should have a hand on the bottle as it is placed into the ground. Words of power to seal the spell may follow. You can choose a litany-style sealing, blessings offered from each member, or you may create and memorize something to say in unison. I like the idea of chanting words of power in unison for this spell, just because this has been a group project designed for the benefit of the group. An example of words you might use follows.

> Witch bottle, vital and strong as an ass,
> Witch bottle, made of precious glass;
> Filled with ashes from the sacred flame,
> It deflects and grounds all harm and bane.
> Witch bottle, warding by the power we beseech,
> Witch bottle, guarding from those who impeach;
> Filled with pins and nails and rust,
> In its warding and grounding we do trust.

By tradition, a witch bottle will protect for a year and a day before it should be dug up and re-created, but mine have seemed to maintain their effect for up to three years. Your coven can decide what works best for itself.

Notes for Spell Alteration: Witch bottles are perfect tools for solitary practitioners to use as warding and protective devices. Using blood or urine is not a health issue when it's only yourself involved, and it gives the practitioner the chance to clean out rusty nails, bent pins, and bits of broken glass from his home. Bury it either near a front door or somewhere away from your home, such as at a crossroads.

◆ WITCH BOTTLE 2: THE TANGLED WEB ◆

Goal: Same as the previous spell.

Subject: To protect the covenstead and its members from harmful intent by grounding and deflecting negative energy.

Items: A glass jar (like a spaghetti sauce jar) and lots of small, 2- to 4-inch pieces of colored string.

Best Times: Same as previous spell.

There is an old belief dating from the Middle Ages that no evil could enter a dwelling to do harm without first counting all the fibers within that place. By putting small pieces of string or thread in a witch bottle, you can tie up harmful intent in a tangled web from which it can never escape.

I made one of these types of witch bottles for myself years ago and only sensed that it was full and had stopped working after about seven years. For my bottle I chose to use pieces of embroidery floss rather than thread. Embroidery floss is not any more expensive than thread, it's easy to cut into small pieces, and its variety of colors addressed every magickal need in reference to protection that I could ever possibly encounter. Any craft store will have a wide selection of embroidery floss. With the assortment of floss shades available, your problem will be limiting your color choices, not finding them.

It's best to select floss colors as a group while keeping traditional magickal color associations in mind. For example, red is the color of war and passion, which gives the bottle these energies when tying up baneful energies. Blue is the color of peace and truth, making it able to sort out true negative intent from harmless energies. Black absorbs negativity, white reflects it back at its sender. Gold protects, and yellow gives the bottle the intellect to sort out and grab onto various energies that enter your circle or meeting place.

As a group you should work together to cut up these pieces of thread while thinking and talking about their magickal purpose. When you're sure you have a pile large enough to fill the jar packed reasonably tight, you may begin loading the jar.

This is an excellent spell to do as a litany. Go in a counterclockwise circle to represent decreasing negative power, and have each person put one single piece of thread in the jar. As this is done that person should recite the next line in the litany, which may be recited dozens of times while the bottle is being created.

An example of a circle of litany you might use follows.

SNOW OWL HPS: Thread of color, tie up the bane.

RED WOLF HP: Keep our coven safe and sane.

MOONDANCER: Tangle up the will of those—

STORMWILLOW: Who send us harm; and they suppose—

RAIN: That they possess the power to pound—

GREENWOOD: And that we cannot protect our ground.

OAKMAN: Thread of color, tangle the intent—

WINDWALKER: That's bent on breaking our faithful bent.

SNOW OWL HPS: We cannot be broken, our will is grave.

RED WOLF HP: The witch bottle assists to make us brave.

MOONDANCER: No harmful spirit, person, or bane,

STORMWILLOW: May enter without finding this tangled mane.

Repeat, et cetera . . .

Repeat for as long as it takes all the cut-up pieces of floss to be placed into the jar. As with the witch bottle in the previous spell, it should be buried within the circle, near a doorway, or placed in a chest or drawer that is rarely opened.

◆ LOVE SPELL FOR GERIENT'S DAY ◆

Goal: To draw to the one or ones who seek true love the best person for them at this time in their lives.

Subject: One or more members of the coven who seek romantic love.

Items: You will need three candles for each member wishing to do the spell. Tapers work best, since this spell will be worked over several evenings. You will also need three candleholders for each person, and several handfuls of powdered herbs associated with love and romance, such as crushed rosemary or myrtle leaves.

Best Times: Monday, Sunday, a waxing or full moon, or a holiday for lovers such as Beltane (May 1), Valentine's Day (February 14), Lupercalia (February 15), or Wales' Gerient's Day (March 16).

Just when Gerient's Day appeared on the Welsh folk or Pagan calendar is unknown. Nothing but apocryphal references are made to it until the Celtic revivals of the late nineteenth and early twentieth centuries. Regardless of its origins, Gerient's Day makes an excellent time to work your own romantic enchantment in the form of a love spell to draw your own sacred partner into your life.

The famous twelfth-century Welsh mythological collection known as the Mabinogion tells the story of the Arthurian warrior Gerient, who fights a battle to avenge the honor of Queen Guinevere. While involved in this quest he falls in love with Enid, a lady in waiting to the Queen. They soon marry. At their marriage the otherworld messenger known as the White Hart appears to them. This white stag, with roots in the most ancient of Celtic mythology, symbolizes the fact that their union is of a sacred nature, one that not only links the male and female principles of creation, but also the mundane realm with the otherworld.

Before embarking upon this or any other love spell, you must fix firmly in your minds the Pagan Rede, which admonishes us to "harm none." Manipulation in the form of attempting to coerce someone to reciprocate romantic feelings is harmful because it violates free will. Everyone in the coven should be reminded to focus only on the qualities of the person they wish to have drawn to them, the one who also seeks them, and not the image of a specific person.

This spell will require that the coven meet for four nights in a row. The candles should be set up on a central altar, three in a row for as many people as are asking for the goal of love. It's best if the candles can remain undisturbed for the four nights of the spell, but it is not required.

Spend some time before the spell begins having those who seek love handle the rosemary (the best choice) or other lover herb such as myrtle, lavender, or jasmine. The seekers should also handle the candles as much as possible to infuse them with their own essence and the energy of their desire.

Once you are in your circle, the seekers should divide their rosemary into four equal parts and tie each part up in a small cloth or handkerchief. Everyone in the group should do something to help pack these so that their energy helps feed the love spell of those who desire it. As you pack the rosemary in, everyone should chant something like the following.

> **Rosemary sweet, your aid we invite,**
> **Show us the face of love this night.**

Have those who seek love step up to the altar and light the first of the three candles as they say something like the following.

> **I start the spell to bring my mate,**
> **The one I seek, my partner, my fate.**

The other members of the coven may chant along if they wish to, adding even more of their energies for success to the spell.

The first of the four packs of rosemary should be passed clockwise around the circle, with each member pouring their energy into it and wishing success for the petitioners. It should then be handed back to the petitioner to take home and place under his pillow before going to sleep. As the petitioner falls asleep, he should repeat the chant over and over to himself.

When the petitioner awakens on the morning after the spell has been enacted, he should take the herb pouch outdoors and release it from its bundle. He should face any one of the cardinal directions—preferably the one moving with the wind—and release the herbs to their task by saying the following.

> **Rosemary sweet, in the far winds now roam,**
> **Seek out my mate and bring her (or him) home.**

On the second night of the spell, the first two candles should be lit and the chant of the petitioners should go as follows.

This is step number two: I now open the way
To clear the path to bring my love to me to stay.

As on the first night, the second pack of rosemary should be passed around the circle, energy added to it, and then it should be given back to the seekers to place under their pillows. Again, as the petitioner falls asleep, the chant from both nights should be repeated over and over.

On the third night of the spell, the petitioners should light all three of their candles and say the following chant.

One and one, they always make two,
Yet two become one, in an act old and true.

The other members of the coven will pass both the third and fourth of the rosemary packets around the circle and hand them back to the petitioner, just as was done on the previous two nights.

One of these should be placed under the pillow of the petitioner, who should fall asleep reciting all three nights' worth of chants.

On the fourth night of the spell, every member of the coven should light the candles, either in fact if there are enough, or symbolically if there are not, relighting the already lit candle. As this is done, each should offer a blessing or wish for a speedy conclusion to the petitioner's spell.

The fourth pouch of rosemary should be passed around the circle as before, only this time each member should take a small handful from it. The petitioners should walk clockwise around the circle while envisioning their desire as the coven members toss the sweet herb over them, saying in unison the following.

Two lights lonely, in darkness entwine,
Two become one and the lights brightly shine,
Two flames united as we see the White Hart,
Bonded forever, the passion does start.
Like God and Goddess incarnate you are,
Soul mates forever, now brought close from afar,
By the power of three times three,
As all will it, so mote it be.

Notes for Spell Alteration: Love spells are very personal goals, and it's not often that a coven will want to spend lots of time and energy working on all the issues of your chaotic romantic life. If you have a coven willing to expend some effort for you, you are very blessed and you should remember their generosity when it's time to reciprocate someone else's personal desire.

This spell can be converted for solitary use with ease. You simply do all the making of the pouches, chanting, candle lighting, and so on, yourself. Repeat the spell once every lunar month until it works.

✦ WITH A LITTLE BIT OF LUCK ✦

Goal: To impart the aura of good luck to all members of the coven.

Subject: Every member of the coven will be part of the spell and will benefit from it.

Items: You will need a place to burn incense. Special censors, iron cauldrons, heat-resistant bowls, and special coals for burning homemade incenses are available at occult shops or through mail order (see Appendix A). You will also need a small bit of dried herbs and oil that make up the ingredients in the incense recipe that appears in this spell.

Best Times: On a Thursday, during the full moon, or on the feast days of any deity of happiness and good fortune. This spell is short and is often best used after other rituals are concluded. The good-luck energies can be absorbed by all during post-ritual festivities, feasting, and dancing.

Fortuna is the Roman goddess of good fortune and Felicitas is the Roman goddess of happiness. They will be called upon to shower their blessings on the celebration during this spell.

The good luck incense should be mixed ahead of spell time. You need only a couple tea-spoonfuls, and each coven member should have a hand in the mixing and empowering.

When the time comes for the incense to be lit, each member should have a small pinch of the incense to place on the hot coals.

The recipe is:

¼ teaspoon frankincense

2 teaspoons small sandalwood chips

⅛ teaspoon allspice

¼ teaspoon hyssop

1 drop nutmeg oil

3 drops vanilla extract

1 teaspoon dried, grated lemon rind

The leader should light the incense coals and, when they are ready, the invocation to the two goddesses should begin.

Important Note About the Coals: Use only incense coals in this or any other spell asking for homemade incense. The charcoal briquettes designed for use in cooking grills contain combustible chemicals that should not be inhaled. They are dangerous if used indoors, and they stink. If you absolutely cannot get your hands on real incense coals, then purchase cone or joss stick incense in a single scent, such as sandalwood, frankincense, or pine, which appeals to the group as one suitable for use in a good fortune spell.

The spell will go something like the following example.

Snow Owl HPS: Felicitas of happiness, Fortuna of luck and joy,
we ask you to impart your blessings on each reveling girl and boy.

Red Wolf HP: Felicitas and Fortuna, we honor you with smoke,
an incense to create a portal, and your presence we do evoke.

Each member should toss their pinch of incense mixture onto the coals. If the coven so chooses, each may offer a blessing or words of thanks to one or both of these goddesses.

✦ THE KITCHEN WITCHES' POTLUCK SPELL ✦

Goal: To have a communal feast that offers all participants a wide variety of magickal blessings.

Subject: Every member of the coven.

Items: Potluck dishes prepared at home and empowered by each coven member, then brought to the covenstead for a ritual feast at a regular meeting time.

Best Times: Immediately following any regularly scheduled coven gathering.

Whether you live in a locale that calls these meals where everyone contributes something a potluck, a carry-in, or a pitch-in, most people enjoy the variety of foods provided from many different kitchens and cooks.

In magick, kitchen witchery is an art unto itself, and entire books have been devoted to its intricacies. The idea behind it is that the ingredients we mix or bake can have magickal consequences. If you think about it, the transformation that occurs when we mix ingredients, add heat, and produce another substance is an amazing act of magick. Our ancestors did not take this process for granted, as we do today in our world with microwave ovens, fine restaurants, and fast food on every corner. The deities of the past illuminate the fact that cooking was once considered a sacred art. Ancient Rome had Vulcan, the god of the oven, and modern Italy has Hestia, goddess of the hearth and domestic chores. The Chinese have a kitchen god who is celebrated in a family festival each year before the new year. Even the chimney, in whose hearth meals were once prepared, still carries magickal connotations in faery tales and in the homes of magickal practitioners.

Many foods have their own magickal associations, just like herbs and stones. Even the individual ingredients within our concoctions have magickal properties all their own that we can use for spellworking. For example, the ginger in your cookies or cakes can be empowered for health, wealth, or lust, just as the end product in which it was included can be empowered for drawing a sweet life or happiness.

Depending on the size of your coven, you may either just wait and see what types of dishes arrive at your feast or you may wish to assign someone to make the main dish, another to make salad, another to provide dessert, and so on. In either case, you need to come to a consensus first on what types of foods will not be allowed. You will need to take into consideration the dietary needs and allergies of each person within your group.

Some people have deadly reactions to nuts or shellfish, while others may be recovering alcoholics who do not wish to consume anything made with alcohol products.

On the day of the feast, each coven member should make their contribution in their own kitchen, or a few may team up and use the same kitchen just for the fun of being together.

Decide before you begin the cooking process whether you will be empowering the whole dish or only specific ingredients. You may need to consult fellow coven members or a guide on herbal magick for ideas. There are two books you may want to consult that can guide you. The first is Patricia Telesco's *A Kitchen Witch's Cookbook* (Llewellyn, 1995) and the other is Scott Cunningham's *The Magic in Food* (Llewellyn, 1990). The following list of common ingredients will help get you started if you are unfamiliar with kitchen witchery or herbal magick:

Apple: Love, romance, health, spirituality.

Basil: Protection, banishing, money.

Carrot: Fertility, stability, lust, sexuality.

Celery: Mental prowess, psychicism, calmness.

Cinnamon: Health, wealth, lust, courage, strength, warding.

Clove: Protection, anti-gossip, money.

Coconut: Purification, protection, spirituality.

Corn: Fertility, abundance, binding, prosperity.

Dill: Money, lust, love, protection.

Flour: Stability, abundance, prosperity, contentment.

Garlic: Protection, healing, passion, exorcism.

Ginger: Health, energy, personal power.

Lettuce: Dream magick, peace, sleep, divination, love.

Mint: Protection, astral projection, dream magick.

Mustard: Mental prowess, protection, courage.

Nuts: Fertility, wealth, employment, partnership, luck.

Oats: Prosperity, money, fertility, grounding.

Olive: Love and lust, peace and trust, truth and justice.

Onion: Protection, health, exorcism, money, nightmares.

Pasta: Comfort, strong family life, peace.

Pea: Money, employment, beauty, fertility, love.

Pear: Lust, love, music and dance magick.

Pepper: Protection, exorcism, anti-negativity.

Pineapple: Friendship, attraction, purification, anti-lust.

Pomegranate: Underworld initiations, fertility, astral work.

Potato: Grounding, fertility, eco-magick, animal magick.

Rosemary: Love, romance, memory, mental prowess, beauty.

Rye: Love, truth, fidelity.

Sage: Mental prowess, wisdom, truth, good judgment.

Salt: Grounding, protection, anti-negativity.

Sugar: Happiness, peace, anti-argument.

Tomato: Love, lust, passion, unity.

Vanilla: Love, romance, beauty, peace, contentment.

Wheat: Fertility, money, prosperity, binding, love.

When your coven has the table for the feast set, each member should announce what their dish is and what about it will provide magick to the coven. This must always be disclosed so that no one is being given magick against her will and so that those with allergies will know if the dish is safe for them to eat or not. This might sound like the following.

> SNOW OWL HPS: I offer a salad with homemade Caesar dressing. I empowered the garlic to bring us protection and the eggs to bring us fertility for all our magickal goals.

> RED WOLF HP: I offer a hamburger casserole in which the potatoes have been empowered to keep us grounded and stable.

> MOONDANCER: I offer a ginger punch, which is empowered to keep our energy levels high.

> GREENWOOD: I offer oranges, which I have empowered to bring us prosperity and abundance.

RAIN: I offer a cream pie topped with nutmeg empowered to bring us health. It is made with a dash of nut oil in the crust, so those of you with nut allergies beware.

STORMWILLOW: I offer a vegetable selection empowered to bring us closer to the spirits of the land. All were grown in my garden and are free of pesticides and chemical growth enhancers.

OAKMAN: I offer a pasta dish for contentment and to keep us a strong spiritual family. It contains green peppers empowered to keep us healthy and lusty.

WINDWALKER: I offer wild venison steaks. They have been seasoned with pepper to keep us protected, and with rosemary to remind us that other creatures must lay down their lives to sustain our own. We must never forget the debt of thanks we owe to them.

It is traditional to offer some type of blessing over both the food and drink before anything is consumed. This custom came into Western mainstream religions from Judaism, which in turn adopted these practices from the Canaanite and Babylonian Pagans living near them in the ancient Middle East. These may be as elaborate or as simple as you would make any other blessing. The character of your coven will determine the style you adopt.

SNOW OWL HPS: (Raising her arms above the table.) **Blessed be the food, gift of the Lord and the Lady. To them we offer a part of this feast, the meal that is their gift to us. May we never forget by whom we are nourished, and may all the positive magickal wishes offered here take root and flourish. By our will, so mote it be.**

At this point some appointed person makes a small plate of food to set aside as an offering to the deities. It can be buried later or left for the wild animals (or domestic pets/familiars) to eat.

RED WOLF HP: **Blessed be the fruit of the vine and all life-giving waters that our deities** (who may be called by name if your coven chooses) **have provided for us. May it quench our thirst in body, mind, and spirit.**

Another person should be appointed to pour a bit of the wine, punch, water, or juice onto the ground as an offering back to the deities. If you are meeting indoors, prepare a separate cup for the deities so it can be taken outside later and offered there.

Notes for Spell Alteration: The ceremony of cakes and ale is a popular Wiccan ritual of unknown origin. That it is ancient is a given, because it shows up in the practices of mainstream religions as communion in Christianity and the *hamotzi*—a very old ritual bread blessing—in Judaism.

In this ceremony, the Earth is thanked for its blessing of food and drink. An offering of wine and a food baked with grain is usually offered as a sacrifice of thanksgiving to the deities of the Earth and left out for animals to consume. This ceremony is perfect to incorporate with a kitchen witches' potluck spell.

If you are unsure of how to create a cakes and ale ceremony, almost any book on basic Witchcraft will have formats you can follow to create your own. Again, if you have not reached this level of expertise within the Craft yet, reconsider attempting spellwork with your coven at this time and learn the basics of the faith first. Take things one step at a time for best results and a long life of happy magick-making.

◆ OVERCOMING AN OBSTACLE ◆

Goal: To help break down a barrier that appears to be keeping the petitioner from attaining either a mundane or magickal goal.

Subject: Any member of the coven who feels there is a block in the path to achieving a goal of any kind.

Items: You will need a hammer and lots of visualization to create an image of breaking through impediments. You will also need a small altar with a lit working candle and enough unlit candles for everyone present.

Best Times: Whenever needed, but a Saturday is best.

This spell works best in a larger coven because the other members are going to literally make up the wall of obstacles that the person feeling stuck must break through in order to achieve his goal. This is similar to the children's playground game Red Rover, in which a person from an opposing line is called on to try and break through the human wall created by the other team.

The obstacle in question can be virtually anything: a job issue, a relationship problem, a health concern—anything a member of your coven has worked hard to overcome by all magickal and mundane means available, but which he still cannot break through. In tarot readings about the problem, the coven member often draws cards that show the frustration of immobility and indecision. These cards include the Eight of Swords, which relates to feelings of isolation and not knowing where to turn, even though an unseen path can lead the petitioner out of his situation. Another card often seen is the Five of Wands, representing a force that is not yet settled. In this case, the energies desired could either be coming together or pulling apart, but the petitioner is unsure how to send them in the direction he wants. The last two cards that often appear are the Four and Five of Cups, which display images of sorrow and contemplation concerning both indecision and loss. In both cards there are cups that are full or that are being offered as a gift that is not recognized by the petitioner, who has become so confused and mired in his difficulties that he now needs his coven's help to break free.

The person needing to overcome the obstacle should stand alone, facing the line of his fellow coven members. The rest of the coven should connect themselves by holding each other's wrists, forming a strong line of defense. They represent the obstacle that the petitioning coven member must break through to find his way once more.

The coven member petitioning for help should state his problem out loud to the group. Coven members may ask questions, playing devil's advocate if need be. Remember, the line of coven members represents the obstacle to be overcome, and your challenges to the petitioner will strengthen your symbolic representation of that obstacle to him.

All members of the coven should be visualizing themselves as the obstacle while still sending their best energies to the assistance of their member in trouble. This type of dual thinking is difficult for newcomers to magick, which is why your most experienced people should be placed in the line alternating with the less experienced. You don't want a long section of weak links if the spell is to work its best.

The dialogue may go on for as long as the petitioner needs it to before he feels ready to break through. He, and not the leader or leaders, will decide when it's time to rush at the obstacle, and the line of members should always be prepared for the petitioner's onslaught. This might sound something like the following.

STORMWILLOW: I've been out of work for two months. I'm a qualified engineer. I have a well-respected degree and a terrific résumé. I have tried magick and physical-world networking, and still no luck. I don't know where to turn next.

OBSTACLE: Maybe people just don't like you.

STORMWILLOW: Not true. I have many friends.

OBSTACLE: That means nothing. Maybe no one likes them either.

STORMWILLOW: Not true. I know I'm making a good impression on the interviewer, but the job always goes to someone else. In one case I was told that out of two hundred applicants the choice came down to me and just one other person.

OBSTACLE: Maybe you really don't want what you say you want. Maybe you want another life—one of leisure or a different career.

STORMWILLOW: Who wouldn't enjoy leisure? But I'm not of that class. I must work, and I love what I do. I worked hard to achieve my status. I worked hard to get through college. This is the life I've wanted since I realized I must work for my living.

OBSTACLE: Maybe you're not as good as you think.

STORMWILLOW: Not true. I've solved many problems others could not, and I've achieved praise and recognition from both peers and superiors for it. I am good at what I do.

When the petitioner feels enough strength—even anger—at his situation, he should charge the line of wrist-locked fellow coven members in an attempt to break through. The coven should not allow this to happen if possible, but don't risk a broken wrist holding him back, either.

The petitioner may make three attempts to break through the line, and on the third attempt he should be allowed to pass through. Three is a number of magickal significance in many cultures, in particular those of western Europe, from where many of our modern Pagan traditions are derived. The number three in those cultures represents completion and fulfillment, and is a number sacred to many of their deities.

The Locked-Wrist Hold

After the petitioner has broken through the obstacle line, he should be congratulated, hugged, and words of encouragement offered to him.

The petitioner and the rest of the coven should stand around the altar. In turn each will take the lit working candle and light an unlit candle while offering a blessing of success to the petitioner. This represents the light of success.

When the spell is ended, the candles should be extinguished and given to the petitioner to take home and use during his own magickal efforts at overcoming his obstacle.

◆ PROTECTION LITANY SPELL ◆

Goal: To raise defensive energy around your circle, dwelling, or other area you wish to protect from any type of harm or intrusion.

Subject: Every member of the coven will work toward this goal, whether the object of protection is the communal circle or the personal space of one of the individual members.

Items: None.

Best Times: When needed, but best on a waxing or full moon, a Sunday or Tuesday, or the Roman holiday of Terminalia (February 23) when, by tradition, boundaries are marked and warded.

This spell strengthens the circle created in each ritual you do and turns it into a spell of protection.

The first step is to open a circle around the space to be protected. Most often this will be your coven's own circle area or covenstead; other times it might be someone's home, possession, or land. The elementals and quarters should be called upon and the deities should be invoked just as if any normal group ritual were about to take place.

Someone in the coven may be asked to call upon the Roman god Terminus, the god of boundaries and portals. A festival in his honor, celebrated around what is now February 23, began in 200 B.C.E. when the Roman emperor declared that all citizens owning property must present a clear outline of those perimeters. The citizens at first resented the dictate, then began marking off the borders of their lands with garlands, flowers, and plants sacred to Terminus. The date soon became an annual festival to him, even as the origin of the festival was forgotten.

Other deities of protection and defense you may wish to invite include England's Coventina or Britannia, India's Shiva, Scandinavia's Thor, China's Kuan-Yin, Rome's Rumina, or Babylonia's Anahita. Deities of places, such as forests and rivers, and their attendant elemental or faery spirits may also be invited to assist.

When all the preparations are made, and any deities—such as Terminus—have been invited, the coven or person who owns the place being warded should make some marking of the boundary. This does not have to be a permanent fixture like a fence, just something that will make clear the visual boundary of the area to be protected. Stones, candles, stakes, flags, and flowers all make good choices.

The coven should began dancing in a clockwise circle around the area, raising the cone of power over themselves as described in chapter 2. The dance should start slow and gather speed as it progresses.

Keeping in time with the dance, a litany that will help feed the spell should be chanted. It may sound something like the following.

SNOW OWL HPS: By our will the wall we raise.

RED WOLF HP: God and Goddess we do praise.

MOONDANCER: Protected, warded, are we all.

WINDWALKER: On the power of fire we do call.

RAIN: Safe from harm from spirit and man.

GREENWOOD: **Summon we the protective hand.**

STORMWILLOW: **We each have power to call our shield.**

OAKMAN: **Protective magick we do wield.**

SNOW OWL HPS: **By the power of three times three,**

ALL: **By our will, so mote it be.**

RED WOLF HP: **The cone we raise, its power set free,**

ALL: **By our will, so mote it be.**

Repeat.

When the leader feels the energy can be built no more, he will direct the coven to stop the dance and immediately send out the energy toward its goal. Each member is usually free to make whatever gesture or use whatever visualization works best for that individual during this process.

> **Notes for Spell Alteration:** If you have a large coven and your goal is the protection of your covenstead, you may dance yourselves into a spiral position to channel the protective energy from the center of circle, which represents all space and time, to the outer boundaries where it is needed.
>
> This litany spell can also be done by solitaries, though more effort is needed and it works best in smaller, personal spaces.

◆ THE HEALING CIRCLE SPELL ◆

Goal: To assist someone to heal by adding magickal energy to the healing process already being given by medical professionals.

Subject: Anyone who asks to be healed whom the coven wishes to help.

Items: A central fire of some kind to symbolize the energy of health, strength, and transformation. You will also need some powdered nutmeg, cinnamon, dill, or other herb associated with healing. These can be easily culled from most people's kitchen cabinets.

Best Times: When needed most, but Wednesday is best.

Healing illnesses has been one of the major tasks of the Witch for centuries. Many women who were not Witches, but who lived in the country and knew about the medicinal value of plants, were accused of Witchcraft and executed for no more than the crime of healing. With the church firmly against what they saw as taking over God's role in the life and death process, and the rise of the male-dominated medical professional in the Middle Ages, women's role in healing was diminished and went underground with the other vestiges of the Old Religion.

The person for whom this ritual spell is being enacted does not have to be present for this spell to work. If they are, they should take their place in the circle with the others rather than be at its center. If this is not possible due to physical limitations from the illness, the petitioner should stand or sit wherever she feels comfortable.

Every member of the coven should have a hand in lighting the central fire, even if only symbolically. It is to be visualized as a fire of strength, healing, and transformative power. Once the fire is blazing, each coven member should toss into it a small bit of one of the powdered herbs associated with the energies of healing. Each should also make a short statement about the healing magick as they do this. Everyone should keep in mind that this statement will be used as a litany later in the spell, so it should be kept to one strong sentence.

Coven members should stand side by side, not touching one other, with their left arms across their stomachs so that the person to their right may easily take that hand when the time comes.

The leader will start the litany by making a statement about the goal of the spell, creating the atmosphere necessary for the visualization to be its strongest. Deities of health and healing may also be invited. These include Ireland's Airmid and Dianchecht, Rome's Minerva and Mercury, China's Yuan-Chin, the Slavic goddess Vila, Greece's Panacea, and the Phoenician god El.

The leader should begin the litany with the words he used when he placed his herbs into the fire. As he does this, he should swing his right arm over his left and grab the waiting left hand of the person to his left. (This is from the spell shown in part at the beginning of chapter 2.) The connection should be forceful but not painful. You are making a link that will pass along magickal energy. You want it to be felt strongly and passed along, so give it all your energy.

The next person will also swing her right arm over her left as she adds her phrase to the litany spell, and take the left hand of the person to her left.

After everyone is linked, the litany chant should still be passed around the circle, the energy building, hands linked, the words coming faster and faster until the leader signals that he feels it has reached its peak. At that point all coven members should turn 180 degrees, or a half turn, to their right, passing under their own right arms. The coven will now be hand in hand, all facing outward. As this happens, each should visualize the healing energy being directed out where it is needed.

If the person for whom the healing spell is being done is present, she should toss into the central flame some symbol of the illness. This can be a doctor's receipt, a drawing of the illness, or some other item that, to that person, symbolizes what she wishes to heal.

Notes for Spell Alteration: Like the protection litany spell already discussed, this spell also works well when the coven dances itself into a spiral formation to channel their energy. To do this, place the person to be healed at the circle's center and channel in the raised energy from the outer edge to the center.

✦ SENDING ENERGY AFTER A LITANY SPELL ✦

Goal: To send the energy built during a litany spell out toward its magickal goal.

Subject: Anyone and everyone.

Items: Depends upon the spell being done.

Best Times: Depends upon the spell being done.

Any litany spell can be used for any magickal goal. When the energy it has created has built to its peak, the litany can be ended and the energy sent out to assist the goal in any number of ways.

1) Coven members fall down, weak-kneed, as if exhausted as the energy is drained from them. They should feel the Earth absorb their energies to be used where needed.

2) Coven members throw up their arms, jump, or start a dance that keeps the energy flowing so that it can be fed even more energy.

3) For spells seeking to banish rather than create, arms can be linked with the left hand over the right, and the turn-out at the end will be done with a left half-turn instead of a right half-turn.

4) Spinning is another ancient practice of sending magickal energy, one still popular with certain Middle Eastern religious sects. Spinning clockwise until one falls enhances creative magick, and spinning counterclockwise until one falls enhances destruction—not to be confused with negative—magick.

5) Coven members can dance themselves into a spiral and channel the energy they've raised into one specific direction.

◆ THE WAND OF WISHES ◆

Goal: To make a wishing stick that stands as a talisman of every coven member's fondest desires and concerns and makes a beautiful magickal decoration for your covenstead.

Subject: Every member of the coven.

Items: A tall stick or dowel rod, about four to five feet in height; markers; colored ribbons about two inches wide and eighteen inches long. A hammer and some nails.

Best Times: The waxing moon, a spiritual new year, the spring equinox, or on a Thursday or Sunday.

During an informal coven gathering, each member should help in cutting up a variety of colored ribbons. Each member should be encouraged while doing this to talk about her greatest wishes and desires, no matter how impossible or fantastic. This is the time to indulge all the best fantasies you've ever had. Forget about whether the magick is realistic or not. All dreams and hopes are beautiful, and they make your wishing wand a talisman of great beauty and power because they represent the dearest hopes of those who create them.

When the ribbons are all cut, each member should take a marker and write on a few of them these dreams, desires, and wishes they have. Those who are more artistic in nature may wish to draw representations of their wishes instead. Do what feels right to you.

When doing this, try to choose ribbon colors for your wishes that correspond to that wish as much as possible. Also keep in mind that color associations are often personal choices and, though traditional color correspondences exist, no choice is inherently right or wrong. If you are unsure as to which color to choose, you may always use white or use the list below, which offers some general guidelines.

Red

For wishes of courage, passion, determination, lust, strength, victory, health, stamina, and sexuality.

Orange

For wishes concerning friendship, attraction, the law, justice, and general success.

Yellow

For wishes of the student, of intellect, good study habits, brain power, employment, and communication.

Green

For wishes of love, beauty, bounty, prosperity, abundance, fertility, faery contact, and money.

Blue

For wishes concerning peace, healing, meditation, sleep, dreams, tranquility, seeking past-lives, and fidelity.

Purple

For wishes of healing, meditation, spiritual pursuits, astral projection, profound change in consciousness, and spirit contact.

Silver

For wishes of psychic matters, the Goddess, dreams, insights, visions, prophecy, and secrets.

Gold

For wishes of prosperity, riches, self-expression, the God, and success.

Brown

For wishes for the home and for animals, and for stopping gossip.

Pink

For wishes of romance, love, stopping gossip, and peace in the home.

Black

For wishes of things you wish to banish or have taken from your life, and for forgetting.

White

For spirituality, purification, chastity, and all magick for which no other color seems suitable. Since white reflects the entire color spectrum to the eyes, you're covered no matter what.

The ribbons should be gathered and nailed or otherwise attached to the top of the stick. At the next coven gathering your wand of wishes should be planted just outside the "doorway" to your circle. In this way it represents the World Tree—the axis on which the universe spins, connecting heaven and earth—carrying your wishes to all worlds.

> **Notes for Spell Alteration:** This spell can be done as a solitary in your own home. Create the ribbons in the same way a coven would, then open a window to the fresh breeze. Attach the ribbons to the window frame so that they blow your wishes in to you. Make sure you attach them so the words or pictures read from the window inward so as to keep the path of least resistance flowing toward you and not back out the window.

✦ WITCH-FINDER TALISMAN ✦

Goal: To make a talisman that will help your coven find other Witches, other Pagan individuals, or other covens to join with for special events and celebrations.

Subject: Every member of the coven will be part of this talisman's creation, if all have agreed to this course of action. If not, the spell should not be enacted.

Items: You will need a circle of orange cloth about two feet across, a string to tie it up with, a small circle of paper, some dragon's blood, a paintbrush, and a single item from each coven member representing what they hope to find in this search.

Best Times: The waxing moon, or a Wednesday or Friday.

Whether your coven seeks new members, newcomers to teach, or another coven to join with for special events, a Witch-finder talisman can help in the search and help weed out the type of people you do not want to meet. I made a similar talisman when I first began studying the Craft and found it worked pretty well, even for someone very new to magick. With the effort of a concerned coven behind it, it should be a powerful talisman for positive attraction.

Before the work starts on the talisman itself, a coven meeting is necessary in which a consensus of exactly what you as a group seeks is defined. Protecting the integrity of a good working group is always your first priority. If someone has a serious issue with newcomers, with teaching, or even with meeting with other covens, their concerns should be addressed in detail lest you risk losing the love and trust you've worked hard to build. You might want to talk on a Wednesday, a day corresponding to communication, and then do to the ritual on Friday, a day corresponding to loving relationships.

Try starting the discussion by having everyone talk about what is good about what you have built so far and in what direction they see the group taking in the future. Be prepared for as many answers as there are coven members. Also be prepared for new ideas to be sparked as everyone has the chance to express themselves. This will help you all get an idea of what you have that is too precious to lose, and what you might have to gain by trying a new direction.

When you have agreed upon what—or who—it is you want to find, each member should be instructed to take a few days to find or make an item that represents what they hope the group finds, or what the group will become in the future. The item should be small enough to fit inside the orange cloth bag that will become your Witch-finder talisman.

When you're ready to begin the spell, the orange circle of cloth should be laid out in the center of your circle. Words chosen by the group during your communication session should be painted on the circle of paper with the paintbrush and dragon's blood. Every member should have a hand in this.

Lay the paper in the center of the orange cloth.

Now have each member step forward and add to the talisman the item they have chosen to represent what they seek. If you recall the blessing spells mentioned in chapter 5, you will also recall that these unplanned speeches are where surprises can occur, especially if one or more of your members was less than thrilled with the consensus. This is the risk you take when you attempt to change your coven's basic structure or format. Change is good and is necessary for growth, but it can be scary—and sometimes things you didn't expect to have change can change forever.

The session might sound something like the following.

RAIN: I place into the talisman a rose quartz. This is a stone of peace and happiness and love. May the Witches we find hold these three things as sacred as we do.

MOONDANCER: I place into the talisman this photo of us taken last Beltane so we will not forget that we are a coven, a family, and so that no matter how our horizons expand and where we end up as a group, we will always be a special spiritual family united by our perfect love and perfect trust.

OAKMAN: I place into the talisman these fresh-picked yellow roses. Yellow roses speak of loving friendship, and friendship based on love is what I hope we find.

SNOW OWL HPS: I place into this talisman the herb dill and a piece of ivy. The dill represents loyalty and the ivy binds us, one to another. May we be one—one coven—even as we reach out to others.

When the talisman is complete, it should be tied tightly and then placed wherever your group feels it will do the most good. It may be buried near your circle site or in front of a coven member's home. It may be kept with a leader or other trusted coven member. It may be hung near a doorway or hearth, or stored in a cabinet with other magickal supplies.

If later on your coven decides it does not wish to continue in this search for other Witches, the talisman should be burned by all members in a central fire and the ashes buried as far way from the member's homes and the covenstead as is reasonable.

◆ A CROSSROADS SPELL FOR BANISHING ◆

Goal: To take something unwanted by the coven and banish it forever. This can be something tangible or intangible.

Subject: The spell works best when the thing to be banished is the goal of every member of the coven. However, it can be done at the request of one person or when each member of the coven wishes to banish something from their lives with the support of the group.

Items: A private but safe crossroads where two or three roads intersect, an offering or gift for the Goddess of the Crossroads, and a small pouch representing what you wish to have the Goddess take from your lives. You will also need a small length of black cord or some black thread and a needle, and a black marking pen.

Best Times: On a waning moon when the dark moon is only a few days away, when the moon is in a barren sign like Aries, or on a Saturday. Another time to select is the Feast day of Hecate, a popular Goddess of the Crossroads (November 7 or 15).

Crossroads spells have been used since there were enough roads to cross one another at some point. They are still popular today. Modern Witches enjoy doing these while evoking the darkly powerful blessings of Hecate.

Hecate is one of the most well-known goddesses within any tradition. She is the image from which the modern Halloween witch with the pointed hat, cackling laugh, and wart-studded nose is derived. Greek legends tell us that on the night of the dark moon she would appear at crossroads with her two large, black dogs at her side. By the light of her single torch she would seek gifts left by her followers. This is why spells crafted for her attention work well at a crossroads; it's Hecate's check-in point, to see what her devotees want from her. Hecate is also envisaged as a Goddess of the Dark and Waning Moon, and spells to decrease, destroy, or banish anything work well under her blessing.

There is no end to the list of things you may wish to banish from your lives. You may even wish to consider doing this spell as an adjunct to another designed to decrease or end something. You can banish poverty, loneliness, grief, a bad neighbor, lack of concentration, illness, an unwanted suitor, gossip, fear, a memory, discord, confusion; it can help you sell a home or other item; it can remove a bad friend from your life; or it can be used to banish a coven member in a final ritual that marks the most drastic action a coven can take against someone who has done something so unforgivable that the group can no longer work with this person. Often the ritual tools of that banished person were buried at a crossroads so they could be given to Hecate to decide that person's spiritual fate.

Because covens are not under one auspice, these banishments do not carry the same weight as excommunication from a church might, but the resulting discord tends to ripple through the entire Pagan community, causing dissension and making us forget we are a spiritual body, not a political one.

About ten years ago, the notion of banishing someone from a coven was overused and it became commonplace to see spiteful notices in Pagan periodicals about who had been banished from what group and why. Most of these banishings were based on pettiness and had nothing to do with spirituality or love and trust. If you think you have a serious-enough problem with another coven member to consider banishing, please consult books on coven dynamics or speak with others who have had extensive experience in covens to fully understand this last-resort step. It should never be undertaken spontaneously or in anger, or to punish someone who just happens to view a spell or ritual in a different light than others.

For this spell blueprint we will assume the coven as a whole has something they need banished from their lives or environment. After that decision is made, everyone should be instructed to take a few days to gather items representing that problem or issue and later, in a ritualized setting, place them into a small pouch.

If the crossroads you have chosen is little-traveled, or it is late at night, you may be able to do this full spell at the crossroads. If not, you may need to do the first part of the spell at your covenstead and then take the pouch to the crossroads for burial and dedication to Hecate. In this example, we will presume the latter is the best course of action.

When you meet in circle at your covenstead for the first part of the spell, have every member, one by one, take hold of the pouch while explaining the significance of his chosen symbolic item. The item should then be passed around the circle for each member to add to it their own energies. When the item has made it around the full circle, it should be placed into the pouch by the person who brought it.

The pouch is then passed along to the next person in line, moving counterclockwise, the direction associated with decrease. The choice of the item is explained by that next person. As before, it is passed around the circle so everyone may help empower it. When it reaches the person who donated it, it is placed in the pouch, and then the pouch is passed on counterclockwise to the next person in the circle.

There should be no judgments made about the items selected by individuals. They may be personal tokens or they may be pictures cut from magazines. They can be herbs, stones, drawings, amulets, poems, or anything else representing what is to be removed from your lives. Allow each person to choose what they see fit to use. The only time a value judgment should be placed on an item is if it is deliberately intended to curse or harm someone. Then the spell should be halted by anyone who chooses to do so, and the matter discussed further before any spell is completed.

An example of this need to stop the spell might be if you are a coven of young people who have a teacher who is clearly not suited to be working in a school environment. She takes pleasure in being rude and surly with her students, she is unapproachable about schoolwork, she assigns grades arbitrarily, and she cannot or will not explain her grading system. As frustrating as she may be, crafting a spell to harm her is not acceptable. However, you may ask that she "go away for the good of all." The result of this might be that she is offered a better job somewhere else that she will accept. It may even be outside of the school environment and, because she is part of the "all" for which you wished nothing but good, she may find she is happy in that job, which would change her attitude toward her subordinates.

Never wish harm on anyone, but always seek to work the spell for the best outcome for all. You'll be surprised how things fall into place when the order of things are reshuffled and people land in situations or places where they are all content.

When the banishing pouch is full, it should be tightly sealed with a black cord, or with a needle and thread that everyone should have a hand in sewing. Use the black marking pen to make a large *X* on the pouch. This is not only the sign of the crossroads but also a symbol to our subconscious of crossing something off our mental list of problems and issues. You may want to pass the pouch and marker around to allow everyone to place an *X* on it to further impress their magickal will upon this talisman.

The next part of the spell must take place at the crossroads and works best if everyone who participated is present. Concrete road shoulders, street signs, or other impediments may dictate in which quadrant you bury your pouch and offering, but if you have a choice use the northwest quadrant. West is the home of the dead and the otherworld in many European cultures, a natural place for deities such as Hecate to reside. The north is the place of cold and darkness in the Northern Hemisphere, the place where the sun never travels, and darkness is a hallmark of Hecate's world. Those covens living in the Southern Hemisphere may wish to choose the southwest quadrant instead.

Though it is traditional to dig holes for burying magickal objects with one's hand, this is not a good idea at a crossroads in the dark. You may encounter broken glass, rusty metal, or other hidden dangers. Once I was seeking specific leaves in a wooded area while barefoot. Many magickal people like to be barefoot to better feel their connection with the earth. Forgetting that I was not in the proverbial "forest primeval," I was not watching where I stepped and I ended up slicing my foot open when I stepped on the sharp edge of a rusty beer can. Being taken to the hospital for x-rays, stitches, and a tetanus shot spoiled the outing.

Even when you use a digging tool, such as a shovel or hoe, you should be aware of exactly where you're digging. Many years ago, while a friend and I were burying a witch bottle at a crossroads in rural south Texas, we were unaware that we were right on top of a fire ant mound until the aggressive creatures began to swarm over our legs. Those who have experienced the itching and blistering of even one fire ant bite will know how awful this was, and how very unmagickal.

The hole you dig does not need to be deep—about six inches will do. When the hole is ready, the leader, or someone else who has been asked to do the honor, should call upon Hecate. Because Hecate is viewed as a Crone Goddess, it is often the eldest female member of the group who is asked to evoke her presence.

STORMWILLOW: (Facing northwest.) **Hear my cry, Hecate, goddess of darkness.**
   I, your sister, and my friends request your favor in our time of need.
   Here at your sacred crossroads we leave you an offering of our homage.

At this point in the speech someone should place the offering near the hole. This can be a coin, a precious stone, a food item, a present for her dogs, or anything else you feel might please the Goddess and curry her favor. Select carefully, for Hecate has always been known as a temperamental deity who can turn her back on you just as quickly as she can grant you favors.

STORMWILLOW: (Continuing her evocation.) **We bury here a symbol of our need**
   that we ask you to carry away with your offering. Goddess of darkness,
   of cold, of night, we pray you take from us (fill in the name of your need)
   for the good of all and with harm to none. We praise your power,
   bless your image, and thank you for your attention.

ALL: **By our will, so mote it be.**

The pouch should be placed into the hole by the one who evoked Hecate. Allow everyone to have a hand in covering the pouch, even if it means allowing everyone to shovel back just one small spoonful of earth. Each member of the coven should make an *X* mark over the spot where the pouch is buried. Again, it is traditional to use a forefinger, but if you're not sure if there is glass or other danger present, then find a small stick or stone with which to make your mark.

Move counterclockwise around the group to make your marks. As each person makes their *X*, they should make an affirmation of the spell and offer their personal thanks to Hecate.

> **Banished be** (insert name of problem to to solved), **and blessed be Hecate, goddess of the darkness and ruler of this crossroads, who assists us tonight.**

✦ LIKE ME, LOVE ME ✦

Goal: To allow the best qualities of your coven, or one of its individual members, to shine through in a situation where this is needed.

Subject: This spell can be done for the coven as a whole when you want to garner the favor of an individual, of the community, or of another coven. It can also be worked on behalf of an individual member of your group who needs his best side to show for a specific event, such as when going for a job interview. Another use for this spell might be when an individual coven member wants to attract the attention of someone in whom they have a romantic interest, but without using manipulative magick.

Items: Pens for everyone, paper, dried herbs, incense coals, and a heat-resistant bowl for burning the incense.

Best Times: Sunday or on a full moon.

As you can see from the opening information for this spell, there are lots of reasons for wanting your best side to show and for needing to get yourself stand-out noticed. You may need to impress a potential boss, landlord, loan officer, or lover, without resorting to manipulative magick. With this spell, your best will come through and you will feel confident while being given a chance to compete fairly or to have a chance to attain your goal with harm to none and with no violation of anyone's free will.

Before your coven gathers for this spell, everyone should have written on a piece of paper the positive qualities they wish to project, either as individuals or for your coven as a whole, depending upon for whom the spell is being worked. For the sake of this example, we shall presume that every member of the coven has some need as an individual to project their best image.

As the spell begins, everyone should toss some of the incense mixture onto the hot coals. An incense for projecting your best and causing others to like you might consist of all or some of the following dried herbs.

Clove: To appear discreet.

Comfrey: To put others at ease.

Gardenia: To appear as a team player.

Ginger: For an aura of success.

Goldenseal: To project confidence.

Lemon Balm: To project calmness.

Linden: To project stability.

Vanilla: For likability.

Vetivert: For appearing happy.

Pineapple: To project congeniality.

Rosemary: To appear intelligent.

Sandalwood: To bring out spiritual qualities.

Sweet Pea: To project trustworthiness.

Vervain: For appearing likable and capable.

Each member of the coven should step forward and state their positive qualities, especially those they wish to project the most. Some people feel awkward expressing what they feel is boastfulness, even within their spiritual family, so please respect the choice of someone who wishes to make their declarations silently, though do encourage the shy ones to speak up if they can.

The written list of good qualities should be passed three times clockwise over the burning incense by each individual while the rest of the coven projects their own energy into the person's goal. You may wish to make a small responsive litany of this.

> **COVEN MEMBER: Incense of air, communicate my will to all the worlds.**
> **Project my desired image to those I need to impress.**
>
> **COVEN:** (State person's name), **you are what you want to be.**
>
> **COVEN MEMBER: May those I need to impress see in me all the good qualities**
> **my spiritual family sees. May I attain my goal.**
>
> **COVEN: With harm to none and for the good of all, so mote it be.**

The paper that was passed through the incense should be kept by its creator as a talisman to draw to each person the success they seek. Whenever a member of your coven is facing a situation where she needs to be impressive, she should carry this talisman on her person, concealed from sight. After the goal is achieved, the deities and spirits of air should be thanked and the paper buried or burned.

> **Notes for Spell Alteration:** Solitaries can work this spell just as well as covens, and they have greater freedom in creating a talisman tailored to fit their specific need. For example, if your goal is employment, add a tiger-eye stone to the center of the paper. If your goal is impressing a bank loan officer, then try adding a coin to project the image of someone capable of repaying a loan or a simple child's marble to inspire confidence.
>
> When passing paper over incense or flames, be careful not to start a fire. This is not only a danger to you, but could alter the outcome of your goal. If possible, keep the paper close enough to scorch, perhaps in a pattern of your choosing, but far enough away not to combust.

♦ FERTILITY SPELL FOR A COUPLE ♦

Goal: To help a couple achieve their goal of pregnancy and childbirth.

Subject: Any couple asking for your help that the coven unanimously consents to work for.

Items: A hard-boiled egg, a small pouch of green fabric, a green cord about five feet long, a chalice, a blade (preferably a chalice and blade belonging to the couple), and a feast dish containing at least one of the following fertility foods: potatoes, carrots, or turnips. The couple wishing to conceive must be present and should bring with them some damiana, bistort, and orris root herbs that they have empowered toward their goal.

Best Times: The full moon, moon in Cancer or Pisces, Beltane (May 1), or on Ostara (the spring equinox).

Modern medical science has discovered miraculous methods for helping couples unable to conceive on their own. Yet, even with all the new treatments available, sometimes couples still fail to become pregnant, often for reasons that cannot be defined. This is where fertility magick can help support and strengthen the efforts of medical science.

In this example, the couple wishing to conceive are coven members Rain and Greenwood. The leaders, Red Wolf and Snow Owl, are standing behind the altar as the ritual spell begins.

> RED WOLF HP: **We are gathered in this sacred place, which is not a place yet is all places, at this time, which is no time and yet is all times, to raise a spell of fertility for Rain and Greenwood. They are the God and Goddess incarnate, and we shall open the pathway to the creation of new life within them—as above, so below; as within, so without.**

> SNOW OWL HPS: **Just as the deities created each of us, so shall Rain and Greenwood create new life. Approach the altar of the deities as the deities you are.**

Rain, the female, approaches the altar and lifts up the chalice. This is the symbol of the womb of the Goddess. Like the Holy Grail of the Arthurian quests, it represents the regenerative powers of the feminine aspect of the divine that would end the wasteland of the Arthurian myths.

Greenwood, the male, also approaches the altar and lifts up the double-edged ritual blade, often referred to as an athame. This is a phallic symbol of masculine potency and represents the masculine aspect of the divine and his powers of regeneration.

When these two emblems are joined, the ritual is known as the Great Rite, a ceremony often performed at spring solar festivals by couples and covens. This rite will be the catalyst that empowers Rain and Greenwood's goal.

Red Wolf and Snow Owl come out from behind the altar. Red Wolf stands before Rain, and Snow Owl before Greenwood. At this point the couple should have their backs to one another and be facing the high priest and high priestess. This is so the spell can work with polarities, with male and female passing their energy to female and male.

> RED WOLF HP: (To Rain.) **Who are you who stands before the altar of the divine?**

> RAIN: **I am the divine. I am the Goddess, the feminine half of the creator.**

> RED WOLF HP: **What do you seek here?**

> RAIN: **My other half. My God, son, lover, and consort.**

> RED WOLF HP: **For what purpose do you seek him?**

RAIN: He is me. I am he. We are two halves of the whole of creation. When I join with him, I shall create new life.

SNOW OWL HPS: (To Greenwood.) Who are you who stands before the altar of the divine?

GREENWOOD: I am the divine. I am the God, the masculine half of the creator.

SNOW OWL HPS: What do you seek here?

GREENWOOD: My other half. My Goddess, mother, lover, and nurturer.

SNOW OWL HPS: For what purpose do you seek her?

GREENWOOD: She is me. I am she. We are two halves of the whole of creation. When I join with her, I shall create new life.

COVEN: (Speaking in unison.) In the spiral that is at the heart of life, turn, turn; find yourself within yourself. The creator is one.

The couple now turns to face one another. Rain holds out her chalice and into it Greenwood places the blade. This symbolizes their roles of two halves of the entire creative life force and the strength of their sexual union. At almost all Great Rites there is an electrical tension that can be felt in the air of the circle when these symbols of creation are joined. Allow your coven a few moments to feel this and to use the time to send back to the couple that energy so they can use it for conception.

COVEN: (In unison.) Blessed be the creator, Lord and Lady, whole, united, eternal, one being ever seeking itself.

SNOW OWL HPS: Union is good. Sex is good. It is the bait by which we are all lured to create. But in this case the union has been unfruitful.

RED WOLF HP: What may we offer to our deities as a talisman to fill their womb with life?

Three people step forward from the group. One bears the hard-boiled egg, another the long green cords, and the last the green pouch.

The one with the cord ties the couple together at the waist. The bond should be snug rather than tight, emphasizing the genital area of the bodies.

COVEN MEMBER WITH CORD: We bind you together with the green cord of fruitfulness and abundance as you stand united in the Great Rite.

Next, the coven member with the egg places it inside the chalice next to the blade.

COVEN MEMBER WITH EGG: (Speaking to Rain.) We, your children, creation to which your union has already given birth, now fill your womb with this symbol of new life. As above, so below; as within, so without. As new life fills your symbolic womb, so shall it fill the womb inside you that is now bound to the body of your lover and consort.

Lastly, the coven member with the small green pouch steps toward them.

COVEN MEMBER WITH POUCH: What offering do you make in return for this gift you ask? What can you give us that we can use as both a sacrifice and talisman for your goal?

COUPLE: (Speaking in unison.) These herbs, with fertile power, used by those who have come before us to assist them in their efforts of creation. From the earth, by the earth, from the fertile earth from where all life flows. We offer damiana for sexual desire. Bistort for fertility. Orris root for love.

The couple places the herbs in the pouch, which is then tucked on top of the egg inside the chalice.

RED WOLF HP: (Placing his hands on the heads of the couple.) Blessed be the minds and hearts of our God and Goddess incarnate, our creators who now create again in a never-ending cycle of life-giving, life-ending, and life-renewing.

SNOW OWL HPS: (Placing her hands on the stomachs of the couple.) Blessed be the creative center of the divine couple from which all life flows. This is how the God and Goddess willed it to be when they separated themselves at the dawn of creation, and how it will always be, even as it is now in Rain and Greenwood. We are the image of our creators and within us we hold the power of creation.

COVEN: By our will, for the good of all, with harm to none, we bless our Lord and Lady and their creative processes. So mote it be.

A feast should be held now in which foods associated with fertility magick are featured. Carrots, turnips, potatoes, and other earth-associated products, or foods found below ground, are always fertility foods. During the feast other members of the coven may offer the couple any fertility talismans, toasts, or special blessings they wish. Randy humor is expected and adds to the atmosphere and enjoyment of the event.

The couple should take home with them the blade and chalice and all the items placed within. They should try to make sure no part of this talisman is separated and they should place it near or beneath the place where they make love.

Notes for Spell Alteration: In some Wiccan traditions, most notably the British Alexandrian Tradition, the Great Rite is often performed de facto with the couple representing the God and Goddess disappearing for some private time while the coven awaits their return. This has never impressed me—or some other outspoken members of the Pagan community—as a valuable addition to this sacred rite. In most cases it seems to detract from, rather than enhance, the sizzling atmosphere of the symbolic part of the ritual. The choice of how this will be done is your coven's alone to make, but think about it carefully before making a decision.

Couples who work together exclusively as a coven of two should always feel free to end the Great Rite with sexual intercourse if they feel in the mood to do so.

◆ PROSPERITY AND CONTENTMENT SPELL FOR GAMELIA ◆

Goal: To create an atmosphere in which there is a feeling of prosperity and contentment. This is not a spell for riches, but one of having enough of all that is needed and having a sense of personal happiness that stems from a personal definition of abundance.

Subject: Every member of the coven, though it may be requested by an individual within the group who feels prosperity and contentment have eluded him.

Items: Each member of the coven will need a green-colored stone or a stone associated with happiness and prosperity (jade, carnelian, jasper, quartz, olivine, topaz, or a heart-shaped stone). They will also each need a single dollar bill, some green thread, an envelope, a pen (green or gold ink is good but not essential), and a piece of blank paper. Each member will also want to find a "surprise" addition to the talismans they make, which will be explained within the blueprint for this spell.

Best Times: A spiritual new year, Sunday, Thursday, Friday, or during the waxing or full moon. Another choice is Gamelia, a Roman holiday that honors Hera in her guise as a deity of prosperity. Her feast day is around January 30, though several other dates throughout the year have been attributed to her honor as well.

Gamelia is a Roman celebration of good fortune and prosperity, one in which a Mother or Supreme Goddess is honored. In this case the deity is Hera, but your coven may choose another if you like. The idea is to honor this deity on his or her feast day, or some other date appropriate to do these honors, so that the blessings of prosperity and happiness will rain down upon the devotees.

Gamelia is one of the many guises of Hera, whose name means "our lady." She was once the supreme Pagan deity of Rome before the people turned their patriarchal hearts to her consort, Zeus. In the oral traditions of Rome, Hera was a benevolent, loving deity, very different from the jealous and moody version recorded in current classical mythology.

On Gamelia, couples carrying palm branches would parade with their loved ones through the streets to Hera's temple, which had been adorned with dates and other Mediterranean fruits in honor. Many of the offerings made to ensure her favor were gilded with precious metals. This was an act of sympathetic magick, where a sacrifice of one kind was made in exchange for a like desire. In this case they are prosperity tokens or charms for a prosperous life.

The festival of Gamelia was also known as Strenia, named for a special type of gift known as a *strenaea*. These prosperity presents functioned as talismans of good fortune and were traditionally given to all one's nonfamilial loved ones.

In this spell, each member of the coven will make a strenaea for another member. To decide who shall make a talisman for whom, place the names of all your coven members in a cauldron or chalice and have everyone draw names.

The talismans should be made between the time the names are drawn and the next coven gathering. This is when the spell will be enacted, though keep in mind that the fact that you are beginning to work for each other's prosperity and contentment right now means the spell's energies have already been put in motion.

To make the strenaea, you must gather all your chosen items and empower them to your will. Use a strong visualization of the good wishes you are having for the person for whom you're making the talisman. As you do this, wrap the dollar bill around the green stone and tie it tightly with the thread while chanting something like the following.

> **Stone of green of the sacred earth,**
>
> **Your blessings now are given birth;**
>
> (Name) **shall prosperity and contentment see,**
>
> **For the good of all, so mote it be.**

Place this inside the envelope along with your surprise item. This may be an amulet, stone, writing, token, or another object that personalizes the strenaea in some way. For example, you might add a lodestone for its magnetic properties with a note for the recipient to place it in his wallet to draw money. Or if you know the woman for whom you're making the talisman is discontented because her domestic partner watches too much television, include a newspaper article about free things to do around town. Naturally, the surprise items should be empowered to the goal of the spell, as is everything else you place in the envelope.

When you're done making the talisman, seal the envelope and write the intended recipient's name on the front.

When the coven next gathers, the envelopes should be passed around the circle so that everyone can add their blessings and pour their energy into them. They should then be placed on the altar.

> SNOW OWL HPS: **Contentment and happiness. They mean something different to each of us. Often they are connected with our sense of our own prosperity, but even that word means many things to many people. What they both have in common is that the person who has them feels like a successful human being.**

> RED WOLF HP: **We must always remember that success is not measured by a bank balance, and happiness does not come from things outside ourselves. It comes from within; from our own balance and harmony. It is the state of having enough, being enough, doing enough, and feeling connected to and satisfied with the lives we live.**

Snow Owl HPS: Tonight we call upon the deities of prosperity, abundance, happiness, and contentment, and we ask their blessings upon these strenaea that we offer one another as gifts of love.

The coven members should move in closer to the altar. If possible, and if there is room, have someone light a green or white candle to symbolize abundance and success. You may even wish to light one of each: a green one for the Goddess and a white one for the God.

Before the spell begins, make sure all the coven members know the names of several deities who are associated with prosperity and contentment. Moving clockwise around the circle, each person will call upon a deity of prosperity with a request to bless and assist in the spell. Deities of the hunt, grains, the home, animals, peace, the harvest, wealth, and protection are all good choices, and there are hundreds of them! Some deities upon whom to call might be any of the following.

Agloolik: Inuit god of successful hunting.

Airmid: Irish goddess of health and well-being.

Bona Dea: Italian goddess of good luck.

Ceres: Greco-Roman goddess of grain and prosperity.

Concordia: Roman goddess of peace and harmony.

Corn King: Euro-American god of grain and abundance.

Daikoku: Japanese god of wealth and good fortune.

Dagon: Babylonian god of crops and abundance.

Demeter: Greek goddess of grain, earth, and home.

Frau Holde: Germanic goddess of hearth, home, and Yuletide.

Gula: Middle Eastern gardening goddess.

Habondia: Germanic goddess of abundance and prosperity.

Hestia: Greek goddess of hearth, home, and contentment.

Isis: Egyptian great mother and protector.

Maat: Egyptian goddess of truth and balance.

Omacatl: Aztec god of happiness.

Shai: Egyptian god of destiny.

Shou Hsing: Chinese god of longevity.

Tien Kuan: Chinese god of happiness.

Urcaguay: Incan god of hidden treasures.

Vesta: Roman goddess of hearth, home, and contentment.

Go around the circle in round robin style—each person speaking in turn—as members call upon specific deities of prosperity until no one can think of any more names to add. Coven members may feel free to pass their turn if they cannot think of any more deities upon whom they wish to call. Your round robin of evocations might sound something like the following.

> MOONDANCER: I ask the blessing of Vesta, goddess of hearth and home and Happiness, to lend her energy to this spell.
>
> STORMWILLOW: I invite the presence of Corn King, Lord of Abundance, to add his blessing to our spell.
>
> RAIN: I call upon Ceres, goddess of grain and prosperity, to be with us tonight and, if she will, bless our spell with her love.

When you are finished with the round robin, each person in turn should draw out the strenaea package they made and hand it to the person whose name they drew from the cauldron. Everyone should open their envelope and, if anyone wishes, they may share their surprise element with the others. Feel free to laugh, cry, and enjoy the surprises.

The strenaea should be kept close to the recipient and envisioned as a talisman to draw in prosperity, contentment, and all their attendant feelings of success and well-being.

Be sure to thank all the many deities who came to bless and assist you with this spell before you bring it to a close. It is best if you can do this by having the coven member who called their name bid them thank you, but if memory does not stretch that far, then feel free to do a generic thank you, hail, and farewell.

◆ GARNERING COURAGE THROUGH ELEMENTAL MASTERY ◆

Goal: To have your coven battle against the wit and wisdom of the elements surrounding your covenstead in order to create courage, be better at magick and ritual, and advance to the next level of your spiritual life.

Subject: Every member of the coven should participate or this spell should not be done. Because this spell works best when all coven members fall within a similar range of knowledge and experience, this is not a good spell for use within a teaching coven or where there are vast differences in the levels of experience.

Items: Only yourselves in comfortable clothing and in shoes appropriate for the season and the area in which you will be working.

Best Times: A spiritual new year or just before or after a solar festival or sabbat. Dark moons are traditional for these type of battles, but full moons offer better night vision and make for a safer spell if you will be working at night.

Those who have been in the Craft for several years know all about the "terror of the threshold." This is the point in your studies when the elements gather to test both your knowledge and your resolve to continue with your spiritual growth. Guided meditations, fantasy books, heroic sagas, Craft initiations, and rites of passage all make conscious use of these thresholds as testing points.

On an unconscious level, such challenges face us daily, though we may not recognize them as such. For instance, the final exams you took—or take—at the end of each school year before you could be passed along to the next grade level were terrors at the threshold of your next step in learning. They inspired fear, tested knowledge, and allowed you to continue in your studies if you were successful.

In Pagan practice we make much of the "terror of the threshold" when it's time for an initiate to make that first pass through a new door to seek a new self. Yet we often forget that the thresholds and the terrors blocking them are infinite in number. We tend to overlook the fact that each new level we wish to achieve must be earned by faith and hard work. The truth is that we find ourselves spiritually tested over and over, whether we seek it or not, and spells such as these merely formalize what we have or will have to endure if we wish to remain on our chosen spiritual path.

The idea behind this elemental mastery spell is to gain the respect of the elements and show that we can face them at their strongest and meet the challenges they offer. To do this, your coven must mentally cordon off an area surrounding your covenstead in which you will begin a quest to battle the elements and bring back a token of your victory from each.

In some fantasy novels, and in at least one book on druidic practice, these elemental challenges are presented as dark and dangerous excursions into the unknown. They include running wild through woodlands and marshes at night while brandishing elemental weapons, burning poisonous plants, and crying out challenges to malevolent spirits. None of these things boosts the effect of this spell in any way, but it could put you in danger of being hurt or even killed.

Get the Hollywood hype out of your head. This is not a spell to do while challenging a malevolent entity to coerce the elements to strike out against your enemies, nor to enact with toxic plants as catalysts. It is not a good idea to do this spell in the middle of the night, in an unfamiliar area, or where predators—the four-legged, two-legged, or two-fanged—may be lurking. It should also be nixed in any place where it is illegal to remove natural items from the area or where first aid is not available should something unexpected occur. The God and Goddess gave us the gift of free will, but they also gave us common sense, and would expect us to use it or, as usual, learn our lessons the hard way.

To begin your spell of elemental mastery, you should start within the safe confines of your sacred circle, with you opening it as you would for any other ritual by calling the quarters and asking the assistance of your Goddess and God. Perform some act to honor each element as you call upon it. Light a candle, burn some incense, or make some offering to its spirits. Let each one know you are ready for your group to be challenged by them so that you can gain confidence and grow in knowledge and spirit. The spirits that rule each element are similar in many Wiccan traditions: undines for water, gnomes for earth, sylphs for air, and salamanders for fire.

If the elements do not wish to accept your challenge at this time you will know it, or your leaders should know. There will be a feeling that the ritual is "off" somehow, that you're not connecting to the elements as you usually do, or you may get a sense that nothing is working right or that you've lost interest in the endeavor. Allow the elements to make this decision. They may know of a good reason why the challenge cannot take place at the time you've chosen. It may be they know of a danger you do not, or perhaps someone in the group is still unready for even the most basic elemental challenge.

When these spells are done with solitary practitioners it is a given that the challenge will manifest at a level slightly above where the practitioner feels capable. In your coven, you will be tested at a level just above that of the least knowledgeable and skilled among you. This is why this spell works best if all of you are working within a similar range of experience.

Before doorways are cut at the four quarters for you to come and go, each member must voice aloud their acceptance of the elemental challenge. If anyone wishes to back out, the spell should be halted. It can always be done again at a later time after the problem—usually one of fear or a lack of confidence in personal abilities—has been talked out. This is a coven exercise and, even if someone backs out later after the spell has begun, it should be started off as a group effort.

The doorways to the circle will be closed behind you until the time comes to reenter. Exit through whichever doorway you feel is appropriate. It is customary to reenter through the same doorway you exited, but if you have felt moved or directed to do differently while on your elemental quest, then you should follow your heart.

The rules of the elemental challenge are simple and similar in many traditions. However, the rules of the "game" must always be read aloud before each adventure so that all participants—including the elements and the nature beings in the selected area—are clear on what is expected. It is only after the reading is finished and all is quiet that the leader will get a feeling if the elements have accepted the terms or not, or if they wish the coven to wait until another time.

Start formally.

> **Snow Owl HPS: Hail and welcome to all the elements and their rulers, to the nature spirits and other entities who dwell in the challenge area, to the deities and heroes of myth and magick who come to watch and cheer, and to this gathering of the** (name of your coven) **coven.**

Your rules will include the following:

1) A boundary will be set for how far each member of the coven may range in their quest for elemental tokens.

2) A time limit will be set for the quest. For example, when the setting sun touches the top of the trees at the western end of the woods, then everyone

must return. Avoid setting "real" time limits. As you no doubt know by now, time has no meaning within sacred space. Time pieces are usually removed or even forbidden in circles, and those that are not removed often fail to work properly.

3) Each member will range the designated area seeking token items that represent the four elements. They will face challenges in both the physical and mental acquisition of these items. This is where our greatest fears will be exposed so that we can learn to overcome them. Often our greatest challenge to magickal skill is the fear of pushing ourselves as far as we can go. For example, if you fear fire or some aspect of it, be ready to be figuratively burned in your quest. If you fear earth or one of her creatures, that creature, or your fear of it, may make getting your token from that element harder. The challenge from that creature may not even be real on the physical plane, but your playing field is between the worlds and anything can appear to happen.

These fears are why you don't want to undertake this challenge in the dark. The chances of being hurt while wandering around in the dark are great enough without adding fear that could cloud your thinking or cause you to behave irrationally. Just like animals, we humans have a well-developed fight-or-flight response to signals of danger and, in the dark, we can risk our safety if we act on impulse.

If you as an individual decide you wish to end the quest, simply state this to all four of the directions, lay down any tokens you have already collected, and then return to the circle to await the others.

4) Each member will bring back the items that she has collected when the time period has expired. If everyone has a token from each element, then the coven as a whole has passed the test of the first threshold and been granted boons by the elements, which will make your magick and ritual stronger and more successful.

If everyone did not achieve their quest, this challenge spell should be repeated at a later time. The tokens collected should not be kept by anyone, even those who found them all. This is a coven exercise, not a solitary one. Replace the items found, but be sure to thank the elements for their participation anyway.

5) If coven members have all found their tokens, thank the elements for their participation and promise to use their gifts wisely and for the good of all.

6) The tokens collected should be taken home by each individual. Have the members of your coven make their prizes into small talismans that same night. These are to be slept with; in your dreams the threshold will continue the challenge.

7) At the next coven gathering these individual experiences should be shared so that you can exchange elemental knowledge or insights. Remember that in the spiritual world we are all always students and all always teachers. There is no end to our learning. Those who feel they've reached a pinnacle are the ones who will be most severely challenged just to press home this point.

8) The small talismans everyone made should then be crafted into a larger talisman, which may sit in your coven's center during magick and ritual to symbolize your courage, knowledge, and will to grow. It may be buried under the circle's center to represent your victory, or it may be burned to transform the elemental power into energy you can draw from for a special spell.

Notes for Spell Alteration: Solitary practitioners can do this spell too. One advantage you have as a solitary is more freedom to cordon off an area you like and set your time limits and tests at the level you need to "pass through" the threshold. In other words, you'll be tested at your level, not at the coven's lowest common denominator.

Solitaries should start this spell with a ritual dedicating themselves to the elements as both master and student. There should be a clear understanding that you are not only there to gain, but to give and to learn.

If you like the fantasy element of this spell and want to be challenged in an exotic setting with all the special effects the elements can produce, try this spell as a guided meditation. Write a script to get yourself into the setting, then take off on your challenge. Always remember that saying the words "I am home" three times will bring you out of the otherworld should you become lost, scared, or feel you're in over your head. At the same time, remember that this is a challenge, and the elements will try to test you just slightly above the level of which you may think you are capable. This is how lessons are learned, and growth and understanding are achieved.

◆ GOSSIP-BE-GONE SPELL ◆

Goal: To stop vicious gossip against your coven and its members.

Subject: The coven itself.

Items: You will need twenty-four whole cloves (more if you wish to use them as an incense to enhance this spell).

Best Times: A waning moon, a Saturday, or during any eclipse.

Whenever I create a blueprint for an anti-gossip spell, I cannot make myself avoid the burial of cloves as its central feature. I have used similar spells twice; once in a coven of two, and once several years later as a solitary practitioner. In the first instance the gossip turned back on the one who began the rumors without us having to do anything but one enactment of the spell. In the second case I did the spell for a friend who realized he was being slandered by a former employer whom his prospective employers were calling for references. Within a month he not only had a job offer, but one at a salary more than a third higher than the others would have offered.

This spell works best when you have not been the one to start the gossip in the first place, and you are truly an innocent victim of maliciousness. If there is any truth in what is being said, or you are merely getting back a threefold blast of a negative cycle of talk you began in the first place, then this spell will have no impact.

Start the spell in your usual ritual manner by calling the quarters and the deities. Next, take the quarter call concept a step further and call the cross-quarters too. These are the in-between directions: northwest, northeast, southeast, and southwest. These areas combine and blend the two elements they bridge and, in the wheel of the year, represent the major sabbats or solar festival dates that fall between the two solstices and two equinoxes: Imbolg (February 2), Beltane (May 1), Lammas (August 1), and Samhain (October 31).

These cross-quarter calls don't need to be any more elaborate than your quarter calls, and might sound something like the following.

Northwest Call: Earth of water. Water of earth. Elements binding fall and winter, old and new. We ask your spirit to be present at this working today to assist us. Thank you and bright blessings.

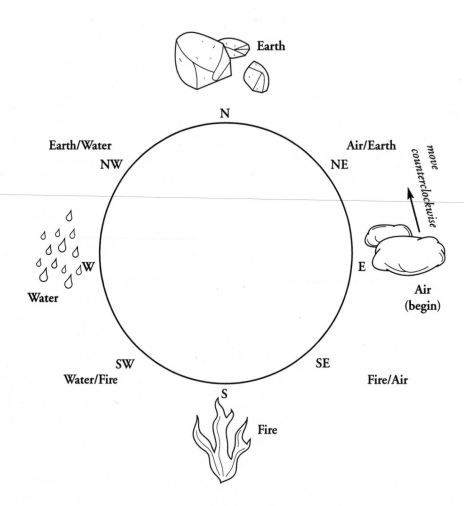

The Quarters and Cross-Quarters

NORTHEAST CALL: Air of earth. Earth of air. Elements binding winter to spring, fallow to fruitful. We ask your spirit to be present at this working today to assist us. Thank you and bright blessings.

SOUTHEAST CALL: Fire of air. Air of fire. Elements binding spring to summer, youth to middle age. We ask your spirit to be present at this working today to assist us. Thank you and bright blessings.

SOUTHWEST CALL: Water of fire. Fire of water. Elements binding summer to fall, light to dark, new to old. We ask your spirit to be present at this working today to assist us. Thank you and bright blessings.

If you have chosen to use cloves as part of an incense to enhance the atmosphere of your circle, they should be placed upon the coals now with any other herbs you've chosen. As this is done someone should make a statement as to the purpose of the spell and ask that the smoke from the incense rise to the ears of the deities whose assistance you require.

One by one, each member of the coven should come to the altar and collect three whole cloves, preferably ones that have been empowered to their task by the entire group. If they have not, then they should be passed around the circle in groups of three so that each person may add her energies to these catalysts.

One of the leaders should cut a doorway in one quarter of the circle—the choice of which one is up to you—and the coven should file out, moving counterclockwise, until each person is standing outside the circle in front of a quarter or cross-quarter point. If you have a coven of less than eight people, then move to the farthest point counterclockwise will take you without passing the doorway to the circle again. Take turns moving backward to work your spell at the other points. If you have a coven with more than eight people, then pair or triple up at the quarter points. The last person to leave the circle should close the door behind him or, if you have an extra person, she can stand guard within the circle and be ready to open the doorway again when the spell is complete.

Have the person standing at the east quarter begin by digging a small hole to bury the three cloves. In lieu of digging, she may press the cloves into soft ground with a forefinger. We start with the east because it is governed by the element of air, which in turn governs communication, which is the realm of gossip.

As the cloves are placed into the ground, everyone should be visualizing the grounding of the gossip that is plaguing you. The words of power will sound something like the following, but your coven should make yours more specific so they can work their best for you.

VOICE OF EAST: By the powers of air, element of communication, I silence the tongues of those who spread harm with their words. May the roaring winds drown out the sound of the chatter.

VOICE OF NORTHEAST: By the blending of air and earth, I bury the harm done by those who gossip against us. The wind shall blow over their words, carrying them away, unable to touch us in the womb of our friend Earth.

VOICE OF NORTH: By earth I restabilize the way of things, calling upon the grounding powers of earth to absorb the evil words hurled against us so that we may feel safe, free, and in harmony once more.

VOICE OF NORTHWEST: By the blending of earth and water, I place gossip into the mud to be sucked in and held. As the floor of the sea holds tight to a downed ship, may the gossip be sucked down as well.

VOICE OF WEST: By water I drown out the gossip, washing away the stain of harm it has done us. May we emerge from the water whole and new, reborn in all hearts who have turned away from the vicious words.

VOICE OF SOUTHWEST: By the blending of water and fire I smoke out the gossip, I steam up pressure on those who would continue to slander us unfairly. By smoke I purify our reputations and by steam I cleanse our hearts to forgiveness.

VOICE OF SOUTH: By fire I transform the negative to the positive, I turn ugliness to ashes and mean-spiritedness to ruins. May the power of change—in the hearts and minds of those who have heard this gossip—be transformed by the power of fire.

VOICE OF SOUTHEAST: By the blending of fire and air, I smoke out the gossip so that it lands on ears that hear common sense. As fire transforms, air communicates truth and opens the mind to think for itself.

When the last of the cloves are in the ground, have the coven file counterclockwise back to the doorway point where the person who closed it will open it again, closing it behind the last person to reenter.

> **ALL:** (Chanting this while filing counterclockwise back into the circle.) **By our will the gossip's gone, biting tongues have been undone; with harm to none we cast this spell, we only ask the truth to tell.** (Repeat until all are again within the safety of the circle and the door has been closed behind you.) **By our will, no more gossip be; for the good of all, so mote it be.**

When you are ready to end your rite you should "dismiss" the cross-quarters first, then the four cardinal points in the reverse order in which you evoked them.

Since you probably know by this point in your studies that the directions and their governing spirits are sentient beings with free will, they cannot be dismissed, as in "ordered to leave." The use of this word is unfortunate because it conjures up images of power-over rather than power-with, but the term "dismiss" remains a tradition just the same.

> **Notes for Spell Alteration:** If your coven wants to work this spell on behalf of one member who is feeling the impact of gossip, you should enact the spell at the quarters and cross-quarters of his home. You could also do this around a school, an office complex, or any other building where negative talk needs to be neutralized, but be aware that the home setting works best to protect the victim you want to help. Tackling a larger setting tends to scatter your energies and doesn't stop the negative chatter at which you're aiming your spell.
>
> If you want to use this as a solitary spell, surround your own dwelling space with the buried cloves. Bury sets of three each at the quarters and, if possible, the cross-quarters and at your front door.

◆ THE SHIP OF TREASURES MONEY SPELL ◆

Goal: To gain money for a specific need.

Subject: This spell works best when money is a need and not a desire. It also works best in group magick when the goal of the money is something that will benefit every member of the group, not just one or a few. For example, you may need to raise money to attend a Pagan sabbat festival in another state or country, or you need to purchase land on which to meet or create a Pagan gathering or burial site.

Items: A toy boat, a coin, a small hat, a key, a coat, a coin purse, a gem, some rice, and another prosperity symbol of your own choosing. You will also need a candle in red, gold, or green.

Best Times: On a waxing or full moon, a Sunday, just prior to a spiritual new year, or a holiday designed for prosperity such as Japan's Three Days (early January).

The prosperity festival called the Three Days is known as Sanga Nichi in Japan. It centers around acts of sympathetic magick designed to draw good fortune and wealth into the home. Because the magick is part of a group effort—the family, in most cases—the festival and its magick translates very well into coven practice.

Keep in mind that good fortune, prosperity, and wealth are not the same animals, even though this festival focuses on wealth as a primary goal. As noted before, prosperity does not necessarily just mean having money. Author Cynthia Killion writes in *A Little Book of Prosperity* (The Crossing Press, 2001) that possessing prosperity is largely a product of your state of mind. It's being thankful for your relative good fortunes and using these tiny blessings to draw in the larger ones. It's being grateful to have a roof over your head, food on your table, good friends, family, and, if you're in debt, being thankful someone trusted in your future prosperity enough to issue you credit in the first place.

During the Three Days, no cleaning of any kind is permitted lest the good fortune be swept away with the dirt. For most women, who are still responsible for the majority of housework tasks, this makes the Three Days a true holiday.

It is essential during this time that no leftover food be thrown away. Food symbolizes abundance in every known culture, the Japanese included, and it must not be disposed of or it could be construed by the powerful kitchen god as your willingness to throw wealth away. The preferred food of this festival is a rich rice stew known as *zoni*, of which a small portion is set aside as an offering to the kitchen god, who will later report to the higher deities on the conduct of the family throughout the previous year.

These higher deities are a septet known as the Seven Divine Ones of Good Fortune. They are honored at shrines and through prayers during the Three Days, while their assistance is petitioned for the prosperity. These deities include one goddess and seven gods who decide what families or groups will be lucky in the year to come and which will not.

Talismans representing the power of wealth and good fortune are placed into toy boats called *takara buni*, which translates into English as "treasure ships." In Japan these toy boats are available everywhere prior to the festival. They are put in a place of honor within the home so that the Seven Divine Ones of Good Fortune may sail in at will and bless the home with prosperity whenever they choose to visit during the coming year.

At the end of the year the old treasure ship is ritually burned so that the divine power encased in it may be returned to the deities. In keeping with the Pagan acceptance that all energy sent out returns to the sender three times over through the wheel of existence, it is believed that the good fortune sent back to the deities will be reciprocated by them in the year to come.

If the Seven Divine Ones of Good Fortune do not appeal to your coven as deities to whom you are comfortable petitioning for good fortune and wealth, there are many other deities and spirits associated with the bringing of good fortune. A few of these follow.

Agathadaimon: Etruscan-based god of good fortune.

Anahita: Persian goddess of propagation and fertility.

Anna Purna: Goddess of food and abundance in old Rome.

Brownies: House faeries who bless good people with prosperity.

Copia: Roman goddess of plenty.

Daikoku: Japanese god of wealth and good fortune.

Fulla: Scandinavian goddess of riches and fruitfulness.

Gandayaks: Native American spirits of flourishing vegetation.

Gollveig: Nordic goddess of gold and excess wealth.

Habondia: Germanic goddess of abundance and plenty.

Inari: Japanese god of rice and prosperity.

Kamadhenu: Hindu goddess of prosperity.

Midas: Mythical king whose touch turned items into gold.

Mokosh: Slavic goddess of health and prosperity.

Nsomeka: Bantu goddess of wealth and riches.

Nuada: Irish god-king of treasures and survival.

Pomona: Roman goddess of food and abundance.

Penates: Roman house spirits who bless with prosperity.

Salamanders: Fire spirits of the south associated with money.

Selekana: African goddess of riches and jewels.

Svontovit: Slavic god of abundance and wealth.

Tamon: A Japanese god of both war and good luck.

Tellus Mater: Roman goddess of abundance and fertility.

Well Spirits: Spirits of wells who bless with wealth and health.

Your coven can make its own treasure ship, filled with talismans of good fortune to attract needed money, by starting with a simple toy boat found in any discount or toy store. You will also need to find or purchase the following items that traditionally belong in the ship: a coin, a miniature hat, a key, a miniature coat, a small coin purse, a gem, and some rice. You are dealing with symbolism and the clothing items need be only representations, such as a doll's clothing. Likewise, an imitation gem or a pretty stone can function as a substitute for the gem. You will also need an eighth item of your own choosing. Eight is the number associated with good fortune in many Asian cultures.

When you have your ship and all the items you need to place inside it, take them into your circle along with a single candle. While Western magicians usually think of green or gold as the traditional colors of good fortune, red serves this function in Asia, where it is the color of life and luck. You may use the color your coven feels is best.

Empower the ship and the items as a group and then begin the main body of the spell. This example uses the Seven Divine Ones of Good Fortune as the deities of assistance, but please feel free to modify this to your coven's taste.

Place the ship and candle in the center of your circle or altar. Light the candle with words of welcome to the Seven Divine Ones of Good Fortune such as those that follow.

> **The fire burns bright this sacred night,**
> **The warmth of its glow is red,**
> **May it guide your way to this humble space,**
> **Our circle wherein wishes are fed.**

> Welcome to you, the Seven Ones Divine,
> Impart your good fortune right here
> Bless now this ship of prosperous days,
> Bring us wealth in this blessed new year.

Allow each member of the coven to place one of the items into the ship. If you have more than eight members in your coven, you can allow people to team up to represent the energy of a specific area. They may work in unison, or each do a different part of any invocation or honoring of their corresponding direction's energies.

Coven members should approach the altar one by one, moving clockwise around the circle. The empowered item being worked with should be passed seven times clockwise over the top of the candle while it is dedicated to the Seven Divine Ones of Good Fortune. This might sound like the following.

> **MOONDANCER:** (Chanting.) **Fire of the Seven Ones Divine, shower good fortune on me and mine; I place in our ship this shiny dime, that it will grow hundredfold in time.**

In this example, Moondancer will place the item inside the ship while everyone visualizes it as both a symbol and an offering of the wealth that is now coming to your coven.

Repeat this procedure with the other seven items. The words of power you speak over each item should begin with the same two lines Moondancer used, but end with two that are suited either to the item being placed into the ship or to the specific money need of the coven. Some examples follow.

> **STORMWILLOW:** (Chanting.) **Fire of the Seven Ones Divine, shower good fortune on me and mine; into this talisman I place a tiny coat, that you sail to us all we need in this little boat.**

> **GREENWOOD:** (Chanting.) **Fire of the Seven Ones Divine, shower good fortune on me and mine; into the ship I place a stone of green, the color of fortune now to be seen.**

> **WINDWALKER:** (Chanting.) **Fire of the Seven Ones Divine, shower good fortune on me and mine; an empty purse I offer to you, that now fills up with money due.**

When all eight items have been placed into the ship, the leader or some other appointed person should pass the entire ship eight times clockwise over the candle while sealing the spell with words of power similar to the following.

> **Red Wolf HP:** (Chanting.) **Thanks be to you, the Lucky Seven, who carry our charge to the highest heaven; your gift of fortune is a blessing that be, wealth as we need it, so mote it be.**

Keep the treasure ship in your circle or somewhere near your covenstead as a visual reminder that you must back up your efforts to seek needed money with physical-world efforts during the year to come.

◆ LEGAL LIGHT SPELL ◆

Goal: To gain favor in a legal proceeding.

Subject: The entire coven, or a single member or members.

Items: A single taper candle in white or blue for each person present. Also some dried anise, carnation, and galangal, and a bloodstone.

Best Times: A full moon, a Thursday or Sunday, when the moon is in Libra, or whenever needed.

Sometimes legal problems fall on spiritual organizations, Pagan ones included. Probably the most famous case in recent years concerns the Church of Iron Oak in Florida, whose members have fought for years for the right to worship as they choose at the home of one of their members. The fight has been costly, but to the credit of those who cherish freedom of religious expression, many have stepped forward to help them in their cause, including mainstream ministers and rabbis who fear that their own home-centered spiritual rituals could be endangered if Iron Oak loses its right to home worship.

This spell may also be used for a single member of your group who is in legal trouble, or it may be used to send needed energy to a group like Iron Oak who needs your magickal assistance and good will.

In this blueprint, we will assume the worst: that there is a legal challenge facing your coven as a whole. We won't specify what that challenge is, which will keep the words of power generic. They will need to be altered to suit the details of your specific case.

Before you gather to enact the spell, you should designate a member of your group to make a brew of the dried anise, carnation, and galangal by simmering it until the water is dark with its essence. He will need to keep the goal in mind as this is done to help empower it with the collective will. It should be strained, placed in a clean glass jar or bottle, and brought to the covenstead at the time of the spell's enactment.

Open your magickal session in the way your coven feels is best. You may ritualize this spell if you like by calling in the four directions and asking the blessing of each element on your cause. Ask air to help you communicate clearly, fire to transform your difficulties into victory, water to give you the intuition to move through the tricky court system, and earth to give you credibility.

You may also want to petition a deity of justice, law, or impartiality. Naturally, doing this works best if you are actually in the right and not trying to win a case you know in your heart would be unfair to your opponent. Some of these deities include the following.

Arete: Greek goddess who personifies justice.

Aeval: Irish faery goddess of justice for women.

Cukulcan: Mayan god of lawmaking.

Djigonasee: Native American goddess of treaties and fairness.

Egeria: Italian goddess of wisdom and foresight.

Eriu: Irish goddess of sovereignty.

Fa: Beninese god of destiny.

Fudumyou: Japanese god of wisdom and mercy.

Genetaska: Native American goddess of justice and judgment.

Kuan Ti: Chinese god of just judgments.

Libertas: Roman goddess of freedom and agriculture.

Litae: Greek goddess prayed to before litigation.

Maat: Egyptian goddess of truth.

Ops: Roman goddess of opulence and abundance.

Var: Scandinavian goddess from whom no truth is hidden.

Weit'o: Chinese god of law and justice.

Candle Cup

When you are ready to begin the main body of the spell, have someone give everyone an unlit candle in a base designed to protect hands and clothing from dripping hot wax (see the illustration, above). A paper cup or piece of round cardboard works well for this.

The leader should light her candle and begin the spell with a statement about the symbolism being employed and about the goal being sought. This is also the time to petition a specific deity of justice, if you wish to work with one in particular. In this example, Snow Owl calls upon many deities.

> Snow Owl HPS: **Blessed deities of fairness and justice—Var, Maat, Arete, Genetaska, in all your many forms and faces—we call upon your assistance tonight to aid us in the fair hearing and judgment of our case** (state nature of case here). **I light this candle** (she lights the candle she holds) **as a beacon of**

fairness in an unjust world. **May it be a light of truth that calls to us your attention, blessings, and favorable judgment on our cause.**

Snow Owl will turn to the person on her left and light that person's candle with her own.

> **Snow Owl HPS:** **I pass to you the light of truth so that justice will burn in the darkness of unfairness. The rightness of our cause shall be a light unto the world that freedom of worship is a blessing for all, and to impinge on that freedom diminishes us all by plunging us into the darkness of ignorance and injustice.**

> **All:** (To be repeated after each passing of the light.) **Blessed be the light of justice in the darkness of helplessness. Our light grows stronger. Our cause is just.**

Moving clockwise around the circle, the coven members should keep passing the light of the candle until the circle is complete. Each person should use the same words spoken by the first person to pass the light. Of course these will have been modified to suit your specific case.

Next, someone should place their candle safely on the altar and take up the bottle of brew. Going around the circle clockwise, that person should anoint the forehead, lips, and solar plexus area of each person with a single drop of the brew while offering a blessing. In this example, Rain will have this honor.

> **Rain:** (Anointing the forehead.) **In the name of fairness and justice, I bless your mind with thoughts of fairness and good judgment in our** (state nature of case). (Anointing the lips.) **In the name of fairness and justice, I bless your lips that they will speak the truth and that the truth will be heard and make sense to all in compliance with the laws of this land.** (Anointing the solar plexus.) **I bless your center of being, your center of will, with the energy to fight the fair fight, always in full possession of your sense of truth, justice, and with a calm air of confidence that inspires those who see us that we are indeed in the right in** (state nature of case).

Rain will bless all members of the coven in this manner, then she will choose someone to do the same to her.

The remainder of the water should be kept and used to anoint everyone again just before appearing before a judge or in a courtroom.

Be sure to thank the elements and any deities upon whom you have called for assistance. If you are using a specific deity, you should offer her a token of your thanks. Bloodstone or malachite work well for this. Have someone carry this token in his pocket during the legal proceedings so that that deity's presence will be with you.

Notes for Spell Alteration: Spells in which light is passed around clockwise can and are used in a variety of spells. They are also features of bonding rituals, in which new covens dedicate themselves to their purpose.

Passing fire represents the growth of light and its triumph over darkness. Use this format for your ritual at Ostara, the spring equinox, when light is victorious over the dark half of the year. Also use it for spells and rituals of purification, spiritual growth, protection, the honoring of a deity, or initiations in which the passing of the light of knowledge is a central symbolic feature.

To the contrary, you can start a ritual or spell with everyone's candles already lit and then have everyone extinguish the candle of the person to their right so that the darkness moves counterclockwise throughout your circle. This is often done at Mabon, the autumn equinox, when darkness is victorious over the light half of the year. It is also a popular feature in passing-over rituals, a right of passage memorializing someone's physical death. The extinguishing of light can also be used to banish someone or something, or for spells involving secrets or the need to be hidden.

You can also use both the lighting and extinguishing of candles within the same spell or ritual. The passing-over ritual is a good example of how this might be employed. You can light the candles to call out to the spirit of the deceased, then extinguish them as you call on a deity to help assist that person into the otherworld, or to wherever he needs to go next. The darkening circle represents the light of that person's spirit leaving you.

◆ THE BRAIN BOOSTER SPELL ◆

Goal: To boost mental prowess prior to an exam, test, or any event that requires quick thinking and good memory.

Subject: All coven members, or one or several members who make the request.

Items: Dried rosemary, dried dill, a lodestone or magnet, and a small cloth in white or yellow.

Best Times: Wednesdays or as close to when needed as possible. It's also best if there is a wind blowing from the east while the spell is being enacted.

This spell creates a talisman that will help you or your coven through a test or trial that requires quick thinking and good memory. In this example, we will assume that all members of the coven need the spell for some test they face—perhaps a test to move on to the next spiritual level within the Craft.

Each person will need to have all the items required for this spell. They will need to empower them on their own and, for the coven spell to work its best, you will need to work out a method in which everyone will have an opportunity to empower and bless everyone else's items. You can do this either before or after the talismans are constructed. I find it's easier and less messy to do it afterward.

The rosemary is for memory, the dill for mental prowess, and the magnet or lodestone to attract back to the one being tested all the knowledge gathered through study that seems to scatter when needed most. Keep the talisman with you during the testing.

You may wish to make a litany of this spell as the talismans are being passed around for blessing.

Notes for Spell Alteration: I have done brain-boost spells as a solitary simply by blowing powdered rosemary into the east wind. This means facing east to empower the herbs and state my words of power, then turning to blow them westward so they don't scatter on my face. I stand and watch them blow away, visualizing them carrying my will to where it needs to go. This method has worked well for me over and over, proving again that spells don't have to be elaborate to be effective. Sometimes the simple ones are best just because there are fewer items to empower and less images to hold in visualization.

◆ THE BALEFIRE DIVINATION SPELL ◆

Goal: To gaze into your central balefire with the power of group mind to see visions or to gather images about a question or issue that's plaguing you.

Subject: Every member of the coven will participate and benefit since this works best when a coven issue is at stake, though it can be done at the request of an individual member in need.

Items: You will need a central balefire, a fireproof bowl, fireplace, or some other place where you can safely burn small pieces of paper.

Best Times: On a full moon, when the moon is in Pisces or Cancer, or on a Monday.

Scrying is the art of gazing into a reflective object to seek prophetic visions. This is what is being done in the old Hollywood movies where a Gypsy fortuneteller is peering into a crystal ball.

Try this divination spell if your coven has a pressing question that other methods of divination have not been able to answer. For this spell, you must first attempt to link your group mind and then you will use fire as your scrying element.

Fire is usually the easiest element for a coven to work with because it is almost always present at any ritual or spellworking. A central sacred fire, known as a balefire, is often present in outdoor gatherings. Even when you're not outdoors or do not have a balefire, there is almost always a single working candle on a central altar or a fire burning in a nearby hearth.

The coven should form a circle around the fire if possible, though a semicircle is fine if you're using a fireplace against an interior wall. Link arms or hands and begin to gaze into the fire. Get a firm image of it in your mind as a living being with its own consciousness and the ability to show you the answers to your question.

Close your eyes.

> **Snow Owl HPS: Blessed be the element of fire. Blessed be its power to transform and change and to capture the images of transformation as they are currently set in motion. We ask tonight that fire show us the answer to our question** (state the question here).

The full coven should repeat the question aloud, adding, "Blessed be the power and spirits of fire."

SNOW OWL HPS: We are a coven, a spiritual family. When we are together we are one. Like the supreme creator, we are made of many parts, but we are also a single being. Our group mind is the force of our commitment to the deities and to each other. It is also a manifestation of the power of our will. See now the connection between us. See the violet-white light of the higher self connecting us as one.

Each member of the coven should visualize a stream of violet-white light linking the area just above the heads of each member of the group. This is the area of the crown chakra, the energy center believed to connect us all to the divine.

SNOW OWL HPS: When we are together we are one. See now the connection between us. See the blue-violet light of our psychic centers connecting us as one.

The coven should now visualize this light connecting the third eye chakra center, that area just above and between the eyes. This is the chakra center associated with psychicism.

SNOW OWL HPS: When we are together we are one. See now the connection between us. See the bright yellow light of our collective will connecting us as one.

This time the visualization links you at the solar plexus, the region just below the rib cage. This is the chakra center corresponding to willpower.

At this point the leader will state again the question or issue you wish to have answered. Everyone should form a clear image of it in their mind and then open their eyes to gaze into the fire.

Scrying can be a difficult art to learn but once the trick to it is discovered, it becomes easier to do every time. The best tip for success is not to stare. Blink when you need to. Also, look into the fire, not at it or beyond it. If you do not see images in the fire be aware of the impressions being made on your mind and, later, in any dream images that seem to stem from your fire-scrying efforts.

The leader will let you know when it's time to stop. You will usually be given fifteen to twenty minutes to scry.

The coven should first discuss what was seen and felt during the scrying immediately after the exercise is complete. It should be discussed again after everyone has had a sleep period, in case any dream images appeared to your members that clarified their mental impressions further. Assess all this information in order to come to a consensus on the answer to your question or issue.

Notes for Spell Alteration: The balefire works well for most covens because some kind of fire is usually featured on the altar or at the center of the circle. If your coven members feel more in tune with earth, they might try scrying into a patch of newly turned earth. If they feel more in tune with water, you might go to a pond or lake when the sun is reflecting off its surface.

You may also have someone who has or will agree to construct a mirror to be used specifically for this purpose, and will be dedicated to coven use only. There are several methods for making magickal scrying mirrors. Some use regular mirrors and others use glass painted black on the back side. Several books on magick and spellwork detail how to make these and empower them to your goal. Some are very elaborate.

The simplest method to make a scrying mirror is to allow the light of the full moon to shine on it while dedicating it to its purpose. Mark the back of it with a positive symbol to seal in your will. Pentagrams or equal-armed crosses are popular for this. Make your mark by dabbing your fingers in a protective oil like cinnamon, bay, clove, or rosemary and "painting" on the symbol.

◆ THE CURSE-BREAKING SPELL ◆

Goal: To collect negative energy that has been deliberately directed at your coven and ground it.

Subject: This example presumes that the coven as a whole is the one being cursed, so every member of the coven will participate and benefit.

Items: You will need a stick thin enough to be broken by hand and long enough to allow every member of the coven to break off a piece.

Best Times: A waning moon, a Saturday, during a solar eclipse, or when needed.

Negative energy that has been deliberately or ritually sent to you is known as a curse. It represents the epitome of negative and manipulative magick and should not be tolerated.

But how do you know if there is a curse on your coven? Sometimes bad luck is just bad luck and it can be changed with a good fortune spell or by doing a divination to see what steps should be taken to improve life. Sometimes the bad period is caused by random energies of those who are jealous or resent you for some reason, and it has nothing to do with magick. These problems can be overcome with simple protection spells. To believe yourselves cursed would mean that you have reason to believe that another group or person has ritually done a spell intended to send harmful energy your way.

As you begin this spell you should call the quarters in your circle and set up as many defensive postures as you can. This includes calling upon protective deities and spirits and pouring extra energy into your circle's boundaries.

When you are ready to begin the main body of the spell, the leader should pass around the stick and allow everyone to do whatever gesture or words they feel best pulls into the stick the negative energy that surrounds you. When this is complete you should pass the stick around again and allow everyone to break off a piece. Be sure to visualize the breaking of the stick as a breaking of the curse that has been placed on you.

The leader should gather the broken pieces together and have someone make a statement that the curse is broken. Toss the stick pieces like garbage to the ground and allow everyone to feel the negative energy being absorbed by Mother Earth, where it can never harm anyone again.

As a group you should bury the stick pieces at a crossroads to ground them away from you for good.

Notes for Spell Alteration: Some Witches prefer to send negative energy that has been sent on purpose right back from whence it came. Others feel this only escalates the cursing game. The choice is yours to make.

Just to be sure that the curse goes back where it's supposed to go, you should never hold the image of a person or a group in your mind as you send it back. Will only that it be returned to the sender. Energy knows its creator and will have no trouble finding its way home once sent on its way.

There are many variations on this type of spell, but one easy way is to have your coven purchase a small mirror to be used only for this spell. You will also need a white candle and some vinegar or lime juice. On the candle, carve the words "GO HOME" starting at the top and moving down the shaft. Light the candle to represent the energy of the one doing the cursing. Visualize that person being ruined by her own efforts without seeing a face attached. Make sure the flame of the candle is reflected in the mirror as you visualize the return of negative energy.

Repeat this over several nights, each time allowing one of the letters you've carved into the candle to be consumed by the fire. Each time you extinguish the flame, use the lime juice or vinegar to sour that person's efforts at magick.

When the entire "GO HOME" has been consumed, you may extinguish the candle and bury it with any remaining vinegar or juice near your home to ground any renewed efforts at harming you. The mirrors should be placed in a glass jar and broken with the blunt end of a hammer's end. Seal it and bury it with the other objects to keep reflecting the negativity away from you.

✦ GOOD GOVERNMENT SPELL ✦

Goal: To open the hearts and minds of those who govern to the will of the people who put them in office, making them responsive and responsible to the public good.

Subject: The "government" as defined by Social Contact Theory (explained further in text). Every member of the coven will participate.

Items: You will need five candles. They may be any colors you choose, but for the example of this spell, we will use one each of white, pink, brown, yellow, and red. You may wish to decorate your circle area or altar with symbols of your school, community, state, province, or nation, depending upon the government in which you wish to focus your spell. These images needn't all be positive. They could be symbols of what the coven wishes to change about the government and, by extension, the society it shapes and serves. You will also need a small, heat-resistant dish for safely burning paper.

Best Times: A spiritual new year, the full moon, a Sunday, on a civil or national holiday, on a remembrance day such as Veteran's Day, December 7, or September 11 in the United States, or on a national independence holiday such as July 4 in the United States or July 1 in Canada.

The beginning of each new month held spiritual significance to the Romans, but when the date of the new year was moved from March, the citizenry was hard-pressed to remember this month was supposed to honor the two-faced god Janus. January slowly lost its religious overtones and instead became a political holiday involving electioneering and government convocations.

The irony of a two-faced deity being linked to politics may at first bring a smug chuckle, but the image also angers the millions who feel increasingly powerless over our government's choices of policies, parties, and practices.

Without unduly bending the free will of people to choose their own governments, effective ritual magick can be worked to turn the government's deaf ears to the voice of those who put them in power in the first place. At least this should be the case in the governments of England, her colonies, and former colonies, which are based on a seventeenth-century concept known as Social Contract Theory as espoused by Oxford-educated philosopher John Locke (1632–1704). The theory states that governments exist through an implied contract with their citizenry to serve the public interests, and that they exist solely by the say-so of those citizens. When the governments cease to serve the people, they, as Thomas Jefferson pronounced in the American Declaration of Independence, have the right to "alter or abolish them."

Many modern covens are using their combined energies to benefit their communities either politically, environmentally, or socially. Though some Pagans balk at the idea of politics within the sacred confines of the circle, keep in mind that many of our detractors, including hate groups, are not above using manipulative ritual or violence to destroy all that free people hold sacred. We should not hesitate to combat this negative force with a positive one.

Its purpose is to open the hearts of those in power to the many plights of those they serve. This ritual is written from the perspective of an American, but those living in other parts of the world should not hesitate to use or adapt the spell as their coven sees fit.

Ask everyone to come to the circle with a few pictures of things they wish to see the government have a hand in changing. This could be racial injustice, homelessness, health care, tax issues, youth violence, et cetera. These disturbing images are all too easily found in newspapers and magazines.

Before beginning the spell, orient your altar to the four quarters and place a pink candle in the west, a brown candle in the north, a yellow candle in the east, and a red candle in the south. Light these four before the spell begins. Place the unlit white candle in the center. You will also need to select four coven members to represent one of each of the quarters. They will become the voice of that quarter's element and will take charge of their respective directional candle during the spell.

One of the leaders, or someone else who has been asked to perform this opening role, should start a chant. The exact wording of it is less important than the fierce desire for change it engenders within the coven. You may want to experiment with what strikes that deep inner-resonance within your group, which tells you that the chant is doing its job. It should be something that sets the tone for what you hope to accomplish, such as the following.

> Home of the brave and land of the free,
> You belong to us, it is we who let you be;
> We are the people, who to you your power give,
> We claim back our right to make our principles live.

Let the chant start low and slow, then build in intensity. When it reaches its peak, the leader should gesture for the chant to slow in volume and intensity until it fades to silence.

Snow Owl HPS: We stand here together in this sacred space, a community within many other communities, poised at the center of them all. We know that no time and place governs the sacred circle, yet a part of us knows that the piece of Mother Earth beneath our feet is part of our homeland: America.

All: Blessed be the United States of America, our homeland, our piece of Mother Earth.

Red Wolf HP: We love our land, though the land is troubled. We have hate.

Moondancer: We have fear and want.

Stormwillow: We have war and poverty.

Rain: We have violence and terrorism.

Greenwood: We have illness and ignorance and pollution.

Oakman: We have crime and children in need.

Windwalker: We have homelessness and hopelessness.

Snow Owl HPS: We have ignorance and apathy.

RED WOLF HP: And we have a great untapped potential. We are Americans. Our legacy has created the myth of the American dream. We gather together to make it happen for all of us—those born here and those called here by hope. Let the healing—the change—begin here, in this sacred space, with us, now.

Continuing from the leader and moving clockwise around the circle, each person should make a wish for the country. It is best to keep these nonpartisan and in keeping with the spirit of the governing document of the country that, in most cases, details the high ideals of a nation, whether they have been realized or not.

After each wish the coven as a whole should make a response such as, "Blessed be the United States," "Blessed be the greater good," or "May the positive will of the people be fulfilled."

SNOW OWL HPS: May our elected leaders, whatever their political ideology, open their hearts and minds to the needs of those they serve, and learn to work together to serve those needs.

WINDWALKER: May our elections be overseen by fair-minded people who are more interested in seeing the will of the people fulfilled than those of their personal agenda.

RAIN: May our elected representatives remember that those they represent are not all the same. There are rich and poor, black and white, male and female. May they remember to serve all the people, not only those who are like themselves.

When all the wishes have been made, the four chosen to be the voice of each quarter should move into their assigned positions near the altar. You may have them begin speaking with any direction your coven or its cultural tradition chooses, then proceed clockwise around the altar. This spell starts in the western quarter.

VOICE OF WEST/WATER: Behold my flame of pink, color of peace, contentment, introspection, and love. What is it you will of me?

Moving clockwise around the circle, allow each person present to voice their west-related desires aloud and how they wish to have things changed. Those who feel one of the pictures they brought with them relates to this directional element should come forward and display it to the group as they speak. When they conclude, they should place it in the heat-resistant bowl near the white candle in the center of the altar.

> **VOICE OF WEST/WATER: I shall carry your wishes with me as I flow through the universe, allowing them to seep into everything I touch. May the wishes you seek manifest now.**

The voice of the West/Water should take her candle and light the pictures in the heat-resistant bowl, seeing to it that as much of them are burned as possible.

> **VOICE OF NORTH/EARTH: Behold my flame of brown, color of our Mother Earth and her creatures, of its fertility and its stability. What is it you will of me?**

As before, all those who feel a picture they have brought relates to the qualities of this quadrant should step forward and display them as they speak. The pictures should also be placed in the heat-resistant bowl when finished.

When there are no more coven members stepping forward, the voice speaks again.

> **VOICE OF NORTH/EARTH: I shall cradle your wishes deep within me, as I am the foundation of all things. I will seek to impart them to all who walk upon my face. May the wishes you seek manifest now.**

Again, the voice of the North/Earth should use the brown candle to burn the unpleasant images placed in the bowl.

> **VOICE OF EAST/AIR: Behold my flame of yellow, color of communication and the intellect, of thought and contemplation, of the person who seeks true knowledge rather than gossip. What is it you will of me?**

Repeat the process used at the other two quarters of allowing everyone who wishes to speak and place a picture in the bowl.

> **VOICE OF EAST/AIR: I shall blow your wishes about, to and fro and here and there, as I travel the universe. Sometimes they will be still on my breath, and other times they will tickle the ears of those who need to hear. May the wishes you seek manifest now.**

The East/Air voice should use his candle to burn the images placed in the bowl.

Voice of South/Fire: Behold my flame of red, color of passion, courage, strength, transformation, and action. What is it you will of me?

This will be the last chance everyone will have to display any pictures they brought that they feel relate to the energies of the south and fire. These, too, should be placed in the bowl until the last person who wishes to has stepped forward to speak.

Voice of South/Fire: I shall transform your wishes with my flames, altering them and carrying them to those who need to hear them. I shall burn in the hearts and minds of those who need to heed your desires. May they listen and may the wishes you seek manifest now.

A litany fits in well here, though some groups may wish instead to sing patriotic songs. Just keep in mind that overt displays of patriotism are uncomfortable for some people, just as they are uncomfortable with any other emotional display.

Snow Owl HPS: Blessed be the four elements, who carry our wishes to the hearts and minds of those who govern our land.

All: May they open their hearts to the plights of those less fortunate.

Snow Owl HPS: By the winds of change, they hear us.

All: Blessed air, open their ears to our cries.

Snow Owl HPS: By the earth on which they build their ivory towers, they notice us.

All: Blessed earth, we can no longer be ignored.

Snow Owl HPS: The flow of the world changes and the tide of the people's will can no longer be held back.

All: Blessed water, they feel our needs and respond.

Snow Owl HPS: The flame of desire to make positive change has been ignited and cannot be extinguished.

All: Blessed fire, transform our world for the greater good.

The voices of the four elements should place the flame of their respective candles on the wick of the unlit white candle in the center of the altar.

COMBINED VOICES: **By earth, water, air, and fire, bring what this coven does desire.**

ALL: **By the power of three times three, by our will, so mote it be.**

♦ THE TREE SPELL ♦

Goal: To use tree magick to obtain a goal your coven seeks in magick.

Subject: Everyone in the coven.

Items: You will need some small bells on lengths of yarn in colors corresponding to your goal, and some pieces of bread.

Best Times: This depends on the goal of the spell. In general, use a waxing moon for things you wish to manifest and a waning moon for things you wish to end. Another time is the Jewish holiday of Tu B'Shevat, or the new year of the trees that came into modern Judaism from its Pagan Canaanite roots. It falls on the full moon of the fifth lunar month of the Jewish calendar, usually in February.

Trees have been venerated in virtually every culture around the globe, and have been honored as sacred symbols of the unity of all realms of existence. Trees live long lives if we let them, and their ancient wisdom and power can be culled for powerful magick if we can communicate to the tree that we mean it no harm.

The coven should select a tree whose energy corresponds to the goal of their spell. This goal can be anything at all. A book on magickal herbalism or tree energy is a good source for help in making this selection. I recommend Scott Cunningham's *Cunningham's Encyclopedia of Magical Herbs* (Llewellyn, 1985) or Yvonne Aburrow's *The Enchanted Forest: The Magical Lore of Trees* (Capall Bann, 1993) as good resources for beginners to tree magick. The following list is a general guideline of correspondences to get you started.

Apple: Otherworld travels, honoring the Goddess, love and romance, healing, cursing, psychic enhancement, beauty.

Ash: Protection, health.

Birch: Purification, love binding, banishing.

Beech: Creativity, inspiration, protection.

Buckeye: Protection, healing, fertility, prosperity, money, overcoming obstacles.

Cedar: Protection, money, purification.

Cypress: Death rituals, consolation, strength.

Elder: Protection, healing, banishing, faery magick.

Elm: Love, faery magick, protection.

Lemon: Love, beauty, purification, lunar magick.

Linden: Love and romance, dream magick, peaceful home life, peaceful sleep.

Magnolia: Fertility, romance, beauty.

Maple: Abundance, prosperity, romance.

Mulberry: Communication, mental prowess, protection.

Oak: Strength, courage, personal power, healing, luck, protection, fertility, wisdom, money.

Orange: Friendship, healing, strength, solar magick, divination, money.

Pine: Money, healing, fertility, banishing.

Pineapple: Friendship, prosperity, luck.

Poplar: Prosperity, employment, astral projection.

Sycamore: Prosperity, communication, mental prowess, music magick.

Willow: Psychic enhancement, binding, love, divination, health, dream magick, astral projection.

Remember that trees have a consciousness, or sentience if you prefer, and are protected by many types of faery life who cherish and protect the tree. Even after you select one you wish to work with, you must ask its permission to approach, stating what you want from it and telling it that you mean it no harm.

Trees have been so abused in modern life that Witches skilled at communicating with plants can feel trees tremble in fear at the approach of humans. If you are not able to calm a tree or gain its trust, then you should choose another. Note here that many Witches who are practiced in faery magick believe that bells frighten away faeries, both the benevolent and the baneful. If this is your belief you may wish to offer decorative crystals or other objects to the tree that do not make bell-like noises. Perhaps if you're feeling turned away by the tree it's only the faeries who live there not wanting bells on their home.

Your coven should let the tree know that you wish only to enact a spell with its help and that you brought the tree a gift of bells for breezes or food for the birds who nest in its branches. If you feel welcome, approach and continue.

When I approach an old tree that seems somehow special or is teeming with faery life, I greet it with the words, "Blessed be, ancient tree." I think I may have read that line somewhere or had it suggested to me in a ritual at some point in my past, but it has become my standard greeting for many years. In most cases, I sense a cautious reply in return until the tree and I become better known to one another.

Have your coven make a circle around the tree and allow your leader to explain to it the details of your magickal need and why you wish to use its energy. Hold hands and dance around the tree while singing a song or chanting your goal. Make sure the words include praise for the tree and the life it supports, both the seen and unseen. As you dance, you should start to feel the tree sending you its energy and lending its efforts to your spell. You may even be lucky enough to have the faery life it supports offer their assistance as well. Often I have seen small flashes of light dancing with me or sparkling with a brighter intensity up in the tree's boughs. These are referred to as faery lights. They often appear when positive magick or ritual is being done in a natural, wild setting.

When you have sent out the energy you raised in your dance, decorate the tree with the offerings you brought by placing the yarn over several of the lowest branches. Don't tie them tightly and never use a nail or pin that will hurt the tree and cause it to reject your spell and any future attempts you might make to work with it again.

Place the bread pieces at the base of the tree as an offering for the birds who live or roost in its branches. Thank the tree and its faeries, if appropriate, then leave the area as clean and undisturbed as you found it.

◆ VICTORY IN EVERY ENDEAVOR ◆

Goal: To achieve victory in a goal that is important to the entire coven. This may be success on an exam in school, a win for the home team, meeting a challenge by doing your best, winning a war, and so on. The spell works best when one single desire is being focused on by the entire group, but it can be worked so that each person can work for their own personal victory.

Subject: It may be every member of the coven with one common goal, every member of the coven with their own goals, or every member of the coven working for a victory goal for one person in the group.

Items: You will need rhythm instruments or a drumming tape that plays a fast and primitive beat. You want to stir up the senses in this spell. Each coven member may also want to bring along a ritual tool they associate with defense or battle, such as a ritual blade or wand.

Best Times: A full moon, Tuesday or Sunday, at noon, Midsummer, or on the old Roman feast day for Victoria, goddess of success (about February 16). Other goddess festivals that work are the Feast of Nike (about July 1) and the festival days set aside for Athena, Greek goddess of war and victory (dates vary).

This spell petitions a goddess of victory to assist you in doing your best to achieve your goal. Victory means different things to each of us. For some, only the total annihilation of the opponent is a victory. For others, it's knowing that they did their best—whether they won or lost—that's important. Victory as a magickal goal is governed, as are all spells, by the Rede of "harm none." In some cases we are just meant to win. We may have to be good sports and settle for doing our best, knowing we were worthy opponents and honorable losers.

Your coven should first meet to select and hone the precise goal in which you want to see victory attained. Then select a deity to assist you. Some choices are listed below if you do not have one in mind that appeals to everyone. It doesn't have to be a goddess. There are many gods of victory to whom you can make your petition.

Aiofe: Irish goddess of defense and patron of warriors.

Ares: Greek god of war.

Athena: Greek goddess of war and victory, one whom many women call upon for strength and success.

Atatarho: Iroquois god who wore a garment of live snakes as his talisman of power as a warrior and magician.

Bellona: Another Roman war goddess.

Boudiccia: English battle queen who defeated the Romans.

Forseti: Scandinavian god of justice.

Hercules: Greek warrior god whose myths have become mutated recently for popular mass consumption.

Hooke: Hittite god of war.

Kali: Hindu goddess of destruction and fear.

Kamu Nahobi: Japanese god who rights things gone wrong.

Luchtain: Irish warrior god who forged the tools of battle for his people.

Mars: Those born under the sign of Aries may have a special affinity for this
    Roman war god.

Maeve: Irish warrior queen who led her army to victory over the Red Branch
    warriors of Ulster.

Morrighan: Celtic triple goddess of war and battle.

Nergal: Babylonian god of war and of the underworld.

Nemesis: The eponymous Greek goddess of revenge and retribution.

Nike: Greek goddess of victory and speed.

Odin: Scandinavian god of war, the dead, magick, and creative inspiration.

Praxidike: A three-faced Greek goddess of vengeance.

Victoria: Roman goddess of victory.

When you are ready to begin the main body of your spell, have your leader light a candle to honor the deity you have chosen to call upon for assistance. Red is a good choice for the candle color since it represents war, courage, lust, passion, and power. Your petition might sound something like the following.

> **Snow Owl HPS: Victoria, goddess of victory, patron of the winners and neme-
> sis of the losers, we request your presence this day to assist us with
> our own need for victory. We light the red flame in your honor and ask your
> blessings upon this spell. We leave the judgment of our petition to you as
> we seek to win. We hope you find our goal worthy and without harm.
> So mote it be.**

Each person in the circle should step forward one at a time and offer their own words of welcome or petition to Victoria, then slowly start to dance clockwise around the inside of the circle.

At this point the rhythm instruments should be brought out or drumming tape started. Those without instruments should dance with any magickal tool they brought with them that represents victory in battle, though blades should be avoided for safety's sake.

Start the dance at a medium tempo and speed it up gradually. The dance should be earthy, with lots of foot pounding, shouting, and primitive gestures. You are connecting with the warrior part of yourself, an ancient archetype deeply embedded in your psyche, yet one our modern world attempts to suppress, especially in its females. Let your warrior self emerge as the beat intensifies. Your dance should not follow a pattern but should be as disorganized as battle itself. If a coven member wants to stop and shout an affirmation, so be it. If another wants to chant to Victoria, let him. You may all even take up the chant, if it's an appealing one. It should go without saying that you should all be keeping your goal in mind and visualizing it as much as possible.

When the energy has reached its peak, the leader will let you know to stop the dance and send out the energy toward its goal.

Before you close your circle, you should have a member of your group thank Victoria for her presence and help.

> RED WOLF HP: **Powerful Victoria, goddess of winners, thank you for your presence here as we wove our spell for success in** (fill in the name of your goal). **Your assistance is invaluable and we respect your judgment upon our cause. We thank you, we honor you, and we offer our blessings of thanks. In victory, so mote it be.**

Extinguish Victoria's candle and send it home with someone you trust to light it on a daily basis to keep the spell fresh until the goal is won or lost. If you all live close enough to one another, you may want to pass the candle along to a different person each day or each three days so that all may participate in keeping the spell's energy alive.

While the candle is burning, the person feeding fresh energy into the spell should be meditating on the goal and should never leave the candle burning unattended. This latter is common sense and is for safety's sake rather than having anything to do with the working of the spell.

> **Notes for Spell Alteration:** These earthy spells that call upon deities of victory also work well for goals of strength, stamina, and personal courage. All are attributes of war deities and are governed by the planet Mars.

◆ CONSOLATION SPELL ◆

Goal: To offer comfort and consolation to someone who is grieving.

Subject: A coven member or someone close to your coven. The person for whom the spell is being done need not be present and, in most cases, it is better if they are not.

Items: An unlit white candle in the center of the altar, a censor or heat-resistant bowl with incense coals burning in it, dried marigolds, dried lemon peel shavings, and dried violet.

Best Times: Whenever needed.

A leader, or someone who is very close to the one in need of consolation, should light a white candle on the altar to symbolize peace and the power of spirit. The words of power that accompany this gesture might sound something like the following.

> MOONDANCER: **We light this candle tonight in the presence of our deities in the sanctuary of this sacred space to help ease the grief of Greenwood, whose father has passed into the otherworld. We ask that this flame burn in his heart and mind, offering him the light of hope for happiness in his own life and that of his family. We also light it as a beacon to help Greenwood's father's spirit make his journey to wherever he is called by the deities he loves. The flame also burns as a representation of the unity of all beings in all realms and stands as a symbol of our belief that we are all one and that someday we will all be united again when we merge with the divine. Blessed be and so mote it be.**

An incense blend made of the dried herbs listed in the opening information to this spell should have already been mixed. You can also have members of the coven bring other dried herbs that would add to the goal of your spell to bring consolation. These include lemon balm, rue, hyacinth, myrrh, myrtle, and vervain. Some may include rosemary, which aids memory, while others may wish to avoid vivid memories of lost loved ones at this time.

Divide the incense blend among those members who did not bring some of their own. As each person steps forward and tosses their herbal offering onto the hot coals, they should offer a blessing to help heal the grieving member's wounds. Move counterclockwise around the circle to symbolize the decrease of grief. The blessings might sound something like the following.

> **Snow Owl HPS:** I wish Greenwood a good night's rest, free from thoughts of guilt, pain, or fear.

> **Red Wolf HP:** I brought lemon balm to ease Greenwood's spirit and calm him in his time of anxiety.

> **Moondancer:** I wish Greenwood and his family the peace of knowing that God—however they view him or her—is in charge of his father's spirit, and that someday they will be reunited.

> **Stormwillow:** I brought myrtle, a love herb, to remind Greenwood that love never ends. May it follow his father into the otherworld and provide a pathway of light to lead Greenwood to him again when it is his turn to pass into the otherworld.

When all offerings have been made, have everyone join hands and mentally send the group energy of consolation and healing to the grieving member. You may need to repeat the spell if the grieving process is prolonged or intense. You may also offer to do a special passing-over or memorial ritual if the member in need of your help requests or needs one.

◆ THE SPELL OF PEACE AND SANCTUARY ◆

Goal: To purge the home of an individual coven member of strife, fighting, anger, abuse, or personal danger.

Subject: A coven member whose home life is in turmoil.

Items: A large pan of boiling water into which peace and harmony herbs such as vanilla, lavender, chamomile, vervain, violet, or myrtle, and a pinch of sugar, have been placed. You will also need enough small, leafy branches taken from a tree who offers them to you for each coven member. Let each member choose their own and bring them to the spellworking.

Best Times: When needed, but should be done when no one but your coven will be in the home where the trouble is occurring. Other good times are on Friday, or on a festival of peace such as Roman's Feast of Concordia (February 22 or January 16), which celebrates familial peace and harmony.

"Familiarity breeds contempt." It's an old saying that is often sad but true. Those we know best are the same people we treat the worst. Family members living under the same roof for years and years sometimes don't get along. This has been the normal course of things for centuries. What is not normal, or acceptable, is when that discord becomes a danger to other members of the family.

During the old Roman feast day of Concordia, symbols of family difficulties would be burned in a ritual fire and the ashes buried far from their dwelling. In our more hectic and difficult world it doesn't seem so easy to overcome these problems.

Keep in mind that this spell is a support for other efforts at solving the family's problems. Physical violence, sexual abuse, substance abuse, or anything else that might put family members in danger should not be left to magick alone. Crisis intervention is needed, and most communities have free or low-cost legal and medical services to address these needs. If you fear for the life or safety of one of your coven's members, then get her out of that home and somewhere safe. The same should go for any dependent children or elderly persons in her care. The first priority is to remove them from the dangerous situation, then make that call to crisis intervention.

The spell you will do is designed to change the vibrations in the house that are buzzing on a low level to a higher one. This helps ease tension and makes it an environment in which negative entities who may have attached themselves to the discord cannot thrive. A friend of mine who was having difficulties with an alcoholic husband actually saw such a negative being enter their home with him one night when he'd been out drinking. She was an experienced Witch, and her psychic eyes met those of the entity, who grinned at her and mentally sent the image that this man was no longer hers, but now belonged to the negativity-feeding entity. In her case, the negative being won the battle, but that does not always have to be the way these problems end.

You should all gather together in the kitchen of the person whose home you are taking care of to simmer the herbs. While doing this, you should all be feeding the mixture your energy of wishes for peace in this house. Encourage the member with the problem to talk about the difficulties. In this environment she will be more willing to open up, and you can get a sense of the seriousness of the problem.

When you have decided the brew is ready, turn off the burner and place a little of the water into small bowls so each member of the coven may have one. Filter out the herbs with a strainer or cheesecloth.

Coven members should wander through the house, dipping their leafy branches into the water and lightly sprinkling the water around them. Use caution not to stain or ruin any item. Only a small bit of the water is needed.

Each person should chant or make an affirmation of their choosing as they go from room to room. These can be simple one-line wishes, rhyming couplets, or entire sections of song or lines of poetry. The contrapuntal sound this produces will help weave a wall of peace and balance around the home. This is the same principle as counterpoint in music, where opposing melodies are all sung simultaneously, but they harmonize with perfection and end on the same chord. The listener of such music is usually transfixed, following first one line of melody, then finding their consciousness dropped into another without realizing they have shifted their focus.

Keep this up for at least fifteen minutes, allowing everyone to go everywhere possible in the home. Pay particular attention to areas that have been designated as problem spots, such as the bedroom or the kitchen table.

When you are finished, pour the remaining water near the entrance to the home to keep out any further negative energies or entities.

If your fellow coven member will not leave her home and come with you, the final thing you should do before you leave your friend is to hide or disable anything that could be used as a weapon by someone in anger. Granted that almost any object can be turned into a weapon, but the obvious ones should be removed. This includes guns, kitchen knives, extra electrical cords, glass knickknacks, statuary, and sharp gardening or household tools.

◆ **THE TALISMAN SEEKERS HODGEPODGE SPELL** ◆

Goal: To enact a fun spell in which each member of the group creates a talisman for a goal they alone seek.

Subject: Each individual in the coven.

Items: Everyone must contribute to this spell so that you will have a collection of colored felt, needles and thread, scissors, herbs, stones, crystals, metals, nuts, glue, sequins, paper, pens, magazines for cutting pictures from, colored markers, and so on. Bring anything that might conceivably be placed in a talisman. Arrange these on a table large enough for everyone to gather around. Donations of munchies and beverages are welcome too.

Best Times: Whenever the group can gather at someone's home.

This is a fun spell that allows each coven member to create a talisman for a desire of their own while still having the support and input of their spiritual family. I have participated in these types of spells and there is little organization to them, but they are fun ways to make magick together and to help bond your group while empowering the talismans with the group's energy.

When all the items are placed on the table, everyone should start making their own talisman while attempting to keep a visualization of their goal in mind. This should be a lively gathering, with items being passed back and forth and suggestions for items asked for and offered. Talking about what you want in a lighthearted way also helps. Some magickal people are very good with words, and story spells work well for them. Be alert for someone who tells a story about their goal as if as already happened. If you like the idea, try it yourself. At the very least, keep this person's talent in mind for future spells your coven may wish to enact.

If you are asked to pass an item, do your friend a favor and pause to empower the item with energy so the person asking for it will have a stronger talisman.

When all the talismans are complete, they should be tossed about the circle. This game of catch and toss should mix up the talismans and the energies. Toss a talisman for fertility to your friend who wants no kids and watch her toss it along like it's poison. It should be energetic and lively, helping infuse the talismans with more group energy. Let it be fun.

Before you leave the house where this spell was enacted, please help your host clean up any mess that was made and wash any dishes that were dirtied. You might even choose clean-up committees before any meeting so there's no doubt about whose job it will be. As someone who has hosted coven gatherings and who has known other coven leaders, it's frustrating and not conducive to good will among members to always get left with the group's mess.

When you're all ready to depart, place your talismans in your right palms and all join hands. The leader should say a word of blessing over the final proceedings, such as what follows.

> **RED WOLF HP:** Dear Lord and Lady who reigned over our merriment today, you who know the deepest wishes of each human heart, we ask your blessings on these spells we have created. We may not always agree with one another's goals, but we agree that we want each other's happiness. We thank you for blessing this circle with joy and laughter as we link hands, feeding each other's strength to the talismans we created. Merry meet, merry part . . .

> **ALL:** . . . and merry meet again. So mote it be.

◆ THE LIGHT OF INSPIRATION ◆

Goal: To offer someone in the group who is discouraged or who has lost hope the chance to find their inner strength through the support and energy of their coven.

Subject: The member who requests the help.

Items: Each person should have a single candle that is unlit. There should be a central candle on the altar that is also unlit. White taper candles work best.

Best Times: When needed. Working on a full moon, when the moon is in a water sign, or on a Sunday or Tuesday can add to the spell.

From time to time, we all fall into depressive states when it seems that no matter how hard we try, we cannot pull ourselves out of our feeling that things are bad and getting worse. For most of us this is a temporary state caused by the pressures of daily living, and it will pass in time. For others it becomes a serious medical condition requiring a doctor's help.

Your coven can help you through these dark times by enacting a spell for you in which they pass the light of inspiration, with all its attendant energies, for you to draw upon and use as you need.

As mentioned in the opening information of this spell, everyone present should have an unlit candle, preferably a white taper. To prevent wax from staining carpet or fabric, or from burning your hands, place these candles in a small paper cup into which a small hole has been cut to push the candle through. If the fit is snug, it will catch 99 percent of the wax (see illustration on page 168).

Ask everyone to come prepared with a simple affirmation, quotation, or other inspirational wish or statement for the person in need. Browsing through a book of poetry or famous quotations can help you find the perfect verbal offering.

When you're ready for the spell to begin, have everyone sit comfortably in a circle together. Make sure the person sitting to the immediate left of the person in need has a match to light his candle. He should light the candle, then look at the person for whom the spell is being done while speaking the quotation, words of encouragement, prayer to a creative deity, or whatever else he has planned to say.

When he is done speaking, he will turn to the person on his left and light her candle with his own, passing the light of inspiration along the circle in a clockwise motion.

That person should now look at the one in need and speak her words of encouragement. When she is done, she too will turn to the person on her left and light that person's candle. The light being passed along should be visualized as gaining power and growing with each person who adds to it. You want it strong and full of all your good energies by the time it gets back to the person who needs it most.

When the full circle has been made, the last candle to be lit will be that of the coven member who requested your help. As the light is passed to him, he should feel the full impact of all the good words and wishes for him charge his candle. In turn, he should allow himself a moment to draw in that energy so it can be used later when needed. He should offer his thanks to you and then invite you all to the center of the circle.

Together you should all light the center candle while the person in need makes a statement similar to the following.

> **Light of the deities of inspiration, of creativity. Thank you for blessing our circle and offering your assistance to me. Bless this gathering, my spiritual family who have given their time and energy to help me in my time of need. May the light of inspiration burn brightly in all of us so that we have creative, happy, blessed lives. By our will, so mote it be.**

Notes for Spell Alteration: This spell also works to help someone in a creative slump find their muse again. This could be a writer, artist, musician, computer programmer, or anyone who feels their creativity has been stymied.

◆ THE GROUP DREAM SPELL ◆

Goal: To cause the entire coven to dream of a solution to a problem, the answer to a dilemma, the right way to work a spell, the proper words for the next ritual, or any other issue that is not able to be resolved thought conversation, consensus, or standard divination techniques.

Subject: The entire coven.

Items: A script that will begin a guided meditation that will set in motion the dream spell. Jasmine or catnip tea and incense, both at the coven gathering and in each person's home, is desirable. You will also need to direct everyone to have paper and pen ready both at the coven gathering and near their beds that night to capture their dream impressions before they fade.

Best Times: When the moon is waxing or in the sign of Cancer.

Before you enter your circle, the script to begin a guided meditation should have been written with everyone's input. However, unlike most guided meditations, it will not take you full circle into the otherworld and back out again. The idea is to lead everyone in by the same path, seeking the same goal, then allow each individual to seek the answer to the group problem on their own, and then find their own way back again.

For example, your coven may be having an argument about the harm that may be done by a spell you're considering. The divinations seem unclear or, worse, at odds with one another. You cannot come to consensus and the spell is important enough to enough of your coven members that you all feel it's worth pursuing. This is when the Group Dream Spell can help.

Each entry into the otherworld is unique. There are many paths: elemental ones, symbolic ones, ships, horses, gateways, and so on. They all lead in and all lead back out again. Choose the one that seems to best correspond to your goal. For example, if your goal is under the rulership of water, use ship imagery. If it is under the rulership of air, fly to the otherworld on the back of a large bird.

Try to frame the meditation with as much symbolism as you can that will both take you into the otherworld and help you find your answers. Someone experienced with archetypes or dream interpretation can be very helpful. If your coven doesn't have someone like this, you might want to find a book on Pagan symbols or dream interpretation to help you.

The spell will be enacted twice on the same night; once in the group setting and again when everyone is home alone. Keep the lights low in the circle area to create a quiet atmosphere. Any music played should be the kind designed for meditation. These have no lyrics and little or no discernible rhythm. Their purpose is to drown out background noise and assist easing your mind into the alpha or theta state needed for a good meditation or dream spell. Jasmine or catnip tea will also help everyone relax, as well as open the dream centers to the psychic impressions you wish to have.

When you're ready to begin the meditation, have everyone get comfortable and close their eyes.

Here is an example beginning script for the lack of consensus situation in which the outcome and possible harmful side effects of a proposed spell are not clear. It should be tailored to your specific needs. It may be read to the group by a leader or it may be pre-recorded so you may all participate.

♦   ♦   ♦

EXAMPLE GUIDED MEDITATION SCRIPT

You are in a place of total darkness—a void—but you are not afraid. The environment is like a large womb in which you float in comfort and safety. You recognize this place as a midway point between the world of form and the world of spirit. It is through this womb that you may be birthed into either place.

You are content here but you know you cannot float forever. All beings must move on into one world or another, sooner or later. That is the way the universe works and we can neither stop nor slow the process. The cycle never ends. Try now to imagine which way you are intended to go.

In a few moments, bit by bit, you remember why you are here. You seek an answer to your coven's dilemma. You must first be birthed into the otherworld of spirit so that you can seek a solution that is too elusive for the physical realm. What will be the outcome of the proposed spell? What, if any, harm might it do to beings in both the seen and unseen worlds? You must go into the otherworld seeking those answers and to find a way—if there is one—to make this spell workable within a positive setting that harms none.

As you think these thoughts, you feel the womb around you contracting, as if trying to expel you. It happens again, and you realize this is no longer a comfortable place to be. It is time to move on and seek your goal.

You see that a light appears in the distance. It is the entrance to the other-world, where your answers lie waiting. You begin to float toward it, moving faster and faster, and the womb pushes you out.

Just before you enter the otherworld, say a small prayer to your personal deities that you will be safe here and guided only by loving and helpful beings who wish you well and want only to assist you in finding your answers.

(The reader should pause for a moment or two to let each person offer their silent prayers.)

In the next moment, find yourself standing in a world that is familiar, yet it is not. Everything around you looks like any other outdoor setting might, with sky and trees and grass, but there is a quality about it that suggests capriciousness, that you see only a well-crafted illusion designed to please the senses. You remember that occurrences here can happen as fast as the speed of thought. This is a place populated by deities, spirits, elements, and faeries. It is the realm of the highest and most benevolent beings, but it is also the home of a trickster being who enjoys leading seekers astray. You know you must be wary. You also know that you do not have to go with any guide who appears to you unless you choose to do so. You may also explore on your own.

In this world are caves, lakes, oceans, forests, libraries, farms, cities, ancient temples, groves, and a host of environments and beings of whom you may ask assistance. Keep in mind the goal you have here and be aware of symbolic images or gifts offered you that may suggest a trap or provide a clue to what you seek.

From the woods ahead of you, you now notice two eyes peering at you. You sense this is the first guide who is going to present itself to you.

(Pause for just a moment to allow everyone to get a feel for the nature of the being who is coming to them.)

The being steps from the trees and comes toward you. It seems to know you and introduces itself. It says it knows what you're seeking and can help you find your answer. You may accept this offer or demand the being leave and another appear, or you can insist on being free to explore on your own.

Remember that you must find out about the proposed spell's outcome and any harm it may do. The otherworld is yours to explore, but keep your goal for being there in mind. The answers are all here for those who want to find them, but they are not easy to uncover. Most people turn back when the terrors of the threshold challenge them or when the trickster spirits make an appearance and send them on a fruitless chase. Be wary. Be smart. Know that you may call upon your spirit guides or deities at any time to assist you. You may also return to your own world at any time by saying the words "I am home" three times in a row.

Good night and good journey. May your travels be blessed and your answers positive.

♦ ♦ ♦

Allow the coven to stay in this altered state of consciousness for twenty or thirty minutes. Some may return before that time, but they should remain quiet and sit still so as not to disturb the others. They should write down all their impressions and experiences as soon as they are coherent so that nothing is forgotten. Guided meditations have the quality of a controlled dream and, like dreams, the details can fade fast once normal consciousness is returned. You want to write down all you can. Leave no detail out. That one image or symbol you happened to see in passing may have also appeared in everyone else's journey and may be the key to solving your problem.

No one should compare notes at this point. The spell is not done and you don't want to put impressions or ideas in anyone else's head that may influence their dreaming that night.

When the coven members return home, they should brew themselves some more jasmine or catnip tea and sit quietly, going over and over the opening script of the guided meditation in their minds. The goal of the exercise should also be kept in the consciousness.

When the coven members go to bed, they should read over a copy of the script and think about the script as they fall asleep, allowing it to take them back to the otherworld.

As soon as each member awakens, they should immediately write down any dreams they remember in as much detail as possible. If no dreams are remembered, they should write down any feelings or impressions they had upon awakening. For example, did they awaken feeling anxious or serene? Did they awaken with a sense of dread or disorientation? Did they feel contentment or dissatisfaction? Did some idea pop into their heads about how to solve the coven's dilemma?

The coven should try to meet again in about three days. This gives those who want to try the spell again three consecutive nights to get a clear dream image from the guided meditation.

When notes are compared in detail, you may be surprised how much alike they are, even if each person's otherworld environment was different. The man who went into a cave with a bear may have seen or experienced many of the same things as the woman who went on her own into a faery forest. Someone else may have seen the outcome of the spell enacted before his eyes, and someone else may have seen the harm that would be done or not done unless changes are made to the spell.

When all the notes have been compared, try to work though the mechanics of your spell again. You may want to do this at another meeting to give everyone time to think about all they learned. This should make reaching consensus easier.

◆ CALLING BACK OR BREAKING A SPELL ◆

Goal: To end the energy flow being directed into a spell and halt or reverse its progress.

Subject: Every member of the coven who helped in the spell's creation should be part of calling it back because their personal energies are part of what is being dismantled. To have someone missing may cause a part of the spell to not be broken if the energies that created it have not melded well.

Items: What you need will depend on how you constructed the spell in the first place. If you used candles, these should be extinguished and buried. If you created a talisman, it should be taken apart, then buried or burned.

Best Times: A waxing moon or a Saturday.

Not every magical practitioner calls back a spell they no longer wish to keep active, but it is a good practice to get into the habit of doing so. It's just the polite thing to do, to clean up after yourself in the astral world as you would the physical.

The energy you fed into the spell will continue to work for you even after the spell is no longer being done. True, it will weaken if not fed fresh energy from your will on a periodic basis. In the meantime, without your guidance, it can act like an unwanted intruder from the astral realm and follow you around, trying to get a fresh energy supply. It will startle and annoy those entering the astral realms too. Eventually it will die on its own, but why not make a clean break? It's the more responsible way to approach magick. We don't need the highways of the unseen worlds crowded with the debris of half-manifested spells and unfulfilled wishes. It's already hard enough to navigate the astral planes and other otherworld realms without haphazard thoughtforms further confounding the traveler.

The first step to take in calling back or breaking any spell is to gather all the items used in its creation. Sometimes these have been destroyed in the making of the spell. Other times it's simply impossible to gather everything. Just do your best.

As you dismantle any talisman, or burn or bury any item associated with the spell's creation, someone in the group—a leader or the one for whom the spell was enacted—should make a statement aloud to let all the elementals, spirits, and deities who were present at the time of the spell's working know that it is no longer a desirable goal and that it is being called back or broken. You don't necessarily need to say why you've changed your mind about the goal, unless you've realized some harm is being done by it, in which case an apology and a statement of being willing to make amends is needed. In either case you should offer your thanks for the assistance.

There are several ritual gestures or ways of pulling back the energy sent out so you can ground it together.

One

Have everyone in the circle face outward with their arms straight out in front of them and their palms facing straight out. As a group, feel your hands drawing in the magickal energy you sent into the universe. This is where a group chant is helpful. The example given here is too generic for most purposes, but will give you an idea of the tone you seek. Make yours as specific to your original spell's goal as possible, mentioning on whose behalf the spell was enacted and what the desired outcome was to be.

> **We sent it out, the power we wrought,**
> **It began to return in the form we sought;**

Yet now we see that harm it did send,
We call it back, this spell we do end.

When the leader feels enough energy has been pulled in, he will stop the chant and direct everyone in the group to ground the energy they have collected. This gesture may need to be repeated several times. Each time the members of your coven will feel less and less of the spell's energy being pulled into their hands. When it seems that nothing else is being collected, ground one last time.

Two

Through directed visualization, your coven can call back any thoughtform or elemental being it has created in the working of a spell that is no longer wanted. This can be done one of two ways.

The first is to have a leader direct everyone in a group visualization in which they enter a meditative state and visualize the calling back or dismantling of these thought-forms. The other way is to have someone in the group who is skilled at astral projection sit in the center of the circle and project herself into the astral world to do the job herself. So that the coven is aware of what is happening, and so they can best lend their energy to the goal, someone should sit in front of the one projecting and ask questions so that the person projecting can talk about what she is seeing or doing. This will not disturb the projection if the person is truly skilled at the art any more than it would disturb someone in a guided meditation or in a directed past-life regression.

Three

If you used candles in the creation of your spell, you can use them again in a ritual to break the spell. Have everyone hold a lit candle. Use the cup shown in the Light of Inspiration Spell to contain the hot wax. These candles represent the energy you each put into the spell. Also have a lit candle on the altar in the center of your circle to represent your group will.

Starting at any point you choose, have each person make a statement about ending the spell. Keep it to one line, brief and simple. Then have them extinguish their candle. Move counterclockwise around the circle until all the candles are extinguished.

At this point a leader or someone for whom the spell was enacted should go to the altar and make a final statement to thank the beings who helped you with the spell so far, and to inform them that it is no longer a desirable goal, and that with the extinguishing of the last candle the light of energy powering the spell is ended. Put out that candle and know the spell is undone.

Four

If you used a cone of power to begin your spell, you can call it back and ground it together as a group. Begin by dancing counterclockwise as you visualize the energy returning to your circle, swirling overhead and spinning in a counterclockwise direction along with your dance. The dance should gain speed and intensity as the cone that is reabsorbing your energies from the unseen world grows.

When the leader has determined that the cone is complete, she will direct the dance to stop. At that point everyone should reach up and imagine they are grabbing the edge of the cone. Together you will all pull it down until it is touching the ground. Keep your hands on the ground as you visualize your hands continuing to force the cone down into the earth. Keep up your visualization until a leader cues you that the last of the cone is buried and your spell's residual energy is grounded.

Resources and References ◆ 111

Appendix A: Resources

Please look first to your local occult supply shops and bookstores when seeking your magickal accoutrements. This not only helps support other members of your magickal community, but these shops are good places to find regional items unavailable or hard to find elsewhere. Another point in their favor is that they are usually good places to begin networking with others who share your interests.

Many occult and Pagan businesses and publications have a prominent presence on the Internet. They are another source for ordering supplies, inquiring about subscription rates, perusing the editorial slant of a publication, or making connections with others. Use your browser's search engines to find anything magickal. I experimented with putting in the words "rosemary oil" and got hundreds of hits for information, medicine, magick, and vendors.

Every attempt has been made to make this appendix accurate at the time of publication, but remember that addresses can change, businesses can fail, periodicals can cease publication, and today's hot website can be tomorrow's cyberdust. Sometimes companies who offer free catalogs discover they must charge for subscriptions or raise prices to stay competitive. If you are reading this book a year or more from its original publication date, it would be wise to query business contacts to check on prices and the availability of goods and services. All prices are quoted in U.S. dollars unless otherwise stated. Always remember to enclose a SASE (self-addressed stamped envelope) when making inquiries to businesses within your own country, or an IRC (international reply coupon) when querying elsewhere. This is not only a matter of courtesy, but is often the only way to ensure a reply.

HERBS, OILS, TOOLS, AND OTHER ACCOUTREMENTS

Aroma Vera
5901 Rodeo Road
Los Angeles, CA 90016
Write for catalog price for essential oils, floral waters, dried products, aromatherapy oils, and incense censers.

Azure Green
P.O. Box 48
Middlefield, MA 01243-0048
(413) 623-2155
http://www.azuregreen.com
Azure Green has almost everything. Request free catalog or order via their website.

Balefire
6504 Vista Avenue
Wauwatosa, WI 53213
This mail-order company carries a large stock of brews, oils, and incenses designed for specific Pagan needs such as scrying, spirit contact, and spellwork. Write for catalog.

Branwen's Cauldron
http://www.branwenscauldron.com
Sellers of magickal accoutrements, jewelry, books, and crafts.

Dreaming Spirit
P.O. Box 4263
Danbury, CT 06813-4263
Natural, homemade incenses and resins, oils, and tools for using them. Dreaming Spirit welcomes queries about custom blends of incenses or oils. The $2 for their catalog is refundable with your first order.

Earth Scents by Marah
Box 948
Madison, NJ 07940
Sellers of herbs, incenses, books, oil blends, and other tools. Catalog, $1.

General Bottle Supply
1930 East 51st Street
Los Angeles, CA 90058
Write for free catalog of herb, oil, and salt bottles.

Gypsy Heaven
115 South Main Street
New Hope, PA 18938
(215) 862-5251
Request catalog of magickal supplies. Currently catalog is being offered for free, but it doesn't hurt to check this information.

Halcyon Herb Company
Box 7153 L
Halcyon, CA 93421
Sells not only magickal herbs, but also staffs, brooms, cloaks, drums, and other items of interest to Pagan folk. Current catalog, $5.

Indiana Botanic Gardens
2401 West 37th Avenue
Hobart, IN 46342
http://www.botanichealth.com
Sells herbal health products, dried herbs, and essential oils.

Isis Metaphysical
http://www.isisbooks.com
Sellers of magickal accoutrements, jewelry, books, and crafts.

Just Wingin' It
P.O. Box 7029
Riverside, CA 92513-7029
http://www.jwi.com
Jewelry, incense, bottles, and other magickal items, both wholesale and retail.

Lavender Folk Herbal
P.O. Box 1261, Dept. SW
Boulder, CO 80306
Medicinal and magickal tea blends, herbs, and herbal crafts. $2 catalog is refundable
with first order.

Leydet Oils
P.O. Box 2354
Fair Oaks, CA 95628
Sellers of fine essential oils. Price list, $2.

Light and Shadows
Catalog Consumer Service
2215-R Market Street, Box 801
San Francisco, CA 94114-1612
Write for their free metaphysical supply catalog.

MagiCrafts
http://www.magicrafts.com
Sellers of magickal accoutrements, jewelry, books, and crafts.

Moon Scents
P.O. Box 1588-C
Cambridge, MA 02238
(603) 356-3666
http://www.moonscents.com
Large collection of magickal paraphernalia and books. Request free catalog.

The Mystic Merchant
http://www.mysticmerchant.com
Sellers of magickal accoutrements, jewelry, books, and crafts.

Natural Impulse Handmade Soap and Sundries
P.O. Box 94441
Birmingham, AL 35220
http://www.naturalimpulse.com
Sells ready-made soaps made of natural oils by a company openly committed to protecting the environment.

Pagan Pretties
http://www.paganpretties.com
Sellers of magickal accoutrements, jewelry, books, and crafts.

POTO
www.poto.com
(310) 451-9166
POTO is short for "Procurer of the Obscure." POTO specializes in stocking or locating rare and hard-to-find occult items. My experience with them is that they are fast and thorough.

Sacred Spirit Products
P.O. Box 8163
Salem, MA 01971-8163
Sellers of books, magickal tools, herbs, incense, and other occult items. Catalog, $3.

Sunburst Bottle Company
5710 Auburn Boulevard, Suite 7
Sacramento, CA 95841
Bottle and container provider whose catalog is $2. Write or call for current price.

Triple Moon Witchware
http://www.witchware.com
Sellers of magickal accoutrements, jewelry, books, and crafts.

Witch's Brew
http://www.witchs-brew.com
Sellers of magickal accoutrements, jewelry, books, and crafts.

GENERAL PAGAN PUBLICATIONS

Accord
Council of the Magickal Arts, Inc.
P.O. Box 890526
Houston, TX 77289
Published by a well-known Texas-based networking organization. As of this writing, sample issues are $4.50.

Blessed Bee
P.O. Box 641
Point Arena, CA 95468
(707) 882-2052
info@blessedbee.com
Publications for Pagan families with younger children. Call or e-mail for rates.

Circle Magazine
P.O. Box 219
Mount Horeb, WI 53572
http://www.circlesanctuary.org
A popular, professional journal for Pagan news and gatherings, contacts, and seasonal celebration information. Sample copy, $5. Write for other subscription information.

The Green Egg
P.O. Box 1542
Ukiah, CA 95482
http://www.caw.org.green-egg
This very popular magazine has been around for a long time. Professionally formatted and always controversial. Contains beautiful artwork. Write for current rates.

Hecate's Loom
Box 5206, Station B
Victoria, BC
Canada V8R 6N4
Another professional-quality journal. Focus on Pagan arts. Write for rates. United States residents should include an IRC to ensure a reply.

PanGaia
Blessed Bee, Inc.
P.O. Box 641
Point Arena, CA 95468-0099
http://www.pangaia.com
Earth-focused general Pagan publication. Professional format and artwork.

ONLINE NETWORKING

The Internet has exploded with Pagan and Wiccan information in proportion to booming interest. Local libraries or public universities often have connections you can use if you're not online at home. Even without a computer, Internet hookups are available through your television with relatively little expense through such devices as Web TV. The resources listed here are national or international in scope, but hundreds of viable regional, state/provincial, local, and campus organizations have been formed. Use your web server's search engine to find these.

British Pagan Circle
http://www.geocities.com/RainForest/canopy/7046

The Church of All Worlds
http://www.caw.org

Circle Guide to Groups and Resources
http://www.circlesanctuary.org/publications

The Council of Magickal Arts
http://www.houston-pno.org

Covenant of the Goddess (COG)
http://www.cog.org

Covenant of Unitarian Universalist Pagans (C.U.U.P.s)
http://www.cuups.org

The Fellowship of Isis
http://www.fellowshipofisis.com

Magickal Education Convocation
http://www.convocation.org

New Age Information Network
http://www.newageinfo.com/res/wicca

Online Pagan Networks
http://www.candledark.net

Pagan Awareness Network, Australia
http://www.paganawareness.net.au

Pagan Education Network (PEN)
http://www.bloomington.in.us/~pen

PagaNet News
http://www.paganet.org

The Pagan Federation, Canada
http://www.pfpc.ca

The Pagan Federation, England
http://paganfed.demon.co.uk

The Pagan Federation, Scotland
http://www.vscotland.org.uk

The Pagan Federation, South Africa
http://www.pfsa.org

Pagan Ireland
http://www.paganireland.com

Pagan Network Webring
http://www.paganprofiles.com/webring

Pagan Paths IRC Chat Network
http://www.paganpaths.org

The Witches' Voice
http://www.witchvox.com

Witches Against Religious Discrimination
http://www.ward-hg.org

Witches' League for Public Awareness
http://www.celticcrow.com

Youth Wiccans and Pagans of Canada
http://www.OypcO.cjb.net

Appendix B: FAQs
(Frequently Asked Questions)

I have found that after over twenty years in the Craft I'm still asked the same few questions over and over again by newcomers, and a few not-so-newcomers. These queries show up in my workshops, in e-mails, and in letters forwarded from the publisher.

There is an obvious hunger for basic Craft and magickal information that, fortunately, is easy to obtain in today's open atmosphere. When I first began my Craft studies, hiding our beliefs in the broom closet was almost an expectation. Only a few brave souls, usually those living in an area where counterculture was a potent force, were able to exercise their freedom of religion. Thank Goddess that is not the case today. We may still have to face down those who do not, or do not want to understand what it is we do, but the information is available in many forms for those with the will to seek it out.

There is power in numbers, and interest in magick and Witchcraft has exploded over the past few years. Today's seekers, like those of the past, are sincere, creative people who seek harmony with the universe and a path to the God and Goddess that makes sense to them within that harmony, and I have loved meeting with and hearing from everyone who has taken the time to write or to stop and introduce themselves. I have learned from everyone too. In the Craft we never stop being students, and we are all always teachers, whether we realize it or not.

This rising interest in Witchcraft also means that I now receive more mail than I can cope with in a satisfactory and timely fashion. When I first began writing about Witchcraft I committed to personally answering each letter I received, remembering the days when I also needed to reach out for answers. The effort to keep this commitment grew more difficult with the increasing volume and, eventually, I was reduced to a form letter with a brief personal line at the bottom, which even I found very uninspiring.

Fortunately, there are alternatives.

Today there are experienced magicians, Witches, Wiccans, and Pagans in almost every city and town across North America and Western Europe. There are excellent books, groups, periodicals, federations, and other resources that were only a dream even a decade ago. Many people who operate occult shops or metaphysical bookstores have been in the Craft for decades and can help answer your questions or recommend books and resources for study. In other words, you have hundreds of resources to turn to for assistance that are faster and easier to reach than you might think.

Don't overlook the Internet as a source of networking and information. There are websites, chat rooms, news groups, vendors, periodicals, and a host of other links that explore magick and Paganism from every angle and viewpoint. They are brimming with lively debate from interesting personalities. If you do not own a computer, your local library or public university probably has one you can use for free to browse the Internet. Try plugging key words into the browser's search engine such as *magic(k)*, *Pagan*, *Wicca(n)*, and *Witchcraft* for a slew of sites you can explore. Also see the listing in Appendix A for the URLs of websites of popular Pagan educational and networking organizations, or for finding supplies.

Free web-based e-mail addresses for receiving answers to your queries can be obtained through most of the major Internet search sites such as Hotmail, Yahoo, and Excite. The beauty of these is that you can receive e-mail on any computer where you have Internet access, not just one that is hooked up to a specific server. Even though I'm hooked up at home to a private Internet service provider, I switched my e-mail address to one of these web-based sites for the accessibility.

There are three tips to remember to give yourself the best chance of receiving an answer if you have a question to address to a specific Pagan author, publisher, musician, artist, or organizer.

1) Use e-mail rather than snail mail.
2) Provide an SASE or IRC when using snail mail.
3) Make your query as specific as possible.

Contrary to popular fantasy, most artists and volunteers for nonprofit organizations hold down other full-time jobs and, with life's other demands, have little time for letter writing. Check out a publisher's, organization's, or periodical's website for the e-mail addresses of writers and artists whose work you admire.

My e-mail address appears below. I'm always glad to hear from others who are interested in Witchcraft. I try to respond to all messages that appear in my inbox. Just be aware that sometimes my backlog of unanswered items can trail back for months.

EDAINMCCOY@YAHOO.COM

If you write via snail mail to a business or to any person unknown to you, you should always enclose a self-addressed stamped envelope or international rely coupon. You should follow this rule both in and out of the Pagan world. It is a matter of both courtesy and economic reality. The tally of hundreds of envelopes, sheets of paper, ink, and stamps make answering large numbers of letters without return postage cost prohibitive.

To make answering a query easier, you should word your question clearly, noting a specific page number if you are asking about a passage in a book. This does not mean you have to reduce your correspondence to one single sentence. It just means that you'll get a better answer if your query is clear and concise. Oftentimes I'm not sure what I'm being asked. It's frustrating for both reader and writer if the communication is not clear or helpful. I think most of us who write Pagan or magickal books enjoy hearing about our reader's lives. We often learn something from them too. But when you're seeking specific information, ask for the specific information, making sure it is something that can be answered within the confines of a brief letter.

I get presented with lots of blanket questions that read like, "Tell me everything you know about Witchcraft." These types of general queries just can't be covered in a letter. They frustrate me because I wish I could do more, and they frustrate the letter writer who really wants to know or he wouldn't have taken the time to write. I usually reply to these types of letters with a list of books I think might help that person get started on a serious course of study, for that is the only sensible answer.

For the sake of saving yourself a couple of stamps, make sure your question has not already been addressed. Most Pagan books contain resource appendices, vendors, websites, bibliographies, recommended reading lists, periodical information, and glossaries that can act as a springboard for the information you seek. I've had readers stop to write me with questions halfway through reading a book I've written. The answer they seek is only a chapter or two away, and they will likely get to it long before a letter from me arrives.

Aside from the fact that your answer may already be close at hand, a book or article on the topic you're interested in will be much more thorough and informative than a paragraph or two in any letter could be, so you will simply get a better answer.

In an effort to address the most frequent queries, I'm providing brief answers here for those who are interested. I hope this appendix will answer many of your basic questions and help direct you to the other resources you need.

1) How do I become a Witch?

A Witch becomes a Witch through study and practice. Period. By tradition it takes a year and a day of reading, working, and learning to know and love the deities you seek to connect with and worship. At this point it is acceptable to do an initiation and call yourself a Witch, Wiccan, or Pagan.

An initiation enacted at this point either by yourself or by someone else does not mean that your learning process has stopped. It has just begun. You've only scratched the surface of the door that opens to all worlds. To pass through it and back at will takes much more skill and effort.

Self-initiations are accepted by virtually anyone within the Pagan community as a valid expression of your commitment to the Craft. No one will question that you're a Witch as long as you display the knowledge expected of an initiate with a year and a day's study behind them. However, know that if you are interested in a particular tradition—or sect or subsect—within the Craft, you will have to be initiated into it through their priests and priestesses, and undergo the requirements of their teaching structure, to be considered a member of the Craft within that specific tradition.

As previously mentioned, this is not a question that can be answered in a paragraph or two. If you are serious about being a Witch, then you must be serious about finding resources. We have no ministers or rabbis to give us our answers, and we believe the best answers for ourselves lie inside each of us. In many cases each of our answers are different, but remain just as true. Only by going deep within ourselves can we go without and be one with the universe. It can be lots of work to learn these processes, and even more to ferret these answers out. Sometimes trying to look deep within ourselves can be the scariest part of all.

There are lots of good books on basic Witchcraft available today. Most of them provide lots of practical exercises that enhance the text and cover your questions in depth. Look for books by Silver RavenWolf, Scott Cunningham, Laurie Cabot, Raymond Buckland, Marion Weinstein, Vivianne Crowley, Starhawk, Gerina Dunwich, Ann Moura, and Stewart and Janet Farrar to start. If your local bookstore cannot find these authors for you, you may want to search an online bookstore or Pagan vendor such as www.amazon.com, www.barnesandnoble.com, or www.azuregreen.com. Out-of-print book searches can be started at www.bibliofind.com.

2) Where can I find a coven in my area?

This is probably the single most-asked question I receive. There have been so many queries over the years that I was inspired to write *Inside a Witches' Coven* to address the issue. Like the previous question, there is no quick formula that produces results. The only answer to this question is that you have to hunt. No coven will ever come seeking you. Many established covens don't even want new members. The only exception to this are some teaching covens who would take you into an outer circle with other newcomers. Your best bet may be to find other solitaries and form your own group, if this is the way you wish to worship.

Not every coven is right for every Witch, any more than every church is right for every Christian. Being in the wrong group can be worse than being in none at all. You must put a lot of thought into not only which coven is right for you, but if being part of a coven at all is the right step for you at this time. Some Witches are better off working alone, and seek out others only for companionship and sharing.

Here's another tip for saving a stamp. Writing to a Pagan author, musician, artist, organizer, or publisher to ask where your local covens are is useless. We often don't know where all the covens are in our hometowns, much less in places we've never been. Even if we did, we would not be at liberty to invade their privacy and put them at risk by giving their personal information to others. Even in today's more accepting atmosphere, covens like to remain private and they will staunchly guard the identities of other members who may be at risk for losing their jobs or homes if their association is discovered. This is why persistent effort on your part is the only way to ferret out the like-minded in your area who are open to working with new people.

I have a basic six-step process for networking for the coven-minded, encapsulated here in points A–F.

A) Seek Resources. No twenty-first-century Witch should ever whine that they cannot make connections. You can almost trip over the resources available to us today. You can find them in the many Pagan publications that are now sold on newsstands in larger bookstores, in the backs of books on magickal or Pagan topics, at the local Unitarian Universalist Church, through national antidefamation or networking organizations, on bulletin boards at occult shops or health-food stores, from the owner of the local metaphysical bookstore, in ads in alternative lifestyle publications, and on the Internet.

I've met other Pagans and Wiccans by leaving notes on cars with obviously Pagan bumper stickers, and once I met someone by making a joke about spellcasting that fell on the ears of someone who I suspected already knew as well as I how spells were cast. The best attitude to have when seeking resources and contacts is to always assume you are not the only Witch around.

B) WIDEN YOUR CIRCLE. You finally meet another Pagan and you're thrilled. You've both worked hard to find each other and now you just can't get enough of talking about the subjects of your passion. This is great, but never assume that the one person you meet who is interested in alternative religious practice is your only chance of having a Pagan or Wiccan friend. Earth and nature-based spiritual practices are the fastest-growing religions in both North America and Western Europe. Take your new friend and use your joint efforts to widen your circle of contacts. You can never have too many friends, and you can never have enough threads connecting to you to the web of Wicca.

You should also attend events of a Pagan nature whenever possible. Sometimes there are local coffeehouses that host weekly or monthly Pagan gatherings. You may also want to travel, either alone or with your new friend, to one of the large Pagan festivals or gatherings. These are well advertised in advance on the Internet and in Pagan magazines, and most often occur around the eight sabbats. These will expose you to the full spectrum of the Pagan/Wiccan rainbow and will help you widen your circle even further.

C) NARROW YOUR OBJECTIVES. Now that you've connected with the Wiccan Web, you should focus on your desire for a coven and narrow your objectives without sacrificing anyone within this circle of contacts you've worked hard to create. You can have lots of Pagan friends, but you probably have fewer good matches if you're looking to find or form a coven or study group. Not everyone works well together, either because their energies just don't blend well or because they have different spiritual needs.

Make a list of the things that are really important to you, such as the focus of your study, the culture in which you wish to worship, the ethics you wish to embrace, the type of ritual dress you prefer, and where and how often you want to meet with a group. Leave off the list anything you don't feel is vital to your spiritual happiness. Allow what's on the list to be your holy grail and go after what you want like a knight on a quest. There is nothing wrong with seeking what you need spiritually, and everything wrong with settling for things you know will only make you—and the group you join—miserable in the end.

D) Let Your Circle of Contacts Know What You're Seeking. People are fussy about religion. All you have to do is turn on the nightly news to realize that some of the brightest and most rational people lose their perspective when discussing the topic, so don't get discouraged during your quest for finding the right group.

On the other hand, you should also not limit yourself too much. Just because people are different doesn't mean they can't blend their energies in perfect spiritual harmony. Keep your list at hand and be clear with everyone about what you hope to find or form.

Make the things you really need and want your priority, and be flexible with the rest. Be prepared to hear all sorts of "holy grails" from others. We all have a few in mind, and it's doubtful that any are wrong. They are unique to each person who seeks a group. You'll find some people, particularly women, who prefer to worship only a Goddess and never a God. You'll find others who want only a Celtic or Germanic focus, never Greek or Roman. Some people want a strict hierarchy with well-defined group leaders, others prefer an egalitarian situation where all participants take on the leadership roles from time to time. Some have a specific tradition they know about or have read about that they want to follow, and no other will do, while others love the mind-expanding experience of eclectic Wicca, where all deities are embraced. Others will want to teach newcomers, while still others feel out of their element in this role. Some people are only comfortable around those in their own age or ethnic bracket, and others prefer a multigenerational, multiethnic melee. Some people are natural crusaders and have to have an overriding cause—such as the environment or antidefamation—to make them feel a group is worthwhile, while others just want a quiet little circle to call their spiritual family.

Once you have a core group you feel can work well together, start off as a study group. All of you should feel free to discuss your needs and ideas in a nonjudgmental manner just to see how they might work together. If things go well for a few months as you talk and study together, you might start to experiment with ritual. If the ritual goes well, you may have the basis of a wonderful coven. Within a year you can be making great magick together, and building a true spiritual family.

E) Assess Your Situation. Several months after you're with your working group, you should take a step back from it and assess it with a critical eye. Is it heading in the direction you hoped? Is the original vision being adhered to? If not, is it heading along a positive path that's making everyone happy? Surprises can be good. Are any members trying to coerce you to do things you don't feel comfortable doing or trying to keep you from seeing your other Pagan or Wiccan friends? Is the group demanding too much time and energy, more so than you can afford to give with all the other responsibilities in your life? Has anyone in the group emerged as threatening or arrogant? Does that person attempt to get their way through vague threats of negative magick? Is the magick you do positive and helpful to all? Are group gatherings fun? Do you have a good time with them? Are these people your friends or people you put up with because you want to be part of a coven? Do you feel you can be a real spiritual family?

There are no right or wrong answers to these questions, but if you find things heading in a negative direction that you feel cannot be redirected, then it's time to step out and try again. There's no shame in this if you've given the group your best effort and worked with the group to solve problems. Sometimes things just don't work out, and it's no one's fault.

F) STAY CONNECTED. If you find you have to leave a group or coven for any reason, you should make your exit in a peaceful and positive way, without casting blame or offering criticism. Sometimes others in the group will feel hurt and not allow you to leave in a positive manner, but this is their immaturity and you should not make it your problem.

Even if there was one person in the group who caused you to leave, this is not the time to bring it up. Chances are there is no one person or reason for your leaving, other than that you need to grow spiritually in a different direction than the group is taking. Even the best people may sometimes not be the best working partners. It just happens.

The possibility that you may need to move on to another group is another reason why it is never good to cut yourself off from your larger networking web just because you've become part of a coven. We all need each other for support and comfort. Remember, no one is ever really alone in the Pagan/Wiccan community—even those who choose a solitary practice—as long as they are connected to others with whom they can share their ideas and concerns.

3) Where can I buy herbs, oils, and ritual tools?

Start by looking in your phone book under "Books" for stores that sell occult or metaphysical books. Chances are they also sell ritual tools and magickal accoutrements.

If you live in an area without such a resource, you can use mail order. I can't overstress how useful subscribing to the major Pagan publications can be in your search for absolutely anything Pagan. *Green Egg, PanGaia, SageWoman, Green Man, Hecate's Loom, Beltane Papers*, and *Circle Magazine* are all professionally formatted journals with wide circulations in North America. Western Europe has many publications just as fine. Information on these can be found in the backs of most books on magick or Paganism, such as this one. Larger bookstores now carry them on their newsstands. Mail-order vendors advertise heavily in these publications, and many have on-line stores now so you don't have to leave your living room to order a new wand. Fire up those Internet search engines and see what you find, or look in Appendix A for a resource list to get you started.

4) We only have three people. Can we be a coven?

Yes, yes, yes! Go back and read chapter 1, then forget every movie on Witchcraft you've ever seen. The fantasy spinners got a few things right . . . but usually just enough to confuse everybody. The Latin root *con*, the basis of the word "coven," means to "come together" or "to be with." It specifies no number. Stop worrying about trivialities that don't matter to the God and Goddess you seek to worship. Your coven of two will run smoother and work better than if you had ten people who weren't as well in tune with one another.

5) My spells aren't working. What's wrong?

This is a hard question to answer without analyzing all the elements of a spell, from its birth as a spark of an idea to its final enaction.

First of all, make sure your spell really has failed. Look back on your words of power and your visualizations to see what it was you asked for. If you asked for a "companion" and got a dog, then your spell worked, whether you were longing for a romantic partner or not. This is where your visualization must be clear and why the generic words of power found in most books on spells and magick, such as this one, are not always appropriate to use exactly as they appear. Spells are not commandments, but suggestions. I think of them like an architect's blueprint. Until the house is finished, you can always make changes to suit yourself.

When looking for spells to use as blueprints, you should seek those whose form and essence you feel in tune with, then hone them to your precise magickal requirements.

This is not to say that they can't work just as they are, but making alterations to suit your needs and affinities will allow you to get the most out of them. If you're not going to get the most you can, why go through the effort of doing the spells in the first place?

There are only two reasons why a spell fails. One, either the proper effort was not put into it in the first place, or two, there is a stronger force opposing your spell.

Keep in mind that opposition doesn't have to come from a concerted magickal effort. It can come from no more than the will of those involved to walk their own paths through life and not bend to the desires of anyone else. There is nothing you can do about this opposing force other than to quadruple your magickal efforts, and even all your redoubled efforts may not be able to get what you want if the opposing force remains strong enough.

You have more options when it's your own magickal effort that has not been strong enough. First, read through that spell and all its words of power. Do some divinations. Is everything spelled out exactly the way you want it? Second, be sure you're doing more than mouthing words and making gestures. Spend time—repeatedly if necessary—doing the spell with all the energy you can project into it. Third, draw in every catalyst you can keep track of and work within the waxing and waning cycles of the moon. Gear your spell to gain on the waxing cycle and to loss on the waning cycle.

6) I want to cast spells and curses like a Witch. Where can I learn?

The first thing to learn is that Witchcraft is a religion. The worship of the God and Goddess is its primary function. Witches accept magick because we have not rejected the natural energies upon which it is based, yet we don't belong to the Spell of the Hour Club. Many newcomers are surprised to learn that magick is often the last subject covered when studying the Craft with a good teacher. Magick is part of our lives. Magick is energy. Therefore it is all around us. It is us. What magick is *not* is a panacea for all our problems or our first line of action in every situation we wish to change.

Because we are a religion, our actions are based on ethics. Ours teaches us that we must harm none in all we do. Cursing is not a good thing, and it's a practice almost all Witches shun. To work negative magick or violate someone's free will will rebound on us in hideous ways and is just not worth the effort. Most of us accept this and enjoy working within this bond of sacred trust with the universe without feeling restricted in any way. Adherents of all religions have their renegades, and sadly Witchcraft has a few who have to learn these lessons the hard way.

The second thing to learn is that the terms *magician* and *Witch* can be mutually exclusive. Folk magick is the inheritance of all people. Anyone can practice it, and many do with good results. If you find you hesitate to give up your current religion for magick, then don't. You can either practice folk magick or study ceremonial magick, which is an old art with Egyptian and Judeo-Christian roots that summons spirits to assist in magickal operations. If you are interested in the latter, look for books by Aleister Crowley, John Michael Greer, Donald Michael Kraig, Israel Regardie, Stephen Skinner and Francis King, and Chic and Tabatha Cicero to start you on your way.

Books on Witchcraft usually include a chapter or two on natural magick. I wrote a book about nothing but cultivating natural magickal skills called *Making Magick*. There are also books on specific types of magick like herbalism, tarot, or candle. Look for books by Scott Cunningham and Raymond Buckland for beginner's guides to some of these.

7) When can I call myself a high priest/ess or elder?

This depends on your tradition, if you have aligned yourself with one. Some traditions within the Craft set time frames for attaining these titles. For example, the tradition I follow deems you are a priest or priestess after your initiation, and you become an elder by being part of the tradition for nine more years. Other traditions prescribe programs of study with other elders to advance. New initiations are performed to mark each rite of passage. These titles are conferred more on learning standards than time factors, though both can apply.

If you are a solitary Witch and want to attain these titles, the best course of action for you is a combination of time and continuing study. If you've been in the Craft for more than three years and work hard at learning, then you ought to consider how you view your spiritual body. Are you a leader, a mediator, a teacher, a counselor, a worker bee, an organizer, a bard? Think hard about what it is you want from your spiritual life. Then meditate on your situation to decide what is the right title for you and how to best attain it—and, most important, live it.

8) Where can I find a Craft teacher?

There is an old magickal adage that says, "When the student is ready, the teacher will appear." Yet, as with any magickal goal, you can't just sit at home doing nothing and expect what you wish for to knock on your door. The worthy student seeks what is needed. You must put the same effort into finding a good teacher as you would into finding a good coven. No one will hand it to you.

I feel the best-educated Witches are both widely read and have worked with several different teachers. Some of the best teaching can now be found in books. To decide what works for you, expose yourself to as many different Wiccan and Pagan ideas as you can. Even if you find a worthy teacher you will probably find she wants you to read many of these books anyway, as well as lots of texts on mythology, history, science, and culture. Use caution when working with a teacher. Ask for references and be sure your teacher is ethical, well-trained, and will help and not hinder your progress.

9) I need (list your need here) really fast. How can I learn to do magick right now?
You can't.

It's just not that simple. If it were, everyone would be beautiful, rich, famous, and have everything they ever wanted. Magick is work. Hard work. It requires physical, emotional, and mental effort, not once, but over and over again.

Magick cannot be mastered in a day any more than any other skill. It requires that you have a solid emotional and mental foundation on which to build and tends to go awry when the person working the spell is feeling desperate or distressed.

One of the most famous modern Witches, the late Sybil Leek, wrote in *The Complete Art of Witchcraft* (Signet Books, 1971) that before making successful magick you must "see to your own house first." In other words, you need some measure of stability and order in your life, and you need to have your major needs taken care of, before you can devote the kind of effort that magick requires to be successful. This is why magick is never the first resort when things go wrong. The Witch is simply not centered and balanced enough, and in the right frame of mind, to focus the magick on the need.

You must also be realistic about what magick can do for you. I've been asked about a variety of spells, from changing one's eye color to changing one's personality. Some things simply can't be done with magick, or cannot be done without other efforts being used to back up the magick. Remember in the first chapter of this book I insisted that nothing supernatural can exist? Magick won't change that fact. It won't make you sprout wings and fly, it won't make you wake up in a different body with a different life, and it won't become a wishing machine that works in an instant, as if it were a genie fresh from a well-rubbed lamp. It will help you find resources such as airline schedules, new friends, tinted contact lenses, and new opportunities.

If you want magick to be a part of your life, then start studying it now. Just don't do so with an eye to solving an immediate problem solely with magick. Even the mainstream religions teach that God helps those who help themselves. Be ready to back up your magick with every effort you can make to manifest your goal. Only then will it be part of your reality.

Annotated Bibliography

Alternatives Press, eds. *The Alternative Celebrations Catalogue* (fourth edition). Bloomington, Ind.: Alternatives, 1978.

This is a counter-culture lovers compilation of unusual holidays and unique ways to celebrate existing holidays. A great resource for inspiring your coven with ideas for creative celebration or for helping mediate a conflict over how to celebrate a specific holiday.

Bonewitz, Isaac. *Real Magic*. York Beach, Maine: Samuel Weiser, 1989.

This is another classic in magickal literature, and the closest thing available right now to a textbook on true "advanced" magick. Bonewitz's probing and agile mind challenges the reader to think in a full 360-degree spectrum—the true hallmark of the advanced Witch.

Buckland, Raymond. *Buckland's Complete Book of Witchcraft*. St. Paul, Minn.: Llewellyn, 1986.

This Craft classic has become known among long-time practitioners as "Uncle Bucky's Big Blue Book." It provides an excellent introduction to magick and divination and contains simple group ritual texts. Ray Buckland has earned his title as "The Grand Old Man of the Craft," and all his books on practical magick should be helpful no matter what your level of expertise.

Cabot, Laurie. *Celebrate the Earth*. New York, N.Y.: Delta, 1998.

This well-known Witch of modern-day Salem has written several books on magick and Witchcraft, and is an active coven leader and teacher. This volume looks at sabbat celebrations and rituals.

Campanelli, Pauline and Dan. *Circles, Groves and Sanctuaries.* St. Paul, Minn.: Llewellyn, 1992.

The Campanellis have compiled a collection that allows the reader into the private ritual space of both solitaries and covens. It's a great sourcebook for garnering ideas for creating or enhancing your own sacred space.

———. *Rites of Passage.* St. Paul, Minn.: Llewellyn, 1994.

This book contains rituals and ritual ideas for life-cycle events such as initiation, passing over, and coming of age that work well within group settings.

Cantrell, Gary. *Wiccan Beliefs and Practices: With Rituals for Solitaries and Covens.* St. Paul, Minn.: Llewellyn, 2001.

A nice sourcebook for ritual ideas.

Circle Guide to Pagan Groups, 2000–2001 Edition (Dennis Carpenter, ed.). Mount Horeb, Wis.: Circle Sanctuary, 2000.

Since first appearing in 1970, this biennial publication attempts to create the ultimate networking guide. If you have an open gathering, group, study circle, or the like, please let Circle know so the information can be made public. See Appendix A for their address.

Circle Network News (now Circle Magazine). "Group Dynamics." Mount Horeb, Wis.: Circle Sanctuary, Summer 1986.

Circle Magazine started out as a small newspaper and is now a high-quality, professionally formatted periodical. Back issues of this issue devoted to group work are still available through Circle Sanctuary as of this writing. See Appendix A for the address.

Crowley, Vivianne. *The Phoenix from the Flame.* Longmeade, UK: Aquarian, 1994.

Chapter 14 ("Becoming a Pagan") contains some good networking tips, and the appendix ("Pagan Resources Guide") lists lots of organizations, magazines, and publishers that have remained fairly up to date.

Eason, Cassandra. *A Complete Guide to Magic and Ritual.* Freedom, Calif.: The Crossing Press, 2001.

This small book explores both ritual and magick and using them for healing one's life and becoming whole.

Farrar, Janet and Stewart. *Eight Sabbats for Witches*. Custer, Wash.: Phoenix Publishing, 1988.

In this popular book, two long-time Gardnerian Wiccan leaders and teachers explain the significance of the solar festivals and provide detailed group ritual texts for each. This is a good "first book" for covens looking for a basic ritual format and for a better understanding of the eight sabbats that spoke the wheel of the year.

————. *What Witches Do: A Modern Coven Revealed*. Custer, Wash.: Phoenix Publishing, 1972.

This book is now out of print, but may still be available through out-of-print book searches. It explores the inner workings of an English coven in the Gardnerian tradition led by two well-known and respected Wiccan teachers.

Grimassi, Raven. *Wiccan Magick*. St. Paul, Minn.: Llewellyn, 1998.

Grimassi has written a solid introduction to Wiccan magick with emphasis on the practical elements and the Wiccan mysteries. I recommend it to any student of natural magick.

Green, Marian. *Elements of Natural Magic*. Longmeade, Dorset: Element Books, 1989.

This is a basic introductory text to the art of natural magick with some practical applications.

Harrow, Judy. *Wicca Covens: How to Start and Organize Your Own*. Secaucus, N.J.: Carol Publishing Group, 1999.

This book contains information and suggestions on forming and organizing a new coven.

Hunter, Dale, and Anne Bailey and Bill Taylor. *The Art of Facilitation: How to Create Group Synergy*. Tucson, Ariz.: Fisher Books, 1995.

This book was written with the business world in mind, but the ideas explored work well in any group setting. An excellent resource if your coven is having trouble creating group mind or coming to consensus on various issues.

———. *The Zen of Groups: A Handbook for People Meeting with a Purpose.* Tucson, Ariz.: Fisher Books, 1995.

This is another book written for the business world, but the business model in this book is so underplayed that any group can apply the ideas. It's a wonderful resource for helping your coven achieve consensus on vexing problems.

Ickis, Marguerite. *The Book of Festival Holidays.* New York, N.Y.: Dodd, Mead, 1964.

This collection covers unusual holidays often celebrated as communal festivals. Use them to spark new ideas for your own coven's seasonal observances.

Judith, Anodea. *Wheels of Life.* St. Paul, Minn.: Llewellyn, 1987.

This is a detailed but easy-to-read introduction to the energy of the chakras. It contains practical exercises for opening and working with their energies that is not available in most books on the chakra system.

K, Amber. *Covencraft: Witchcraft for Three or More.* St. Paul, Minn.: Llewellyn, 1998.

Amber has written a meaty volume that covers virtually every aspect of group ritual work and coven organization. Seasonal and life-cycle ritual texts are included.

K, Amber. *True Magick.* St. Paul, Minn.: Llewellyn, 1991.

Kaner, Sam, et al. *Facilitator's Guide to Participatory Decision Making.* Philadelphia, Pa.: New Society Publishing, 1996.

This book was written for the business world, but it can help show covens how to allow all members to participate in the group's decision-making process and achieve consensus.

Libera, Caitlin. *Creating Circles of Power and Magic: A Woman's Guide to Sacred Community.* Freedom, Calif.: The Crossing Press, 1994.

This book is part how-to and part biography. Libera traces her all-female coven from its origins as a metaphysical discussion group into a full working coven. She creates a good model for organization by showing how her group came to consensus and handled difficulties on its way to becoming a sacred family.

Marks, Diana F. *Let's Celebrate Today.* Englewood, Colo.: Libraries Unlimited, 1998.
This is a nice reference book for discovering little-known holidays. The text is short on specifics, and has somewhat of an ethnocentric focus, but it can provide ideas for coven celebrations.

McCoy, Edain. *Celtic Women's Spirituality.* St. Paul, Minn.: Llewellyn, 1997.
Chapter 20 ("The Bonding of Soul Friends") discusses ritual ideas for a coven of two and contains the text of a soulfriends bonding ceremony.

————. *Astral Projection for Beginners.* St. Paul, Minn.: Llewellyn, 1999.

————. *Inside a Witches' Coven.* St. Paul, Minn.: Llewellyn, 1997.
This book details how to find or create your own coven or Pagan study group based upon my experience with a Texas coven and several study groups and networking organizations. It contains an initiation ritual in the Wittan tradition and expounds on coming to consensus and dealing with problems, including a banishment ritual to use as a last resort.

————. *Making Magick: What It Is and How It Works.* St. Paul, Minn.: Llewellyn, 1997.
This is a detailed text of the natural magickal arts, from basic steps to advanced work. It focuses on building magickal skills and understanding the structure of spellcraft.

————. *The Sabbats.* St. Paul, Minn.: Llewellyn, 1994.
Contains detailed group rituals for the solar festivals.

Modrzyk, Stanley, J. A. *Celebrating the Times of Change: A Wiccan Book of Sharing for Family and Coven Growth.* York Beach, Maine: Samuel Weiser, 1995.
This slender book contains ritual texts for sabbats, esbats, and rites of passage. A good source for those who need to understand the basics of these rituals before moving on to magickal work.

Morwyn. *Secrets of a Witches' Coven.* West Chester, Pa.: Whitford Press, 1998.
This book presents rituals from the British Alexandrian Tradition of the Craft.

Pals, Ellen M. *Create a Celebration: Ideas and Resources for Theme Parties, Holidays, and Special Occasions—Activities for All Ages*. Golden, Colo.: Fulcrum Publishing, 1996.

As the lengthy title suggests, this is a book for developing ideas for doing things together as a group outside of the ritual circle. Activities like these help build spiritual groups into true extended families. As the bonds between coven members tighten, group mind is strengthened.

Sabrina, Lady. *Reclaiming the Power*. St. Paul, Minn.: Llewellyn, 1992.

Now out of print, but likely available through out-of-print search services, this is an excellent guide to ritual purpose and format for Witches.

Scabaro, Allen, and Nancy Campbell and Shirley Stave. *Living Witchcraft*. New York, N.Y.: Greenwood Publishing Group, 1994.

This high-priced book is advertised as the first scholarly ethnography to delve into coven dynamics. Using a large Atlanta coven as its subject, it probes the religious beliefs, sociology, and personal freedoms of a small focus group. It is worthwhile reading but does not always make clear that the experience of one coven can be vastly different than that of another.

Simms, Maria Kay. *The Witches' Circle*. St. Paul, Minn.: Llewellyn, 1996.

Maria is not only a skilled Witch and priestess, but also a professional astrologer. Her book is full of coven practices and rituals based upon the astrological year.

Slater, Herman. *Book of Pagan Rituals*. New York, N.Y.: Magickal Childe, 1983.

This book contains ritual texts of all types for modern Pagans.

Starhawk. *The Spiral Dance* (Twentieth Anniversary Edition). San Francisco, Calif.: HarperSanFrancisco, 1999.

Starhawk has created a classic in Pagan literature with this book. She provides blueprints for coven rituals and suggests ritual ideas that have been used in hundreds of group settings for two decades.

Valiente, Doreen. *Natural Magic*. Custer, Wash.: Phoenix, 1985.

Weinstein, Marion. *Positive Magic: Occult Self-Help* (revised edition). Custer, Wash.: Phoenix Publishing, 1981.

Chapter 9 ("Widening the Circle") discusses group dynamics. This is also an excellent introduction to the basics of magick and divination.

Ventimiglia, Mark. *Wiccan Prayer Book: Daily Meditations, Inspirations, Rituals and Incantations.* New York, N.Y.: Citadel Press, 2000.

Though written for the solitary practitioner, the ideas in this book can easily be adapted for group use.

SPELL INDEX

INDEX

☽ REACH FOR THE MOON

Llewellyn publishes hundreds of books on your favorite subjects!
To get these exciting books, including the ones on the following pages,
check your local bookstore or order them directly from Llewellyn.

Order by Phone
- Call toll-free within the U.S. and Canada, 1-877-NEW WRLD
- In Minnesota, call (651) 291-1970
- We accept VISA, MasterCard, and American Express

Order by Mail
- Send the full price of your order (MN residents add 7% sales tax)
  in U.S. funds, plus postage & handling to:

  Llewellyn Worldwide
  P.O. Box 64383, Dept. 0-7387-0261-7
  St. Paul, MN 55164–0383, U.S.A.

Postage & Handling
- **Standard** (U.S., Mexico, & Canada). If your order is:
  $20.00 or under, add $5.00
  $20.01–$100.00, add $6.00
  Over $100, shipping is free

  (Continental U.S. orders ship UPS. AK, HI, PR, & P.O.
  Boxes ship USPS 1st class. Mex. & Can. ship PMB.)

- **Second Day Air** (Continental U.S. only): $10 for one book + $1 per each additional book
- **Express** (AK, HI, & PR only) [Not available for P.O. Box delivery. For street address delivery only.]: $15 for one book + $1 per each additional book
- **International Surface Mail:** $20 or under, add $5 plus $1 per item; $20.01 and over, add $6 plus $1 per item.
- **International Airmail:** Books—Add the retail price of each item; Non-book items—Add $5 per item

Please allow 4–6 weeks for delivery on all orders.
Postage and handling rates subject to change.

Discounts
We offer a 20% discount to group leaders or agents. You must order a
minimum of 5 copies of the same book to get our special quantity price.

FREE CATALOG
Get a free copy of our color catalog, *New Worlds of Mind and Spirit*. Subscribe for just $10.00 in the United States and Canada ($30.00 overseas, airmail). Call 1-877-NEW WRLD today!

Visit our website at www.llewellyn.com for more information.

Making Magick
WHAT IT IS AND HOW IT WORKS

Edain McCoy

How do I raise and send energy? What happens if I make a mistake in casting a spell? What is sex magick all about? What is the Moon's role in magick? Which magickal tools do I need the most?

Making Magick is a complete course in natural magick that answers these and hundreds of other questions. Through exercises designed to develop basic skills, *Making Magick* lays a firm foundation of elemental magickal wisdom. The first chapters begin with an introduction to magick and how it works. You will study Craft tools, learn to connect with the elements—the building blocks of magick—and delve into the intricacies of spell construction and timing. The last half of the book will take you into the advanced magickal arts, which rely on highly honed skills of meditation, astral projection, visualization, and sustaining of creative energy. A special chapter on the tattwas will show you how to use these ancient Hindu symbols as gateways into the astral worlds.

1-56718-670-X
304 pp., 6 x 9, illus., photos $14.95

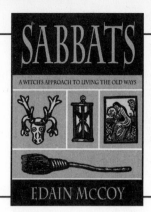

The Sabbats
A New Approach to Living the Old Ways

Edain McCoy

This book may contain the most practical advice ever for incorporating the old ways into your Pagan lifestyle!

The Sabbats offers many fresh, exciting ways to deepen your connection to the turning of the Wheel of the Year. This tremendously practical guide to Pagan solar festivals does more than teach you about the "old ways"—you will learn workable ideas for combining old customs with new expressions of those beliefs that will be congruent with your lifestyle and tradition.

The Sabbats begins with background on Paganism (tenets, teachings, and tools) and origins of the eight Sabbats, followed by comprehensive chapters on each Sabbat. These pages are full of ideas for inexpensive seasonal parties in which Pagans and non-Pagans alike can participate, as well as numerous craft ideas and recipes to enrich your celebrations. The last section provides sixteen complete texts of Sabbat rituals—for both covens and solitaries—with detailed guidelines for adapting rituals to specific traditions or individual tastes. Includes an extensive reference section with a resources guide, bibliography, musical scores for rituals, and more.

1-56718-663-7
320 pp., 7 x 10, illus., photos $17.95

Celtic Women's Spirituality
ACCESSING THE CAULDRON OF LIFE

Edain McCoy

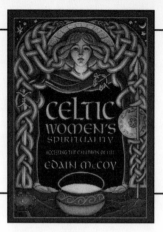

Every year, more and more women turn away from orthodox religions, searching for an image of the divine that is more like themselves—feminine, strong, and compelling. Likewise, each year the ranks of the Pagan religions swell, with a great many of these newcomers attracted to Celtic traditions.

The Celts provide some of the strongest, most archetypally accessible images of strong women onto which you can focus your spiritual impulses. Warriors and queens, mothers and crones, sovereigns and shapeshifters, all have important lessons to teach us about ourselves and the universe.

Celtic Women's Spirituality shows how you can successfully create a personalized pathway linking two important aspects of the self—the feminine and the hereditary (or adopted) Celtic—and as a result become a whole, powerful woman, awake to the new realities previously untapped by your subconscious mind.

1-56718-672-6
352 pp., 7 x 10, illus. $16.95

Astral Projection for Beginners

Edain McCoy

Enter a world in which time and space have no meaning or influence. This is the world of the astral plane, an ethereal, unseen realm often perceived as parallel to and interpenetrating our physical world. *Astral Projection for Beginners* shows you how to send your consciousness at will to these other places, then bring it back with full knowledge of what you have experienced.

Explore the misconceptions and half-truths that often impede the beginner, and create a mental atmosphere in which you become free to explore the universe both inside and outside your consciousness. This book offers six different methods for you to try: general transfer of consciousness, projecting through the chakras, meditating towards astral separation, guided meditation, using symbolic gateways, and stepping out of your dreams. Ultimately you will be able to condition your mind to allow you to project at will.

1-56718-625-4
256 pp., 5³⁄₁₆ x 8 $9.95

Inside a Witches' Coven

Edain McCoy

Inside a Witches' Coven gives you an insider's look at how a real Witches' coven operates, from initiation and secret vows to parting rituals. You'll get step-by-step guidance for joining or forming a coven, plus sage advice and exclusive insights to help you decide which group is the right one for you.

Maybe you're thinking about joining a coven, but don't know what to expect, or how to make contacts. Perhaps you already belong to a coven, but your group needs ideas for organizing a teaching circle or mediating conflicts. Either way, you're sure to find *Inside a Witches' Coven* a practical source of wisdom.

Joining a coven can be an important step in your spiritual life. Before you take that step, let a practicing Witch lead you through the hidden inner workings of a Witches' coven.

1-56718-666-1
224 pp., 5¼ x 8 $9.95

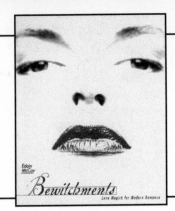

Bewitchments
LOVE MAGICK FOR MODERN ROMANCE

Edain McCoy

The simple act of braiding your hair can be a potent spell for love—that's why Celtic women had to wear their hair loose at their weddings. Eat a pineapple, long a symbol of friendship and unity, and watch new friends come into your life. Whether you're looking for a new friend or a lifelong mate, *Bewitchments* can help you narrow the focus of the search and show you how to attract, sustain, or refine these relationships with its grimoire of over ninety spells.

Drawing on both multicultural folk magick and new scientific discoveries about the chemical process known as "falling in love," *Bewitchments* shows, step by step, how to bring the ancient spells into the present and make them work.

1-56718-700-5
264 pp., 7½ x 9⅛, illus.   **$14.95**

To order, call 1-877-NEW WRLD
Prices subject to change without notice

Ostara
CUSTOMS, SPELLS & RITUALS
FOR THE RITES OF SPRING

Edain McCoy

Shelve your inhibitions and dance wildly upon the face of the reborn Earth!

Whether you're breaking into the seed catalogs or taking off for spring break, the lure of the vernal equinox is impossible to ignore. Called Ostara or Eostre in nature spiritualities, it is one of the most primitive and "earthy" of the solar festivals.

Many of the symbols and customs surrounding the Christian celebration of Easter come directly from Euro-Pagan practices. Why is the humble egg such a potent trademark of spring? And what about that Easter bunny? This book discusses such universal symbols that have survived intact for thousands of years.

From coloring eggs with natural plant dyes, to spring cleaning rituals, to spells for love and lust, *Ostara* will help you connect with the spirit of the festival and incorporate its rituals and customs, both ancient and new, into your own Ostara celebrations.

- Of interest to Pagans and Christians alike, as many of the symbols and customs surrounding Easter come directly from Euro-Pagan practices.

- A sourcebook for understanding the spiritual aspects of the vernal equinox.

- Full of rituals, spells, recipes, crafts, and customs to celebrate spring.

0-7387-0082-7
240 pp., 7½ x 9⅛, illus.

$14.95

To order, call 1-877-NEW WRLD

Prices subject to change without notice